T0163562

Parables and Fables

PARABLES AND FABLES

*Exegesis, Textuality, and Politics
in Central Africa*

V. Y. Mudimbe

The University of Wisconsin Press

The University of Wisconsin Press
114 North Murray Street
Madison, Wisconsin 53715

3 Henrietta Street
London WC2E 8LU, England

Copyright © 1991
The Board of Regents of the University of Wisconsin System
All rights reserved

5   4   3   2   1

Printed in the United States of America

Library of Congress Cataloging-in-Publication Data
Mudimbe, V. Y., 1941–
    Parables and fables: exegesis, textuality, and politics
in central Africa / V. Y. Mudimbe.
    260 pp.   cm.
    Includes bibliographical references and index.
    ISBN 0-299-13060-6   ISBN 0-299-13064-9
    1. Luba (African people)—Politics and government.   2. Philosophy,
Luba (African people)   3. Luba (African people)—Religion.
4. Structural anthropology—Zaire.   5. Marxist anthropology—Zaire.
6. Zaire—Politics and government.   7. Zaire—Religious life and
customs.   I. Title.
DT650.L8M83   1991
306′096751 — dc20   91-12498
                                CIP

To the Reverend Father Vincent Mulago

Est operae pretium nebulosi dogmatis umbram prodere, quam tenues atomi compage minuta instituunt, sed cassa cadit ventoque liquescit adsimilis, fluxu nec se sustentat inani.

Prudentius, Apotheosis 952–55

Contents

Preface

This book bears witness to and, I would hope, also provides insight into the unfolding of an intellectual odyssey that began in the academic year 1968–1969. With other young teachers, I joined the Faculty of the University of Paris–Nanterre, the site from which the *révolution manquée* burst forth in May 1968. Although I was assigned to the Department of Ethnology and Comparative Sociology, everyone knew that I was completing a doctoral dissertation in comparative philology and finishing a complementary thesis on the political philosopher Ber Borochov. The university, in fact, seemed to need younger scholars who could, on the one hand, speak and understand the students' language and in so doing provide an alternative discourse to what was being questioned by the 1968 students' uprising. On the other hand, we were supposed to believe in the mission of the university as established by French tradition and as stipulated by the French government. I personally accepted the challenge of meeting these contradictory demands and began to share my weeks between Louvain in Belgium and Paris–Nanterre. At Louvain, I was quietly reading ancient Greek, Latin, and French texts, and from time to time, I would direct Professor Willy Bal's seminars and correct undergraduate theses in Indo-European philology. I enjoyed, in brief, an atemporal peace. At Nanterre, however, I had to be a believer in the vocation and grandeur of the French university system, and at the same time, I had to be capable of entering into dialogue with even the most extreme leftist theories. I did not hide the fact that I was then a practicing Catholic, although, philosophically, agnostic.

The intellectual atmosphere of Paris was then explosive. Jean-Paul Sartre and Simone de Beauvoir were on the streets helping the cause of Maoists. Claude Lévi-Strauss was a god dominating most of us in the department, appropriately called the "Laboratoire d'Ethnologie et de Sociologie Comparative." When in 1973 Lévi-Strauss was elected to the *Académie Française,* some of my colleagues and students went into mourning. They were convinced that such an election to one of the most elitist institutions could only be a sign of betrayal toward what Lévi-Strauss had been teaching about otherness. Yet, Claude Lévi-Strauss' choice could be understood: in effect, why should he despise institutions of his own country while he was, by vocation, describing and celebrating those of remote cultures? Louis Althusser's articles were published for the first time as a book. This, entitled *For Marx,* was regarded as a sort of leftist bible, which unveiled new possibilities in Marxian and Marxist interpretations. In order to face my own students at Nanterre, I was, the first year, participating at Louvain in a rigorous interdisciplinary seminar, "Reading Capital," that scrupulously followed the syllabus conceived by Althusser. Jacques Lacan was still, despite his problems with the French university and the French Orders of physicians and psychologists, initiating his students into a rethinking of Freud. Focusing on the little object *a,* as that which silently manipulates us and as that which we repress, he demonstrated that it nonetheless marks us and our choices.

Such an intellectual context could not but force me to articulate a number of questions about myself. Here I was, so to speak, the margin of margins: black, Catholic, African, yet agnostic; intellectually Marxist, disposed toward psychoanalysis, yet a specialist in Indo-European philology and philosophy. How could all this relate to myself, my origins, and my transcendence as a human being? I presented at Louvain my dissertation on the concept of *air* and my complementary thesis on Ber Borochov's language in 1970. Five years later, I was, after a sojourn in Africa, in Geneva, Switzerland, dying of bone cancer. In Africa, as well as in Switzerland, doctors had given me a maximum of six months to live. A misdiagnosis. In a surge of defiance, I wrote three books in five months. The first, a collection of poems, *Entretailles,* was published in 1973 by Editions Saint Germain-des-Prés in Paris. It is dedicated to Jean-Pierre and his fiancée, Patou. Both had just passed away in a motorcycle accident. Jean-Pierre had been my student. It happened that he was also the son of Dr. Jacques and Madame Madeleine Bassot, who are my French "parents" and who served more than twenty years ago as witnesses when I married Elizabeth Boyi, my life's companion. The collection of poems speaks about impossible conjunctions between day and night, men and women, nature and culture, north and south, etc. In them, I wanted to express the tension of a communion which in the very project of its expression would supersede its warring elements. The second book, a novel, *Le Bel immonde,* published by Présence Africaine in 1976 (translated into English as *Before the Birth of the Moon,* and published by Simon and Schuster), patiently conjugated the "French Nouveau Roman" techniques with a critical yet impatient reading of 1960s Central African politics. Finally, I wrote *L'Autre Face du royaume,* published in Lausanne, Switzerland, in 1974, by L'Age d'Homme.

The objective, in this last book, was to interrogate the paradoxes of social and human sciences and, specifically, to address the aims of anthropology. Naturally, the arguments of a dying young man unjustly went against those he admired the most. Yet despite such a bias, for the first time I really understood and felt that social and human sciences do not produce inoffensive, abstract identities and rules as do, say, logic or mathematical systems. Eight years after, with my *Odeur du père* (1982), I was more circumspect in my evaluation. The subordination of the other to the same still obsessed me. On the other hand, I had moved from the Lacanian horizon to what Etienne Perrot, a maverick and unorthodox Jungian psychoanalyst, was expounding from Marie-Louise von Frantz's analyses and interpretations of Jung's hypotheses and affirmations. Although published when I was in the United States, *L'Odeur du père* belongs to my African experience. For nine years, I had lived in my own country, teaching African students and facing mythologies on science, tradition, and everyday life in a degrading social context. With this book, I wanted to reformulate, from a radically new perspective, the naive challenge raised by *L'Autre Face du royaume*. The process meant, among other things, a reevaluation of structuralism, whose method grounds, at least for me, the most stimulating ways of understanding human cultures; and on the other hand, against structuralism, I wished to invoke the rights of the subject and focus on the still-compelling soundness of a philosophy of subjectivity.

Two main questions imposed themselves: How does one think about and comment upon alterity without essentializing its features? Second, in African contexts, can one speak and write about a tradition or its contemporary practice without taking into account the authority of the colonial library that has invented African identities? It seemed obvious to me that one could easily transcend ethnographic discussions about what is false or true by facing local speeches and texts in themselves as simple contingencies. In effect, these can be interpreted from their own organization and instability. This also implies that it should be possible to read them without necessarily confronting them as true or false historical documents. The myth of historical roots so widespread in African studies leads, as we all know now, to the constitution of an alienated and alienating bibliography.

I thus thought of using my own education as a framework in which I could, thanks to some methodological lessons from Sartre's phenomenology and Claude Lévi-Strauss' structuralism, rewrite my personal readings of some beautiful African fables and parables. Concretely, I was caught between Sartre's existentialist philosophy and historical perspective (which claim that we are completely free, fully responsible, and universal lawmakers) and Lévi-Strauss' masterful ahistorical demonstration that seems to negate such a position and, in any case, questions the tension between the "savage" and the "scientific" mind. It became important to position myself vis-à-vis the Cartesian cogito and reconcile the impossible dialogue about the cogito which simultaneously separates and unites Lévi-Strauss and Sartre.

Jean-Paul Sartre has some critical pages in *Being and Nothingness* (1956) in which he discusses the meaning of the Cartesian cogito. In the famous expression *Cogito ergo sum,* the consciousness which states "I am'' is not and cannot be the subject's consciousness. The cogito, in fact, reflects and indicates Descartes' thinking upon his own thinking, rather than the thinking of Descartes pinpointed by traditional understanding. In sum, strictly speaking, the Cartesian *Cogito ergo sum,* Sartre notes, is reflective: its object cannot be itself but rather is the original consciousness of doubting which has made it possible. And this prereflective cogito is a nonthetic, nonpositional consciousness. In other words, the consciousness of the object (thinking) is a consciousness of being conscious of the thinking as object, that is, of being aware of it. Thus, in this cogito, Descartes states an awareness. Consequently, the paradigm should be understood to mean I am aware that I am thinking, therefore I am.

Following Sartre further, one's being is tension between *l'en-soi* (being in-itself), which simply is being in the absoluteness and contingency of its existence, and *le pour soi* (being for-itself), which is both nihilation of the in-itself and its transcending. This for-itself names its complexity through three scissiparities that initiate three *ekstases,* or modes of being: temporality, reflection, and *le pour autrui* (being for others). There is residual tension, which may construct the question: What reveals the for-itself vis-à-vis the massive passivity of the in-itself, that is, the affirmation of an object transcending itself and capable of critically perceiving itself as both consciousness of being and being of consciousness? Or to put it a different way, this tension signals a basic truth, that of a consciousness which becomes aware of itself (Sartre 1967:51). The case of Antoine Roquentin in Sartre's *Nausea* (1964) is exemplary here. While meditating on his being and that of things, he discovers that he is what he is not and he is not what he is.

In this framework, one understands that it is always before an other, outside of the self, that one is intelligent or stupid, ashamed or innocent. The other is the occasion by which one unveils previously unknown possibilities of one's own being and apprehends oneself as subject and object. This stranger manifests himself or herself in my experience by his or her forms, and I experience them as contingent. Ontologically, there is no way of proving the necessity of the other's being, yet my existence is profoundly affected by his or her presence to the point, thinks Sartre, where I can say to the other: "I need you in order to realize fully the structures of my being" (1956: pt. 3, chap. 1). Actually, the for-itself is not fully without the for-other. In a more metaphoric way, I am, as Sartre writes, a language: "Whatever I may do has an outside, a meaning which escapes me." It is in this sense—and in this sense only—that Heidegger is right in declaring that "I am what I say" (Sartre 1956:485–86).

The integration of the other in my existential experience is dramatic. It always signifies an opening up of what I am and reduces me to the status of a sign-object, to be reflected or commented upon. Moreover, it uncovers completely new types of consciousness which "even while themselves remaining strictly for-itself point to a radically different type of ontological structure. This ontological structure is 'mine,' it is in relation to myself as subject that I am concerned about myself, and yet this concern reveals to me a being which is my being without being-for-me" (Sartre 1956:301). Thus outside of the structure of my for-itself, there is a field which is mine and, at the same time, in a fundamental manner, is not mine. I could possibly pass judgment about its construction, since it claims to reveal me, yet I know that its modes, as well as its very being, depend upon and express the other's power of representation and his or her capacity for objectifying me. An existential necessity—the other in his or her interaction with me—actualizes new structures which, simultaneously, involve me, mark my own perception of my being for-others, and definitely objectify me.

One might think of dramatic examples, such as Antoine and Annie in *Nausea,* or Goetz and Hilda in *The Devil and the Good Lord.* Looks mark and even, I would say, unveil the extent of both objectification and appearance of a new type of ontological structure. At any rate, one can just focus on the ambivalence and the ambiguity of what dialogues bring about. The conversation of Goetz and Hilda toward the end of *The Devil and the Good Lord* shows in a clear way how the other's look sustains the reality of one's being and existence in a godless world: "I can tell you," says Goetz to Hilda, "God is dead. We have no witness now. I alone can see your hair and your brow. How real you have become since he no longer exists. Look at me, don't stop looking at me for one moment: the world has been struck blind; if you turned away your head, I should be afraid of annihilation" (Sartre 1969:143).

We could claim that speech as a means of dialogue allows one to read the other's mask, penetrate and comprehend the other's mystery. Yet as Maurice Merleau-Ponty notes: "This reading seems to be in fact an interpretation of one's own projection" (1973:140). If speech is "the locus of meditation of the same and the other" and, therefore, a concrete reference, thanks to which one can think of the pertinence of concepts such as "community of being" and "community of doing," it nevertheless remains the excellent means by which I can generalize myself and project myself into the other (1973:140). Speaking to, conversing with, the other, "I make the other in my own image" (1973:134), and yet, in this mysterious and polysemic exchange, the other and I "realize the impossible agreement between two rival totalities not because speech forces us back upon ourselves to discover some unique spirit in which we participate but because speech concerns us, catches us indirectly, seduces us . . . , transforms us into the other and him into us, abolishes the limit between mine and non-mine, and ends the alternative between what has sense for me and what is non-sense for me, between me as subject and the other as object" (1973:145). This communion of the same and the other in the verb brilliantly emphasizes the virtues of dialogue: Am I one or two? Am I the other, and if so, who am I? On the other hand, in this sharing of speech, I clearly bring the other to life and thus produce myself.

Can one relate this perspective to Jean-Jacques Rousseau's principle, the I as the other, which Lévi-Strauss takes as one of the founding paradigms of his anthropological project? Let us begin by noting that Rousseau's statement is in both its own formulation and Lévi-Strauss' commentary a complete negation of the Cartesian cogito. Lévi-Strauss states that "To Montaigne's 'What do I know?' (from which everything stems), Descartes believed it possible to answer that 'I know that I am, since I think.' To this Rousseau retorts with a 'What am I' without a definite solution since the question presupposes the completion of another, more essential one: 'Am I?' Intimate experience provides only this 'he' which Rousseau discovered and which he lucidly undertook to explore" (1976:37).

This is, according to Lévi-Strauss, the end of the Cartesian cogito that Rousseau indicates in his *Confessions*. Rousseau's statement clarifies itself from his double principle: first the identification of the I with the other (even to the most other among others, even to an animal—"le plus autrui, de tous les autrui, fût-il un animal") and, second, the refusal of identifying oneself with oneself, that is, a rejection of whatever can make the I acceptable. And Lévi-Strauss grounds his belief on this radical lesson of Rousseau's *Confessions*. "In truth, I am not 'me' but the weakest most humble of others"; "En vérité, je ne suis pas 'moi,' mais le plus humble des 'autrui.' Telle est la découverte des *Confessions*" (1976:39).

This lesson, thinks Lévi-Strauss, can be rationally founded. Its possibility arises as a correction. Descartes, he believes, made a mistake of believing that one can go from human interiority to the exteriority of the world (*l'extériorité du monde*) without crossing human achievements (*des mondes d'homme*). This perspective, stemming from the cogito, would account for the fact that Descartes could posit a physics but not a sociology or even a biology. Second, in linking the "I am" to the "I think," Descartes put aside an unanswerable question, that of knowing the I am, which implies another major issue: Am I? The only way out of the circle of these questions seems to be in Rousseau's proposition that personal identity is acquired by inference. What unveils the most intimate and profound experience is not an I but a thinking he or she in me, who is so clear and explicit that I should doubt whether or not it is me who is thinking; "Il

existe un 'il' qui se pense en moi, et qui me fait d'abord douter si c'est moi
qui pense'' (Lévi-Strauss 1976:49). In other words, my existence can be
defined only as an inference from and a reference to an other. On the basis
of this lesson, Lévi-Strauss credits Rousseau with the foundation of the
ethnological spirit. In effect, notes Lévi-Strauss, confronting for the first
time the "savages he has chosen for himself" (''considérant pour la premi-
ère fois les sauvages qu'il s'est choisi''), the ethnographer can always
repeat Rousseau's invocation. Here you are, "unknown strangers, non-
beings to me, since I wished it so! And I, detached from them and from
everything, what am I? This is what I must find out first'' (1976:36). For
Lévi-Strauss, Rousseau's anti-Cartesianism provides both the philosophical basis and the founding motto of ethnology. He goes on to make the
claim that the anthropologists's work is no more than a confession
(1976:39). One of his own books, *Tristes Tropiques,* serves as good evidence.

Tristes Tropiques can be read in at least two ways: as an anthropologist's
saga and as a spiritual journey. The text's strategy offers them in complementarity. There is no doubt, however, that the intellectual complexity of
the saga and its achievements do not make sense without the postulations
of a confession and its significance. It is a discreet, yet imperative, voice
which speaks about being simultaneously "potential fodder for the con-
centration camp" and a French citizen (Lévi-Strauss 1977). He served his
country honorably, and here he is defining himself as part of an "endan-
gered species" that the Rockefeller Foundation is trying to protect and to
salvage. Fundamentally, the story, from the first to the last page, is about
a "strange stranger" (1977:23–25). He had been trained in philosophy,
but he rejects it as a gratuitous intellectual game; he chooses anthropology
as a vocation (1977:47–51) and claims that he has "a neolithic intelligence." Yet he has made sure that we understand that he, unlike Sartre, got
his "agrégation de philosophie" the first time he went through the examination. Nevertheless, Lévi-Strauss is a lost soul in an absurd world, discovering that some people can identify Hitler with Jesus Christ and that
others suspect him of being a Jewish Freemason (1977:23) or a German
spy (1977:25). Is he completely rejected from his French tradition? In the
Brazilian jungle, the main object of his meditation is not the remote Indian
communities he visits, but primarily himself and his own culture. On the
plateau of the Western Mato Grosso, he recalls that "what came to [him]
were fleeting visions of the French countryside or snatches of music and
poetry'' (1977:429). More significant, he is haunted by Chopin's Etude no.
3, opus 10, and after a highly self-intrusive reflection on why he should be
colonized by this particular construction, he concludes that "perhaps then,

this was what travelling was, an exploration of the deserts of my mind, rather than those surrounding me'' (1977:429–30).

Lévi-Strauss' structuralist project as illustrated in his ''Mythologiques'' series might not, at first sight, seem to bear witness to the mystery of a meditation on oneself. Looked at carefully, however, it does actualize practical deductions from the paradigm ''I as an other.'' Its pivotal moment comes as a revelation, the discovery of the double articulation of language, finding the existence in language of two complementary systems of relations, one of units of significance and a second of units of distinction (1967:31–54). This revelation organized methodological implications graced by three metaphors that Lévi-Strauss calls his ''three sources of inspiration'' (1977:50). They cover the totality of the geography of life: geology, or the study of profundities of a natural space; Marxism, or the analysis of functional structures of the human space of a social formation; and psychoanalysis, or the study of the individual unconscious. ''All three demonstrate that understanding consists in reducing one type of reality to another; that the true reality is never the most obvious; and that the nature of truth is already indicated by the care it takes to remain elusive'' (1977:50). In sum, the three metaphors project the symbolism of three essential truths. First, the master-meaning is always discreet, invisible, beyond the apparent rationality and the logical constructs of the visible surface. Second, the passage from the visible to the invisible is discontinuous and represents a rupture. Third, despite its connections with the visible and despite its determining impact on it, the invisible is an autonomous system whose activity has its own reason. In Lévi-Strauss' structural anthropology, this invisible order becomes the unconscious. Unlike Freud's ''floating energy'' or ''set of impulses under pressure and striving for discharge,'' this unconscious is a self-intelligible structure and refers ''to a form or an aggregate of forms, empty of any content.'' What it reveals would be the functioning of human mind in general and not idiosyncrasies of the I's thinking vis-à-vis the other's, nor the reverse.

Mythology, Lévi-Strauss writes, reveals how to understand the apparent arbitrariness of the mind (1969:10). In the same text, the Overture to *The Raw and the Cooked,* he insists: ''I am not concerned with the classification of what is in myth but with the system of axioms and postulates defining a code, giving a significance on unconscious formulations which are the work of minds, societies and civilizations'' (1969:12). To those who accuse him of destroying the dignity of consciousness and the creativity of the subject, he answers: ''The social sciences, following the example of the physical sciences, must grasp the fact that the reality of the project they are studying is not wholly limited to the level of the subject apprehending it. These appearances are underlaid by other appearances of no greater value, and so on, layer by layer, as we look for the ultimate essence of nature which at each level escapes us, and will probably remain forever unattainable'' (1977:638).

It becomes obvious that the centrality and primacy of the consciousness for Sartre can only be opposed to the reality of Lévi-Strauss' unconsciousness. Sartre's concept of consciousness expresses the continuation of Descartes' rule on the necessity of conquering oneself rather than the world (Sartre 1965:46). He postulates human existence on the one hand as an absolute freedom and a radical anguish, since to exist is to be a lawmaker. On the other hand, he describes existence as forlornness and despair insofar as God does not exist, and thus, ''we confine ourselves to reckoning only with what depends upon our will'' (Sartre 1965:45–46). For Sartre it is only realism to claim that humans are nothing else than their plans and that there is no reality outside human action. His psychoanalysis shares with Freud's a major principle: the search for the meaning of behavior through the reconstruction of the human as ''a situational being.'' Yet it rejects Freud's emphasis on the role of the libido and the unconscious psyche itself. For Sartre, in effect, ''human action and ways of appropriating the in-itself and the other express in a particular situation, an already concrete choice of being. Each action is the entire human being existing in a way'' (1956:716). This affirms a powerful paradigm: human action and behavior always reflect a freedom and its pattern. It follows that, in order to account for the truth of its being-in-the-world, existential psychoanalysis should look for the ''prereflective choice'' (1956:722–31) of the being, not for a mythical unconsciousness.

It is not only Freud's unconscious which is being challenged here, but also Lévi-Strauss'. If the unconsciousness does not exist, then, by analogy, unconscious mental structures become unthinkable. Sartre formulated this critique in *The Critique of Dialectical Reason* and *ad concretum exemplum* in his monumental study of Flaubert. The reinterpretation of freedom, which in the *Critique* ceases to be the absolute absoluteness in the collective process of building a ''we-subject,'' does not belittle the majesty of the consciousness. Against historical dialectic, Sartre emphasizes the primacy of consciousness as absolutely intentional and dialectical, and individual praxis as the ''only ontological reality'' and basic and unique source of all dialectic. Thus, according to him, history should be conceived as a critical dialogue between human praxis and the practico-inert (Sartre 1956:18). To use, analogically, the founding concepts of *Being and Nothingness,* one could subsequently define history as constructed by the interaction of the for-itself and the in-itself. In the last chapter of *The Savage Mind,* Lévi-

Strauss methodically criticizes this imperialist ambition. The key to his position can be summed up in his evaluation of the relationships existing between the science of the concrete and the science of the abstract (1966: chap. 1). In Sartre's philosophical anthropology, according to Lévi-Strauss, the choice — be it prereflective or not — as well as the freedom of the for-itself signify a "sociologization of the Cogito." The ego's society is set apart from all others as an absolute model, and "each individual's group and epoch are the center of consciousness in lieu of the timeless consciousness."

Strictly speaking, the dialogue between Sartre and Lévi-Strauss seems impossible. Yet, from a Sirius' viewpoint, I can formulate some of the conditions of this difficulty and elaborate on both the austerity of differences and their accessibility. These, then, are my three main positions. The first concerns the objective of Lévi-Strauss' enterprise. The reality and the power of his concept of an unconscious claim to uncover "hidden forms," in principle, should lead to a good understanding of how, in a given context, being relates to itself and not, as Sartre proposed, in relation to oneself. The postulation of the unconscious has thus a demonstrative function.

My second consideration concerns the reading of myths as search for the discreet, unconscious, and constraining structures. Myths, Lévi-Strauss teaches us, indicate how we should understand "the apparent arbitrariness of the mind," but beyond the surface of their textuality, they also unveil ways and techniques of dealing with "unwelcome contradictions." In fact, as Edmund Leach put it, "the function of mythology is to exhibit publicly, though in disguise, ordinary unconscious paradoxes" (1980b:78). As such, mythology accounts for regional manners of treating and manipulating basic contradictions of human life and, in this sense, speaks also about local histories. Jacques Maquet nicely touches upon this when he notes: "When a Bororo listens to a narrative concerning the origin of tobacco, the myth provides him with a verbal equivalent of a past event. In an oblique way, the tale discloses for him some important meaning of the tobacco in the Bororo social life. Lévi-Strauss' reader, when he perceives the homologous relationships linking in a corpus hundreds of New World myths, understands much better the stories themselves, their place in the Indian cultures, and one of the ways of the human mind" (1986:131–32). Why, therefore, cannot one add that this understanding is about the dynamics of a particular history, of human praxes related to both their physical and sociocultural environments?

My last consideration is a deduction about Lévi-Strauss as subject and his own enterprise as a purposeful action. If empirical categories, as he masterfully proves in his "Mythologiques," can be used as a key to a silent code which unveils universals, then, when analyzed, such a project in the social sciences can say its own name only in the intentionality of its inventor. In our case, it is Lévi-Strauss' praxis expressing itself within a cultural and human environment, which is an obvious practico-inert as illustrated by the confession of *Tristes Tropiques*. The cry which closes the book—the golden age is not behind nor before us but in us—expresses the power of a consciousness and its liberty. In sum, the structuralist method that Lévi-Strauss brought into being and convincingly applied is an intellectual tool whose condition of possibility resides in an epistemological field in which the relative strength of the cogito has led to the right of an absolute human freedom and, consequently, to systematic meditations on the comparative virtues of the same and the other.

At any rate, one might radically reflect upon the grave moral and, I am afraid, too-strong conclusion that ends *The Origins of Table Manners*. Lévi-Strauss demonstrates that the ambiguous authority of Sartre's pronouncement Hell is other people has not been entertained by Indians who, modestly, state that Hell is us (1979:507–8). This closure illustrates the lesson of Rousseau, without negating or suppressing Lévi-Strauss' freedom of meditating on and comparing these paradoxical statements. In this particular situation, he occupies—to use an expression he likes—the situation of an astronomer looking at stars. To claim I am another would be, in this case, to propose a symbolic identification. Even so, the I who pronounces the sentence is in anguish, thinking on how to apprehend himself: is he the subject of the praxis that the sentence expresses symbolically or a pure reflection of the other as meant by the copula? I would invoke here a magnificent image proposed by Merleau-Ponty: "Myself and the other are like two nearly concentric circles which can be distinguished only by a slight and mysterious slippage. . . . Nevertheless the other is not I and on that account differences must arise" (1973:134).

I would like to maintain this quotation as an invitation to clarify Lévi-Strauss' project, not as means of integrating him into a phenomenological or existentialist perspective. He says that he profoundly dislikes these: the former, because "it postulated a kind of continuity between experience and reality" and because it does not recognize that "the transition between one order and the other is discontinuous"; the latter, "because of its overindulgent attitude towards the illusions of subjectivity" (1977:50). What I have been attempting so far is solely an interpretation of Lévi-Strauss' founding principle from the viewpoint of a philosophy of the subject. I feel comfortable about doing this, despite his harsh rejection of existentialism, since the guidelines of *Tristes Tropiques* as well as those of the two volumes of *Structural Anthropology* and the ethical presuppositions of the "Mythologiques" indicate explicit links between Lévi-Strauss' own subjectivity and the imperative necessity of postulating, against the Cartesian cogito, an I as an other. In any case, it is noteworthy that the urge to explain the other in the experiential dimension if being forced Merleau-Ponty, years before Lévi-Strauss, to question the dialectic of the ego and the alter and to conclude that this dialectic is possible only in the case of a philosophy culminating in a return to the self. What this implies is a clear critique of the cogito that Merleau-Ponty formulated in his *Phenomenology of Perception* (1962), in which one finds statements such as: "The Cogito must reveal me in a situation and it is on this condition alone that transcendental subjectivity can, as Husserl puts it, be an intersubjectivity"; or "The Cogito depreciated the perception of others, teaching me as it did that the I is accessible only to itself, since it defined me as the thought which I have of myself, and which clearly I am alone in having, at least in this ultimate sense."

There is without doubt not only pertinence in Lévi-Strauss' rediscovery and promotion of Rousseau's paradigm but also validity in its explication as a founding rule for discourses on others. At the same time, the very choice of such a philosophical norm, which means a wrenching away from the cogito—"C'est bien la fin du Cogito que Rousseau proclame ainsi, en avançant cette solution audacieuse" (Lévi-Strauss 1976:38)—presupposes in a manifest way a prereflective choice of the for-itself in the most specific Sartrean sense. On the whole, this choice actualizes itself as reflection which, to use another of Merleau-Ponty's magnificent expressions, "steps back to watch the forms of transcendence fly up like sparks from a fire" (1962). In this feast, both Sartre and Lévi-Strauss bear witness to the grandeur of the I thinking about itself vis-à-vis the other. And it is from the least phenomenological of existentialists, who happens to be also the most tolerant of existentialists, Simone de Beauvoir, that I draw the frame within which Sartre and Lévi-Strauss can fit with their irreconcilable differences and their complementary ambiguities concerning Descartes' cogito. In *The Ethics of Ambiguity* (1980), de Beauvoir demonstrates that one's being should be grounded within freedom of choice as the means of constructing one's own existence vis-à-vis the other who is always a mirror of one's significance. Her perspective seems close to Sartre's. But there is a major difference, for de Beauvoir emphasizes liberty as that which is objectified by the other, rather than the complex and contradictory self-perception of the for-itself. At this level, Sartre meets Lévi-Strauss, and they can, at least, share without tension the continuation of the verses from *De natura rerum* that Lévi-Strauss placed as an epigraph to *Tristes Tropiques:* "Sic alid ex alio numquam desistet oriri, critaque mancipio nulli datur, omnibus usu."

What does this have to do with Africa? All and nothing. Or, to refer to my *Invention of Africa* (1988), it relates to the fact that *poiesis* is, generally, *mimesis;* and, specifically, to the very tension between the I and the other, the same and its negation, which belongs to metaphysics. In fact, in this book, one can read my own passion and doubts about such concepts as identity, sameness, and otherness, since, fundamentally, I am illustrating a paradoxical statement of Sartre's in *Being and Nothingness:* "I am what I am not, and I am not what I am." In doing so, I distance myself from essentialist positions that still dominate African studies. The concepts are there as a means of bringing together what I have learned from Claude Lévi-Strauss, Jean-Paul Sartre, and Vincent Mulago. The latter is a specialist of African religions and was the only African professor I had at the university level. I took one of his courses, because I thought I could make it through without working much. He proved me wrong, and at the same time, thanks to him, I began to look at African cultures with a new interest, long before my intellectual crisis in the aftermath of May 1968 in Paris.

The title of this book means what it spells out. The concepts of parable and fable should be understood in their very ordinary meanings. My own text might be only a fable or a parable about other fables. In effect, a fable is a fictitious story that claims to teach a lesson, and a parable is also a story that pretends to illustrate a normative lesson. Cannot we reduce interpretations in any culture to these two simple basic lines?

Chapter 1 of this book introduces the problematic of religious "revelation" as political performance and situates it within the African colonial context. Chapter 2 clarifies the issue by analyzing the background from which the concept of African philosophy has been conceived and how, from the beginning, it was linked to that of African theology as envisioned by Catholic missionaries in Central Africa. Chapter 3 reviews some of the mythical founding events that led parabolically to the concept of an African philosophy and theology. The two following chapters continue this exploration, elaborating and commenting on a particular and well-documented experience, the Luba's, as offered by marginal ethnographical descriptions. These are questionable, insofar as, explicitly or silently, they situate themselves in the dynamics of a cultural conversion. In Chapter 6, I converse with a Marxist anthropologist, Peter Rigby, in order to interrogate an alternative. A coda concludes the book.

It should be obvious by now that the project of this book is a subjective one and is profoundly marked by my own intellectual autobiography. As Jan Vansina put it, I deal more in probables and with what a particular person reads in them than with certainties. In doing so, I have been following old and respectable guidelines provided by Descartes: namely to be as firm and resolute in my actions as I am able, and not to adhere less steadfastly to the most doubtful opinions, when once adopted, than if they had been highly certain. Indeed, such a position does not mean that I would deliberately deny or falsify facts. In actuality, the sense of this Cartesian maxim forced me to check all details as carefully as I could. On the other hand, I am quite aware that the interpretations I am offering constitute a mingling of discursive practices. I do not apologize for this. In effect, to refer again to Descartes, the best metaphor to use would be his description of a traveler lost in a forest who chooses the probable way out because there is no other certainty that could direct him.

Parts of some chapters, including this preface, were published elsewhere. I have, however, in most instances revised them. The bibliography indicates the books I have consulted in my explorations and includes the works cited. When the titles are in a language other than English (French, German, or whatever), the English quotations from the works included in the text are my translation and responsibility.

This project would have been very difficult without Luc de Heusch's work and even more so without his friendship. Thanks to him, I patiently learned how to reread anthropological texts and to make sense of Claude Lévi-Strauss' masterful enterprise. The late Michel de Certeau also aided and encouraged me in this project. In 1984, during the Twentieth Century French Studies Conference that took place in Ann Arbor, we worked together for the last time. We debated the influence of fables and parables on human existence. Finally, I would like to note my indebtedness to Willy Bal. Thirty years ago, he taught me how to read a text with a philologist's eye, and later on, at Louvain, he patiently introduced me to the art of reading as a demanding undertaking.

I am also grateful to all those who helped me to shape this book. The critiques of Bogumil Jewsiewicki, John Middleton, Allen Roberts, and Jan Vansina allowed me to better it. Ivan Karp's encouragement stimulated me. Arnd Bohm, Gaurav Desai, Elizabeth Eames, David Newbury, Peter Rigby, and Faith Smith read sections of the manuscript. I thank them for their valuable criticism. None of them is responsible, however, for the ideas advanced.

Finally, special thanks are due to Mary Moessinger, my research assistant, for her forbearance and efficiency; to Angela G. Ray, for superlative copyediting; and to Barbara Hanrahan, my editor, for her patience. I am grateful, too, to Rita Henshaw, who typed several drafts of the manuscript, and to the Duke Romance Studies for its support.

Parables and Fables

1

Revelation as a Political Performance

Codes and Systems of Representations

> Non solum quod unus Deus est sed etiam quod Trinitas est, naturaliter
> verum est; propterea ipse verus Deus in personis Trinitas est, et in una
> natura unus est.
>
> Ex libro S. Fulgentius, *de Fide ad Petrum*

The question of the relationship between God and human beings in African
experience presents itself as a contradictory and paradoxical sign. Nothing
about it seems obvious, definitive, or clearly founded, and the very concept
of God is not transparent. Various manifestations of this concept in the
anthropological and the theological literature of the last eighty years indicate a deep conceptual disorder. One looks in vain for a unifying sense.
The fertility of scholars' imaginations as well as the complexity of cultural
data make every decision of interpretation a doubt-laden choice between
opposed and controversial hypotheses: a Deus Africanus (African God) or
Dei Africanorum (Africans' gods) as a mirror or as a negation of a Deus
Christianorum (Christians' God).

Methodologically, the main problem for an analysis of these issues lies
in the plurality of discourses which sustain, express, repress, or avoid
them. In order to specify the body of discourses to which I am referring,
let me say that using Michel Foucault's suggestion (1982:41), they are
defined by three systems which map their existence and strictly account for
their characters, registers, and orientations.

The first is the *surface of the emergence*. In the West, at the beginning
of this century, the nineteenth-century ideological space of rationalization
of otherness strongly confirmed itself as both a model of cultural orthodoxy
and a sign of normativity. The modalities of this autodefinition spring from
a method of positing the *demonstrandum* as being, in essence, what it is

3

not, that is, that very difference which it should conquer, reduce, or domesticate. West is not East; North is North and cannot be South. Three major types of discourse contributed to limiting and solidifying this space. First, the exteriority of certain speculations on civilizations could not but bear witness to "pre-logism" and "savagery" (e.g., Evans-Pritchard 1980:78–99). Second, political manifestos and exegeses based a presumed European nobility on descent from the superior race of Aryans rather than the Gaulois or other Latins (Boulainvilliers' and Montlosier's theses). Such theories of the inequality of races (e.g., that of Gobineau), in which class-thinking theories meet class- and race-thinking propositions (see Arendt 1968), explicate both the "aristocracy" of European nations and the "barbarism" of all non-Western societies. Finally, the Christian theses comment upon God's integration in Western historicity and his divine plan for the salvation of the world. Culture-bound methods generate explanations for why God's chosen ones are no longer Israel's descendants but rather Western Christians, whose history and reason have become both the paramount signs of an eternal providence as well as the universal conditions for salvation (e.g., Bowman 1958:5).

Next, the *authorities of delimitation* incarnate three overlapping powers: the colonial state, science, and Christianity. They ground three principal arenas of conversion: the colonial commissioner's transmutation of "savage spaces" into "civilized settings"; the anthropologist's codifying of humans, institutions, and beliefs by their particularity vis-à-vis a functional model; and the Christian missionary's self-sacrifice among "primitives" in the struggle between the "true light" and local tradition. In the action of these three powers, one could analyze rules for the transformation of physical and human spaces and notice in these procedures the pathologization of Africans, as I tried to show in my book *The Invention of Africa* (1988). In any case, these powers decided the adequacy or inadequacy of the organization of African territories and, accordingly, promoted such inventions as "natives," "tribes," and "colonial states," modeled on thematized classifications.

Finally, the *grids of specification* map the existence of discourses. Adapting to my topic what Foucault says of the psychiatric discourse (1982:42), I would note that these grids are the systems according to which "savage" beliefs are "divided, contrasted, related, regrouped, classified, derived from one another as objects" of the anthropologist's or missionary's discourse and framed in a universal system of binary oppositions which founds and accounts for the grand dichotomy between "civilized" and "primitive."

The discourses with which I am dealing belong to this colonial library created by the colonizer, the anthropologist, and the missionary. These discourses are circumscribed and determined by the three systems of power and knowledge I have just presented: the nineteenth-century Western surface of emergence of discourses on a Deus Africanus; the authorities of delimitation that situate themselves in the frame of historical, scientific, and theological rules as concrete events; and finally, the grids of specification which differentiate types of methods, validity of discourses, and techniques of describing and converting cultures. Thus, we have, first, a religious methodology whose validity is founded on a philosophical postulation: the existence of a canon which unites in the Christian interpretation Judaic revelation, Greek rationality, and Western historicity (Eboussi-Boulaga 1981). Second, we follow anthropology and ethnology as sciences with epistemological roots (Hodgen 1971) in Montaigne's sixteenth-century form of curiosity about "savages," but they have only been thematized as disciplines since the nineteenth century. They were established analogically to the natural sciences, particularly with regard to the principles of evolution and biological inequalities of species and beings. Finally, there is the political methodology or colonial science in the strict sense. It is a global, totalizing science, neatly encapsulated by the reality—and unintended irony—of a Colonial University which, in fact, functioned for years in Antwerp, Belgium. The vivifying effects of this science on more specialized practices that are its auxiliaries indirectly (anthropology, theology, etc.) or directly (applied anthropology, missiology, etc.) come from a fabulous thesis: Western history is the only space of human history and of God's fulfillment and revelation.

These systems constitute, in fact, historical and sociological events. They had or have humans as subjects and objects of their practices and discourses. One can state that they actualize themselves as performances, that is, as institutional exercises regulated by specific rules of method and demanding a specialized competence. The colonial commissioner has a mission to colonize and civilize, and it is accounted for by a scientific discipline, the natural law. This right delivers knowledge and a concrete technique for programming its activity. The missionary conforms the meaning of his or her action and generosity to both the theological implications of the extension of the *Heilsgeschichte* (the history of salvation) to non-Western peoples and the procedures of missionizing.

Grid of Transformation-Conversion

Actors	Object to Act Upon	Aim
Colonial Commissioner	Savagery	Civilization
Missionary	Paganism	Christianity
Anthropologist	Otherness	Sameness (in difference)

The anthropologist's role seems more complex. Thus, for instance, it is clear that prefunctionalist scholars were mainly concerned with evolutionary schemata, with thinking through historical paths from otherness to sameness, a task applied anthropologists perceived as a political objective within the framework of colonial Africa. On the other hand, one observes that the functionalist or the structuralist simply claims to examine and interpret comparatively or not, as the case may be, the paradoxes of otherness and those of sameness.

At any rate, if what is implied by the concept of competence varies, then at least one common trait unites the performances of the three actors (the colonial commissioner, the missionary, and the anthropologist): the principle of "reenacting" the Western experience as a sign of knowledge, of human experience, and of God's revelation. To this thesis, Africans would tend, nowadays, to oppose a different sign, that offered by the notion of difference.

I am proposing here to read, in a very general way, Christian revelation as a political performance in Africa. Human actors who thought and think about God's message and incarnation proposed or are proposing what seem to this observer to be political processes. On the one hand, they assert an integration into Western culture as a means of participating in the messianic and paradigmatic extension of the message of the Deus Israel (God of Israel) to Gentiles, thus promoting sameness. On the other hand, there is, as I shall explain later on, an approach to revelation from a contextualist method which is, in this sense, an affirmation of the virtues of the other. I have chosen not to choose between the infallibility of the same and the tolerance of the other. I shall try to use my own subjectivity as a center and as a way of transcending the tension between the same and the other. Should it be necessary to defend this choice, one might think of Paul Ricoeur's proposition in *The Reality of the Historical Past:*

> I propose, more for didactic than for dialectical reasons, to place the idea of historical past under the incomparable categories that Plato, in the *Sophist,* called the "great classes." For reasons that will become more apparent as our work of thinking progresses, I have chosen the three great classes of the Same, the Other, and the Analogue. I do not claim that the idea of the past is constructed dialectically by the very interconnection of these three great classes, I merely hold that we are talking sense about the past by thinking of it, in turn, under the sign of the Same, then of the sign of the Other, and finally under that of the Analogue. (Ricoeur 1984:4–5)

Speech from Within versus Speech from Without

The surface of emergence of Western colonial responsibility explains and makes necessary colonization as a global activity for converting a non-Western space into a Western-marked area. The inscription of Western Christianity and its African incarnation grounds the power and the meaning of these systems and the explanatory effects of political actions. Thus, a missionary arrives in an African village. He or she meets the local chief, amicably negotiates a sojourn, and, in most cases, is accepted without problem. The event immediately degenerates into a pattern repeated throughout the continent. The missionary first establishes in the village a network of friends and sympathizers by recourse to generous initiatives and gifts. Second, he or she makes familiar his or her presence by associating it directly with the efficiency of a serving power. The mission, from its beginning, offers its meaning as a vocation of service and promotes schooling and caritative institutions such as dispensaries and hospitals. Third, the missionary inflates the spiritual and political sacredness of his or her own enterprise: the beard of the Catholic priest is identified with wisdom, the white cassock and celibate life of priests and nuns symbolize purity of heart, and missionary activity in general is conflated with God's will and politics.

It is, however, by means of more specific symbols and concepts that this political performance achieves its aims: the integration of regional liberties and customs (labeled in advance as negative) into the positivity of Christianity's universals. The most dramatic actualization of this dimension is in the building of a Catholic church as soon as possible and, daily, at dawn, the performance of the Mass. These are two constant affirmations of a miracle, in fact the unimaginable one, the *miraculum miraculorum* (the miracle of miracles), from a human viewpoint, that of God's incarnation. From an analytical viewpoint, one observes that this symbolic actualization of a divine power explicitly means and is intended to bring about major spatial and spiritual alterations. The center of life and hope shifts from the *grand place* of the village or the chief's court to the church and its appendages which now correspond to an axis of modernization. All traditional socializing events, such as the assembly in the evening around a central fire or the weekly social ritual of exchanges of goods in the market, where they exist, lose their absolute pertinence. In terms of social value, they become relative to and dependent upon the socioeconomic model exemplified by the parish and its prescription about a modernized way of life. Third, traditional rites of passage, by the very fact that they take place outside the visible place colonized by a new intentionality and a dialectic whose center is the church, are bypassed and rejected as devilish.

The conjunction of the politics of missionary integration with techniques of manipulating symbols of divine power signifies a reordering of a social map. It constitutes the kernel of missionizing as a political performance. More important, it obscures the local struggle of cultures in the name of assimilating virtues of a universal Christian revelation. African Christianity grew up, strong and conquering, from this framework: it counted 149 million Christians in 1974, 203 million in 1980, and will probably represent, with Latin America, more than 50 percent of the world's Christian population in 2000 (de Meester 1980:215).

At the same time, the colonial state solemnly tried to westernize the continent. Capital installed new processes of production, extending new economic techniques and establishing transformations of social relations of production. Everything thus intermingled in a quite serious "historical drama" indicates the universalization of the Western paradigm made intelligible and familiar by the colonial library. Development equals the extension of the capitalist mode of production, while education and social norms necessarily assume the profundity of Western experience and religion means conversion to Christianity as incarnated and propounded in the colonizer's culture.

It is a paradox to note that African discourses which correct, critically reread, reinterpret, or challenge the colonial library or the missionary performance are possible and thinkable only insofar as they actualize themselves within those same intellectual fields which nowadays permit political, anthropological, or theological exchange with or refusal of earlier statements. Partial shifts of authorities since the 1950s, as well as a greater sophistication of grids of specification, account for the fact that, for example, J. S. Mbiti can, on the same epistemological ground, oppose E. B. Tylor's concept of animism, H. Spencer's ancestor worship, Durkheim's propositions on magic, and various hypotheses on totemism, fetishism, and naturism of the late nineteenth-century and early twentieth-century authorities: "African religions and philosophy have been subjected to a great deal of misinterpretation, misrepresentation and misunderstanding. They have been despised, mocked and dismissed as primitive and underdeveloped. . . . In missionary circles they have been condemned as superstitious, satanic, devilish and hellish. In spite of all these attacks, traditional religions have survived, they dominate the background of African peoples, and must be reckoned with even in the middle of modern changes" (Mbiti 1969:13).

Similarly, using G. Granai's definition of religion as a language that allows humans to insert themselves into intimate relationships with the universe, Louis-Vincent Thomas could relativize the notion of religion itself and bluntly state that all existing religions necessarily include totemism (expression of the communion existing between humans and animals and, through sexual symbols, search for a parental phylum), ancestor worship (institutional means of reproducing social order and the cornerstone of the authenticity of beliefs), naturism (natural and healthy tendency toward integration into the cosmic order), fetishism (manipulation of the sacred), and paganism (or local cult marked by peasants' understanding of religion). It follows, according to him, that "the traditional Negro-African religion results in a balanced synthesis of organized attitudes which vary according to the ways of life. These attitudes were probably constructed throughout time according to historical contingencies that are now lost and that diversely express the African soul" (Thomas, Luneau, and Doneux 1969:6).

In his *La Religion traditionnelle des Bantu et leur vision du monde* (1973), Vincent Mulago simply rejects the theses of a progressive evolution of religions (Tylor), ignores those of regression of monotheism in some cultures (R. E. Denett, A. Lang, W. Schmidt), and celebrates Bantu monotheism (Mulago 1973a:16). Quite recently, A. Shorter has gone so far as to indicate ways of overcoming prejudice and conceiving cultural pluralism within a universal Christian church (1977:130–43). A leading African theologian, Alphonse Mushete Ngindu, of the Faculté de Théologie Catholique in Kinshasa, Zaire, while commenting on Christ as cosmic action, has challenged the thesis that Christian churches are the sole loci of salvation and the sign of God's kingdom: "The church does not possess Jesus Christ nor eternal salvation. Essentially, the term salvation is synonymous with the Kingdom. That is to say, it expresses the presence of God the Savior who acts through Christ in the cosmos and throughout history, particularly within the secret of each human's desire for God" (Ngindu 1981b:98).

How could one understand the variety and apparent contradiction of these discourses on religion and God? Are we dealing with a consistent evolution of ideas about, and perceptions of, God and his signs, or simply with disparate assumptions and rhetorical artifices noted in the margins of the colonial library as commentary upon its own ironies?

Let us relate the question of these discourses to the more general one concerning African cultures and traditions, that is the larger framework in which the notion and reality of religion make sense. Paulin Hountondji proposes to distinguish two groups, or more exactly two types, of discourses describing these cultures. The first sees, describes, and speaks of African tradition from without and, thus, "inevitably leads, either to rejecting it on behalf of reason, or to systematically justifying it in all its aspects" (Hountondji 1983b:141). The history of anthropology, from Frazer to Tempels, would witness to this type. The second type—discourses from within—have so far been essentially and historically responses and challenges to the first type. Take, for example, the paradoxical reaction to reason in Aimé Cesaire's *Return to My Native Land,* or, alternatively, that cultural nationalism which tries "to show the internal rationality of one's own traditions" (Hountondji 1983b:142). When looked at closely, this distinction means two things. First, the usefulness of separating the authorities of delimitation by their cultural and geographical origin: are they from without or from within? Second, Hountondji implies a genealogical link between the first type and the second. The latter is a response to the preceding discourse: it either values "insanity above reason, by conceiving the former as the real source of all creativity and spiritual fruitfulness and the latter as equivalent to conformism" (Hountondji 1983b:141) or, in its celebration of otherness and distance, searches for its identity in any positive statements elaborated by discourses from without.

What we get is a surface reuniting contradictory, yet related, codes, that is, specialized systems of manipulating knowledge, expressing it and communicating it. All of them, in the name of the power of knowledge or the truth of strategic choices, claim to formulate the deployment of traditions in their specificity. These codes are pure abstractions, since the real discourses which actualize them only reveal the contingency of the general theoretical systems or frames regulating the practice of interpretation, rules of enunciation, and possibilities of elaborating valid models. It is thus acceptable to consider the intrinsic mutations and transformations of languages on otherness and traditions as both history and metahistory, as dialectic. They simultaneously constitute the foundation of codes affirming, reviewing, correcting, or reinterpreting their raison d'être and contribute to the establishment of theoretical performances and concrete modalities for using individualized discourses in accordance with specific norms. Hence, for example, Max Müller formulated his circular thesis on primitive religion as religious instinct and the latter as sign of the first, Spencer considered ghosts, Tylor described animism, J. Frazer and Durkheim commented on the centrality of magic. On the other side, A. Lang criticized the ghost theory, Marret reasoned on "savage religion" as "something not so much thought as danced out," and Lévy-Bruhl invented prelogism (see Evans-Pritchard 1980). They cannot be dissociated from a well-defined code about what civilization is and what anthropology should be or from the cultural *a priori* on which they rest. Yet they witness to the foundation and organization of a scientific model of discourse on otherness in the same way as the succeeding theories will do, but from the perspective of a different code. Tempels' *Bantu Philosophy* (1959) achieves and negates Lévy-Bruhl. Books on African religions by H. Deschamps (1954), D. Nothomb (1965), or E. G. Parrinder (e.g., 1961, 1970), and others install new approaches to the same object. These are not, fundamentally, different from discourses coming from within, such as J. B. Danquah's study *The Akan Doctrine of God* (1968), J. S. Mbiti's *New Testament Eschatology in an African Background* (1971), or O. Bimwenyi's *Discours théologique négro-africain* (1980).

I would say that, first, the nineteenth-century *a priori* assumption about primitive images as contemporary and as symbols of Western prehistorical experiences is challenged. Second, a new and somehow relativistic *a priori* provides the scholars, be they Westerners or Africans, a new frame for the understanding of the paradigm: Western culture is different from non-Western culture, and vice versa. Let us note that "this *a priori* is what, in a given period, delimits in the totality of experience a field of knowledge, defines the mode of being of the objects that appear in that field, provides man's everyday perception with theoretical powers, and defines the condition in which he can sustain a discourse about things that is recognized to be true" (Foucault 1982:158).

This being so, some may argue that the epistemological continuity of discourses seems here more important, in any case more pertinent, than any opposition between discourses from within and those from without. In the nineteenth century and at the beginning of the twentieth, it was obvious in terms of the historical *a priori* that African expressions of God did not and could not really fit into the Judeo-Christian model of God. They were part of a language (*langue*) whose arbitrariness seemed absurd and, consequently, pagan in both meanings of the word *paganus:* as marginal, someone living on the edges of "civilization" and cut off from the culture of cities; and as someone whose beliefs, opinions, and behavior are unsound from the viewpoint of the dominant language. On the other hand, by the 1940s, a new *a priori* detached itself from the very experience of the normative language, and it became accepted that all languages, all civilizations, are arbitrary *a priori* (see Braudel 1980:177–217), and meaningful orders only *a posteriori*. The counterpart of this was, among other things, the recognition of a possible respectability of a Deus Africanus or, if one wishes, Deus Africanorum (see, e.g., Parrinder 1970; Mulago 1973a; Shorter 1977).

It is now possible to theorize upon the pragmatics of these recent readings. They can be classified according to two main orientations. Cultural anthropology tends to focus on empirical facts and to render an image of African divinities, their names, features, properties, attributes, and functions, as signifiers of a particular, localized, and self-sufficient religious revelation (e.g., Danquah 1968). Conversely, theologically oriented renderings, although sustained in socioanthropological contexts, promote linkages between African beliefs and Judeo-Christian revelation on the postulation of the universality of revelation and subsequently present characters and structures of regional experiences of God as *praeparationes evangelicae,* that is, as stepping-stones wanting a providential fulfillment (Mulago 1965a; Mbiti 1971; Nothomb 1965).

The two orientations bring about two different representations of the Deus Africanus. Strictly speaking, in anthropological interpretations, God is often a Completus Deus (complete God) within a language and a regional culture (Forde 1976; Abraham 1962:51–69). He is, despite the multiplicity of his signs, a well-perceived signifier whose signified witnesses to its own meaning, truth, and existence within the language and culture. At the other extreme, the African theologians' God is, at best, a symbol coming from pluralist and dominant representations of a concept of God (Mbiti 1970; Mulago 1973a; Bimwenyi 1981). As a consequence, God's local signs become simply symptoms that can contribute to the construction of a universal model which pretends to account for the classical statement *Anima naturaliter christiana est* (The soul is naturally Christian). In this realm of metaphysical allusions God's African presence seems to unveil itself as imperfect, as reducible to the completeness of a Deus Christianorum. To put it in a different way, the Africans' "wise ignorance" of the real and true revelation unveils a Deus Incompletus (incomplete God), whose finality consists in his necessary metamorphosis into the Judeo-Christian God.

A particularly good example is given by the God of the Central African Mongo. His names are numerous and vary from village to village (Hulstaert 1961). They all, ultimately, suggest attributes of a concept of God which, according to G. Hulstaert, a long-standing specialist on Mongo culture, is purer than the Old Testament's images of God: "He remarkably transcends the anthropomorphic images of the Old Testament" (Hulstaert 1980:80). I do know, indeed, that some scholars have accused Hulstaert of inventing the Mongo. The fact does not perturb me. In effect, all anthropologists, as well as historians, invent the object of their discourse (see Veyne 1984; Wagner 1981). On the other hand, the Mongo exist in reality. I have met some of them who question a number of Hulstaert's interpretations. In any case, my discussion here is not about the tension between a cultural reality and its scientific transcription, but rather about the method of translating correctly from one cultural experience into another the human "incarnation of God." This God of Mongo combines all virtues of a Deus Praesens et Remotus (present and remote God) and draws together the order of his divine majesty and that of the universe. Creator, source of life, he is the Sovereign, the Lord, the Providence, the Legislator, and the Master of Life and Death. Everyday happenings and accidents witness to his power and presence and dramatically suggest his concern, impulse, or action. By definition, he is the Invisible, a pure spirit who cannot be imagined as having some kind of material body. He is Elímà, Bongóli, Bokáli. Metaphorically, he is also known as Mother of Spirits (Nyang'e a Bilímá), and more frequently, he is referred to as the Invisible Shrubby Tree (Njakomb' éy itámbá el', a ngonda efen' anto). Strictly speaking, he is the Absolute and, as such, does not need sacrifice. According to Hulstaert, Mongo emphasize the mediation of inferior gods or guardian spirits between this supreme divine Majesty and the human.

For Hulstaert, however, the Mongo's God cannot be identified with the incarnated Word of a resurrected and reviving Christ. Indeed, the polysemy of some of his names diffuses his very reality and being into both nature and culture indistinctively, and one would tend to think of Evans-Pritchard's "fractions of divinity." Mongo, according to Hulstaert, call the praying mantis Njakomba (God). Among the neighboring Ekonda, attributes of God (Wai, or Wabi) can also designate a fortunate person. For the southern Mbole and the Booli of Salonga, Nyonyi (God) also signifies death, and the Kutu use this word to mean sickness. For Christian scholars such as Gravrand, Mbiti, or Mulago, it follows that, at best, the Mongo's concept of God witnesses to a Deus Absconditus (hidden God) who should be completed in Jesus' revelation.

With adaptation theology, such authors as John Mbiti (1971), Vincent Mulago (1965a), or Dominique Nothomb (1965) take this as their main thesis. Its method suggests a policy of "retrodiction," by which I mean to indicate that it is the opposite of prediction. It establishes an analogical parallel between the missionary performance under colonial rule and the future of Christianity under African initiative. It insists on the necessity of looking into traditional systems of beliefs for unanimous signs or harmonies which might be incorporated into Christianity in order to Africanize it without fundamentally modifying it. Politically, the method accepts the universality of a Deus Christianorum yet questions the results, both statistical and psychological, of missionary performance. In fact, given the spirit and global strength of this adaptation theology, the missionary enterprise could and should have been more successful had its aim been to raise the African Deus Absconditus to his fulfillment into the Deus Christianorum.

Here resides one of the major problems of present-day African cultures. The notion of tradition which has replaced the concept of primitiveness still identifies itself as marginal (see, e.g., contributions in Fashole-Luke 1978). The problems of tradition may indeed be critically discussed (see, e.g., Eboussi-Boulaga 1977), yet they tend to be perceived once and for all in the ambiguity of a signified which valorizes both spatial and epistemological remoteness. African tradition—and thus the Deus Africanus—is dated before, or at least situated outside of, the historical experience in which God became Word. We can see, then, why nationalistic objectives of indigenizing the Gospels and contextualizing Christianity in Africa are still part of a Western *a priori* and, at the same time, how these enterprises of fusing the Deus Christianorum and the Deus Africanorum, or, more precisely, of mirroring the latter in the former, remain more a problem than a solution. Hountondji is probably quite right when he states: "I term this particular attitude, theoretical extraversion. In my opinion, though the issue of self-identification is justified in its own way, it should nevertheless be, first, disconnected from this extraverted, outside-oriented problematic and reformulated in the framework of a dialogue internal to our own societies, and secondly, "relativised" so as not to exclude or leave out other kinds of problems which may also be of great importance, direct or indirect, to our people" (Hountondji 1983b:142).

When one analyzes carefully the historical transformations of paradigms, it becomes even clearer that the distinction between speech from without and speech from within constitutes a problem. Most of the thinkers of foreign origin (like Tempels, Nothomb, etc.) who took part in the political process of transforming these theoretical paradigms were or are, in fact, Africans at heart and often by choice. Thus, the geographical distinction of speeches seems problematic. When one considers that Kagame is Tempels' disciple and that Mbiti and Bimwenyi represent a dialectical effort of going beyond Tempels' discourse, the distinction becomes wholly questionable. It would be more pertinent, then, to look at the progressive change of discourses from the 1940s to the 1960s as a political generalization of the sign of the other. The modalities of conversion, commentary and interpretation of cultural symbols, as well as God's presence, could then be thought of through a new canon, the sociocultural context from which the witnesses speak. In 1973, Vincent Mulago echoed Tempels' 1945 invitation to profoundly indigenize Christianity as a condition of evangelization: "The Church follows the law of incarnation: she originates in the peoples' cultural experience and traditions, by purifying and saving them. So we should not fear that in remaining faithful to the Church, our authenticity, our rights and obligations in the heart of the Father, could be wronged'' (Mulago 1973:154).

The Decentering of God's Signs

> Haec dicit Dominus Deus Israel: Ego eduxit Israel de Aegypto et erui vos de manu Aegyptiorum et de manu omnium regum, qui affligebant vos.
>
> Infra hebdomadam III post Pent. *Breviarum Romanum*

It has been said and written that through the conversion of Africans, Christian churches intended to ensure their salvation. Others have argued that this is nonsense and that the churches, because of their historical and cultural *a priori,* were nothing more than expressions of the politics of subordination during the colonial period. We have in the 1950s an emphasis on promoting Christianity on the basis of local contexts (see, e.g., Taylor 1963; and mainly Hastings 1979:5–34). This gave birth to theologies of alterity whose main currents were, first, the adaptation approach with its search for African cultural elements that could be considered as *praeparationes evangelicae* (local preparations for the Gospels) and then, in the late 1970s, the incarnation approach, which attempts a translation of African religious experiences into a language that could adequately express Christianity. There exist two projects in these approaches: the critique of traditional policies of evangelization along with their theology of salvation; and the establishment of a regional capacity for adapting the Deus Christianorum to, or integrating this God into, a new cultural order (see Hastings 1979).

Two examples of religious performance will indicate the differences between the two types of theologies: the famous Missa Luba could serve as an illustration of adaptation theology, while the new liturgy of taking solemn vows in a feminine religious order is an example of the ongoing search for incarnating Christianity.

The Missa Luba by "Les Troubadours du Roi Baudoin" (directed by Father Guido Haazen) is a sound musical composition whose structure assumes two radically different, yet harmoniously interacting, lines. The Luba-Katanga rhythmic in its responsorial mode and sensitivity parallels the Latin text. The rhythm is here a pictorial event. It has been partially reorganized and stylized in such a way that it strongly recalls the supposed exoticism of a "tribal setting" and, at the same time, has been arranged to fit the seriousness of the Lord's epiphany. In fact, the musical line vividly calls upon senses, and it is up to the Greek (Kyrie) and Latin (Gloria, Credo, Sanctus, and Agnus Dei) to keep alive the spirit of the Christian tradition and the testimony of the sacrament. In brief, regional musical features and patterns have been summoned in order to serve as decoration for the Roman rite of the Mass.

Of the same order and project would be some earlier compositions, particularly the hymns of Father Stephano Kaoze. In the late 1950s, the most renowned musician working in this sense was Joseph Kiwele. A former seminarian, he was for years a teacher at the Catholic School of the Parish Saint Jean in Elisabethville. With independence in 1960, he became the first minister of education in Moise Tshombe's provincial government in Katanga. The normative conception in Kiwele's compositions is fundamentally similar to that of Father Haazen. It substantially aetheticizes traditional rhythm, or, to put it more exactly, traditional inspirations. Studs Terkel, who wrote the presentation of the Missa Luba version that circulates in English-speaking countries, notes that "in listening to this Missa Luba, I am reminded of another performance: a Harlem congregation singing out, 'Joy to the World.' It was the only time I had heard this buoyant carol sung as it was meant to be sung—with joy." In this case, as well as in Father Kaoze's or Maître Kiwele's, the composition and, indeed, its performance become intelligible and fit the mystery of a Christian celebration, insofar as they have been domesticated by a determining something else, yet keep an air of an exotic and moving strangeness.

A different type of deployment is given by evocative experiments of incarnating Christian symbols. The order of Sisters of St. Theresa in Kinshasa uses a highly original and controverted ceremony for taking religious vows. It takes place during a special liturgy of Mass, and its central moment duplicates one of the most constraining of African symbols, the pact of blood, which means friendship and fidelity to death (see, e.g., Tegnaeus 1954). The formula consists of three complementary steps. The priest first makes an incision on one of the candidate's fingers. Then the blood is spread on a white tissue, which remains on the altar throughout the ceremony. Finally, all the sisters participating at the moment of communion (may) share "the Blood of Christ" from the chalice used by the priest.

A Catholic theologian nun has recently reexamined this formula and proposed a series of variations which, according to her, should more effectively symbolize the constraints of belonging to God and the state of a born-again person (Bwanga 1981). One of the formulas consists of four moments, all of which take place in a church during a special liturgy presided over by a priest: the priest performs the incision; the blood of the candidate to the perpetual vow is put in the chalice; this blood is mixed with the wine, which, during the consecration, will become the Blood of Christ, and remains on the altar, a vivid sign of the public pact; and all the candidates during the sacrament of communion can share the contents of the chalice. There is also a five-moment variant of this formula: the priest performs the incision; the blood is put into the chalice (or simply spread on a tissue); participants share Christ's Blood, that is, the consecrated wine; the blood is given to a member of the candidate's family, who publicly drinks it and thus recognizes, as witness, the decisive and eternal pact between Christ and the candidate; and the new religious community of the candidate and her family exchange gifts.

The Missa Luba and these special rites for taking vows exemplify two starkly different politics of conceiving an African presence in Christianity. In the first case, the emphasis is on maintaining the essential symbolic lines of the Western vision and Christian tradition. Referring to the conditions of possibility of this political performance and, more particularly, to its grids of specification, one might say that the praxis of adaptation, of which the Missa Luba is just an illustration, intended to rectify the forms without transforming the axial line of traditional Christian symbols. It was a program for adapting to a new climate what was considered to be the Christian universality without regionalizing its representational meanings: the Credo, the Roman rite, and the canon of symbols. On the other hand, the incarnation program tests a searching out of the very nature of regional symbolisms and experiments with mediations for reconciling Christianity and local cultures. This search is potentially a questioning of the Christian message itself and an interrogation of its basic symbols (Bimwenyi 1981). The symbolic narrative of the pact of blood, for example, tells of the individual's absolute possession by God, if necessary *ad damnationem*. It is, therefore, slightly different from the individual's privileged commitment to God *ad aeternitatem* according to the traditional Roman ritual.

The incarnation policies have led to a fabulous inventiveness in arts. I shall signal here just one example, that of the chant of Benedictine monks of Keur Moussa in Senegal. The fusion of cultures is here remarkable. Indeed, one can hear balafons, koras, and tom-toms accompanying the chant, yet the instruments have no longer an exotic significance. They figure a project, a correspondence with highly educated human voices for the celebration of the canonical hours. The chant is sometimes in Wolof. During Advent and Christmas time, one can enjoy listening, for example, to "Wis ma ndoh" ("Sprinkle Me with Water"), sung with two tom-toms; "Dyebal na la," with two koras; or "Ndav su gnul," a hymn to the Virgin

Mary, sung with two tom-toms. Aesthetic and religious levels that, some years ago, opposed each other by duplicating the tension existing between Christianity and African cultures seem to fuse. And a new creativity represents in musical narratives a mode of expression to which we were not accustomed. As in the case of Plato's mixed narratives, the most common, and thus dominant modes begin to reflect what was uncommon. They have registered each other and produced a genre of musical expression that we, by remaining in the tradition of the Gregorian chant, can already compare, say, to that of Clervaux, Solesmes, St. Wandrille de Fontenelle, or Montserrat, or to the Magyar Gregorianum.

The methods of adaptation and incarnation indicate modalities of indigenizing Christianity. As intellectual or pragmatic exercises, they properly belong to mainstream Christian churches and somehow reveal processes of rationalizing concrete advocacies of otherness implemented by Christian sects and nativistic movements since the 1920s. By the expression *Christian sect,* one should understand "Jesus Christ plus something else, especially adult baptism or the Sabbath." Nevertheless, "while most of the Christian sects are literalistic and fundamentalistic in their interpretation of scripture, the nativistic movements again are also fundamentalistic, i.e., they wish to restore aspects of the traditional African religion" (Sundkler 1976:306). Today all these orientations are generally unified under the term *independent churches.*

We should thus distinguish the spirit and philosophy of mainstream churches (Anglican, Catholic, Methodist, etc.), characterized by the liberal legacy of the West, their norms of religious orthodoxy, and an international constitution, from those of independent churches (sects and nativistic movements) founded by local prophets protesting or opposing the power, the teachings, or the religious rules of mainstream Christianity. Analyzed in sociopolitical terms, this distinction implies the existence of two ideological systems. We have the mainstream bourgeois churches which assume an experience of acculturation and, on the other side, independent, popular, small communities following charismatic prophets who proclaim holy utopias. This distinction, however, does not mean a division of the African society into two parts with, at one side, a Western-educated class belonging to internationally respectable churches and, at the other, masses of peasants and working-class people believing in local prophets' inspiration and projects. Yet a careful analysis shows that, up to the 1960s, at least in Central Africa, the so-called city bourgeoisie was generally—at least, officially—in mainstream Christianity, which was, for most of its members, the religious counterpart of the profane processes of westernization. While some founders of independent churches are intellectuals who could have succeeded elsewhere (e.g., Simon Kimbangu), one observes that most of the members were generally and until the 1970s blue-collar workers and peasants. This line of separation can thus be used as a methodological tool indicating the degree of deference to, and access into, the space of power organized under colonial rule.

It should be evident that if, in the 1950s, the mainstream churches signified privileges of sociopolitical power and orthodox knowledge and, hence, could circumscribe social respectability as well as both political and intellectual leadership, then a decade later things had changed in a radical way. The political structure that, in the 1960s, replaced the colonial relation (ruler versus subject) completely blurred the distinction between motivations based on sociopolitical power or religious orthodoxy. Subsequently, the hierarchy of Christian churches was altered. By that time, elite status was equated with a nationalism which set out to challenge the colonial heritage, its values and ideals. It is this shift which, metaphorically, is represented in the passage from adaptation theology to incarnation theology. It expresses new strategic motivations for, and modalities of, power and values, as related to political and cultural responsibility.

The geographical space of power was thus reorganized. New normative themes imposed themselves upon consciousness, and the *mot d'ordre* of contextual authenticity, coming out of postexistentialist theological hypotheses, replaced the concepts of westernization and adaptation theology (see Eboussi-Boulaga 1977). They drove the mainstream churches to indicate new methodologies of conversion which, by and large, were similar to the signs that independent churches had been servicing since the 1920s. The most important paradigms concern God's revelation as a universal phenomenon, the necessity of a break with the self-interest within Christianity's mission, and, finally, the formulation of an eschatological order in which representation of salvation would be based on signs and symbols existing within local cultures. Thus, the African prophet's consciousness became a significant event witnessing to God's mysterious plans (Eboussi-Boulaga 1981). Indeed, African traditional wisdom appeared to equal, at least in valence, some Western horizons. And A. Shorter, among others, could state: "No single culture has a monopoly of God, just as no single culture has a monopoly of human experience" (Shorter 1977:132).

Even the most orthodox theories and opinions at times confront this ambiguous reversal of the Western historical *a priori* and search for a pertinent illumination of Jesus as fulfillment of African traditional religions en bloc (Bimwenyi 1981). This is a major problem. Above all, interpretations of what is happening explicate the emergence of a new *a priori* concerned with the significance of a new political challenge: "The majority of current articles and books insist on the necessity of building a Church fully African with its own characteristics. The rule is Africanization, and as it emanates from the highest authorities: sociologists, theologians, bishops and popes, it would be superfluous to debate the legitimacy and urgency of Africanizing the Church'' (de Meester 1980:14–15).

On the visible surface of this new promotion, events as well as speeches, endeavors as well as texts, depend, now, on a new legitimation. It spells out that all humans are determined by three objective and complementary facts, always already given and in any case determining: time, space, and the (un)consciousness of the subject. Experiences as well as beliefs should, then, be understood from their locus of emergence, that is, at the junction of these three factors which, taken together synchronically, can, *a posteriori,* define the individuality of a person, an ethnic community, or a culture.

Revelation, according to this contextualist presupposition, traces itself within a human context and the memory of both its epistemological and sociohistorical fields. As Michel de Certeau once put it: ''No one speaks from nowhere'' (1969:224). In a more concrete manner, I would say, to use a powerful image, comments and interpretations on the central Christian theme of *Et verbum caro factum est et habitavit in nobis* (And the Verb became flesh and did inhabit among us) are now referred to, and understood from, the specific cultural context which is the condition of Christ's possible incarnation and the figures of both its symbolic and theological meanings. The procedures of God's revelation are part of, and strictly derive from, human events which, since the beginning of the world, have differently marked and constituted social environments and nowadays still define the processes of being human, living in a given community, and believing in God. The human context, therefore, is always both a providential text and a sign of God's presence. It speaks about the human condition and unveils a regional history of God's strategies. God is thus part of human contexts, of various languages. They are what, diversely, find God, make God thinkable, and establish salvation as promise of a necessary fulfillment: ''It is through its culture that a people does dim itself or is reborn throughout the ages, and finally, it is through its own culture, which is to say on the level of its interpretation of the universe, that one faces the problem of development and salvation'' (Ngindu 1981a:96).

The concepts of Deus Africanorum as well as those of Deus Israel or Deus Christianorum root themselves at the beginning of all beginnings in regional traditions. It is, I suppose, obvious that I am referring to regional actualizations of an *Ens Causa Sua* (a being who is the cause of its being), an absolute source and significance. Hence the notion of God does not seem to make sense any longer out of the particular history of an environment and the human culture which produces it and then colonizes it. In the case of Africa, this dynamic process would have been questioned by the intrusion of Christian missionaries who brought Jesus' message with its cultural genealogy. The metaphor unanimously accepted today, despite the fact that its economy rearranges Jesus' duplication of regional orders, is that Jesus signifies the fulfillment of all existing regional revelations (see, e.g., Bimwenyi 1981).

The anthropological foundation of this reading is spelled out in the effort to understand oneself as human subject facing God's presence and acting upon it. That implies an explicit claim of one's identity and a critical reading and perception of differences vis-à-vis the order of the same (Buakasa 1981:196). First, it means an integration into a living cosmology and anthropology, constituting an existential experience and offering a conceptual schema in which fundamental human invariants recount themselves in the richness of local variants. Second, the biblical testimony is apprehended as both a tool and a social function for the totalization of a regional human fate (Ngindu 1981a:66; Bujo 1981:24–26). It is in the truth of this process that the new Christian subject claims to affirm his or her being and existence as culturally and geographically determined stepping-stones in a dynamic interaction with God's activity. God always precedes his messengers. As a Zairean theologian writes: "I thought that I was going to meet pagans, the *"bena diablo,"* that is, Satan's subjects, members of Demons' clan, as people say in Kasai. It is exactly the contrary: I find saints, at least those saints St. Peter talks about in Acts 10.34, those who respect God and practice justice" (Bimwenyi 1981:55).

This understanding of theology as a cultural discourse commenting upon and revealing God's performance in a regional milieu is in itself neither equivocal nor scandalous. In effect, one would easily agree that a theological discourse is always "a cultural reality comparable to others. It searches for implications and sequences (of the unthinkable); it establishes order: order among the themes of life (and death) for the believer (sinning, justification, sanctification, hope for the end), order among the (meanings) of absolute events (Incarnation, Cross, Resurrection, Parousia); in short, order among a totality of experiences and a totality of events" (Ricoeur 1984:179). In its most credible aspects, the African theology of incarnation is a discourse of the analogue. It brings together God's historical signs of incarnation—"This God is incarnated somewhere and comes to us by and through history" (Bimwenyi 1981:53)—and the multiple and various traces of revelation (*multifariam multisque modis*) within African cultures: "That which God had created before genesis . . . This focus is capable of welcoming him, since the context has been previously fertilized, labored by his action as Verb, as generating Word'' (Bimwenyi 1981:54). Theology intermingles with cultural praxis. As a consequence, African myths, for example, can stand for God's secrets (Neckebrouck 1971:241).

Here are, for example, two capsules from which one can see how it becomes theologically possible to shift from an anthropological reading to an analogical interpretation.

1. The Tower and the Musicians (Luba)

   At the beginning of time, men lived in the same village as God. Tired of the noise of their quarrels, the Creator dispatched humankind to earth. There they suffered from hunger and cold, and came to know sickness and death. A diviner advised them to return to the sky to find immortality. So they began to build an enormous tower of wood, with its foundations in a *lusanga* tree. After many months of labor the builders arrived at the sky. They entered the celestial domain, beating a drum and playing a flute to make the news known to those who remained on earth. But these were too far away to hear. When He heard the noise God became angry and destroyed the tower, killing the musicians (de Heusch 1982).

2. An African *Anastasis* (Luba-Kasai)

   One day Maweja Nangila (God) decided to save his creatures from death. He decided to sacrifice his own son, his own First Born Spirit. The Son became human, was sacrificed and died. The following day, he resurrected, manifested to them as Spirit. Since then, we say that there is covenant between us and God, and we know that death shall never overcome.

Luc de Heusch (1982:54–63), has noted that the tower episode is a very well-distributed theme in Central African cultures. One finds also numerous narratives and scenarios presenting the classical motifs of genesis, original sin, universal flood, etc. throughout the Congolese savanna. The question of a possible ancient Christian influence has been often formulated. Although symbolic resurrections are not rare in Luba-Songye mythology, the Luba *anastasis* might seem to some observers as an enigma if a Christian connection were not posited. Let us remark that the strong dependence, both structural and ideological, existing between such narratives and founding myths dating from before the first contacts with Europeans in the sixteenth century complicates the hypothesis of a Christian influence. The difficulty is a major one when one keeps in mind that the Luba tradition has, so far, refused to open the doors of its religion (de Heusch 1982:34). At any rate, against the hypothesis of a Christian influence, one could, more realistically, face de Heusch, who, after Frazer, invokes the universality of the image of the tower (de Heusch 1982:34). I tend to consider the African *anastasis* as well as the motifs of universal flood and original sin to be signs of something else.

The concern with drawing regional myths to a Christian hermeneutical interpretation does not, at least in principle, imply the presupposition that the myth is Christian, nor that it has been marked by Christianity. It is in its own textual autonomy and regional sets of cultural indexes that, for Christian theologians, the Luba *anastasis* can be understood as both a metaphoric prefiguration and a local apprehension of the real *anastasis*. In the same manner, they would say that the semantic structuration of the tower story offers a plot which, in regionally specific cultural terms, makes accessible and reenacts another lesson also present in the biblical myth: the dialectic of human limitation and God's power, mortality and immortality, continuity and discontinuity.

This contextualist orientation would seem to propound a relativistic line. Yet the perspective changes completely once one accepts the hypothesis of some contemporary theologians that there is such a thing as African traditional religion. In effect, the reality of African religion can impose itself, if one uses a minimal definition and considers as religion all systems of beliefs which organize problems concerning the antinomy of life and death, the meaning about the imperfection of this world and its significance vis-à-vis the perfection of another world. Once this is accepted, another hypothesis must be examined. It has become evident, at least among practitioners of structuralism, that beyond oppositions and discriminations manipulated by religious stories and myths, there is a quality which is not observable. It strictly expresses what Lévi-Strauss termed an unconscious, that is, an aggregate of forms imposing norms and laws upon humans' mental life and as such accounting for universal invariant structures (Lévi-Strauss 1969, 1981).

By advancing these two hypotheses, my aim is to think about the contextualist line as the "beyond" of relativism. Religious myths unveil mechanisms of the human mind and, more concretely, the quality of techniques for dealing with fundamental human paradoxes. This quality directly impresses all levels of a culture on which, as Ngindu (1981b) put it, the question of salvation complements that of interpretation of the world. By propounding this or similar perspectives (e.g., Eboussi-Boulaga 1981), African theologians in mainstream churches appear willing to rank revelation as a cultural performance which witnesses simultaneously to its own regional variety and to the paradigmatic universality signified by the tradition of the Deus Christianorum. The thesis, in fact, can be equated with a more radical generalization of Gerhard von Rad's classical work on the historical traditions of Israel: significant events in all human traditions constitute a regional *kerygma* deployed in a particular *Heilsgeschichte* whose achievement resides in the coming of a Messiah. This clearly supposes faith.

By contrast with these highly intellectual interpretations, syncretic and nativistic movements allegorize revelation to signify the union of Old Testament sagas with African performances. The concept of performance is to be understood here as expressing both a theatrical dimension (conversion, baptism, inspiration, etc., as holy games) and a political one too, insofar as it tends to bring about social transformation and, in any case, implements policies of cultural rupture. "Let us not place Jesus in the hard forehead, but in the stomach, where he can lie nicely and softly, just as Jesus lay in Mary's womb. Jesus finds his resting place there. That is where the power is; that is where Jesus is. The belly is the powerstation of the body. . . . The glory and power of Jehovah is to be found in the stomach. . . . From a person filled with Jesus, power and blessing will flow" (Chiliza, in Sundkler 1976:90).

It is clear in this quotation from a popular preacher that the Deus Africanus has been subsumed in the theatricality of a field of representation which is the locus of articulation of the Deus Israel and his cultural expansions in the Deus Christianorum. In fact, we are facing a central issue that, I think, has been so far overlooked by theologians and specialists of traditional religions: God who, in Africa, according to anthropologists' studies, for centuries has been silent—a Deus Silentius Remotusque (a silent and faraway God)—becomes talkative once Christian missionaries arrive. This is a decisive event. Before the arrival of Christianity in Africa there is not really such a thing as prophetism, religious renewal decided by God, or the divine direct message for a transformation of societal structures. Let me be specific. As already noted in preceding pages with reference to Hulstaert's study on the Mongo's God and confirmed by my own experience with some Central African cultures (particularly Bemba, Luba, Lulua, Rwanda, Sanga, and Songye), God, who is a known concept, is a pure idea, benevolent and interested in the human experience, but completely detached from it. In order to reach him, humans pass through lesser gods or spirits to whom they address prayers and offer sacrifices (see Hulstaert 1980; Van Caeneghem 1956). Indeed, as Allen Roberts writes me in a personal note of 14 October 1988, referring to the Tabwa context of eastern Zaire: "God (as Leza, Kabezya Mjungu, or other praisenames) certainly appears in pre- or early colonial invocations and myths, as is still the case." It is the style of the apparition that I am concerned with. In chapters 4 and 5, I shall focus on God's creation of the world. The soundness of this intervention—direct, through action or communication; indirect, in dreams for instance—belongs to the logic of mythological narratives, which functions as both a foundation of a tradition and its explanation. Another type of God's appearance presents three main characteristics: God speaks directly to an individual and gives to him or to her a specific mandate in order to cut off what is going on in a cultural tradition and thus transform a society and its history; the confrontation, as in the case of biblical revelations and Christian mystics, opposes God to a given individual, and it is generally about human behaviors falling short of divine expectations; finally, the activity of the chosen one after the communication with the divine generally seems to escape the common political responsibility of a tradition, and the way a society has transcribed it, and thus often leads to prophetism.

I would tend to hypothesize that it is with the arrival of Christianity that things change: God begins to speak. He communicates directly with humans through dreams and explicates to his chosen ones the poles of religious knowledge and his own being, and his Spirit emancipates itself and dwells in the performances of prophets. Rigorously speaking, God anthropologizes himself. This is a major conversion. Yet it is unthinkable out of the field of Christianity, in which by his incarnation God proclaims himself as the culmination of life and sacrifice.

Transplanted into Africa by missionaries, the human miseries of an anthropologized God do not destabilize the particular, specific, and absolute concept of Deus Christianorum, which posits itself as the foundation of eschatology. In any case, God speaks now and perhaps too frequently, if one keeps in mind that the Deus Africanus, as paradigmatically illustrated by the Mongo's God, was, by definition and experience, a Deus Silentius (Hulstaert 1980). It is thus easy to imagine that nowadays God is supposed to create a discursive economy of salvation in which negotiations between him and Africans are now conceivable, particularly in charismatic groups. On the other hand, by the very fact of his incarnation, the daily experience of humans is not autonomous any longer, from the Supreme Being—it has been, indeed, always dependent upon minor spirits and ancestors. But now God immerses himself in empirical positivities and speaks to humans.

We have several studies telling us that things are not so simple (e.g., Douglas 1970; Thomas, Luneau, and Doneux 1969). On the other hand, it is only too easy to reject en bloc racially ambiguous propositions which, before the 1920s, negated the very being of a Deus Africanus and thus, directly or indirectly, required an African amplification of Deus Christianorum. Today, in fact, the general celebration of his existence invariably brings back the problems that in early studies contributed to his negation as Deus Completus et Universalis (e.g., Mulago 1973a:19–28). "Animism" writes Thomas, is not "revelation," and in it there is no such thing as God's Word: "Here, the sacred word does not have the significance that the important revealed religions give it. Animism is not a revelation, and in it the word is not God's word" (Thomas, Luneau, and Doneux 1969:384).

Or to put the argument in a more evolutionary and classic form: "Religion at this stage of its development polarizes itself around the notion of an All-Creator and the notion of effective life-giving power. Neither of these can be accurately described as an object of worship. The first is almost completely ignored. The second is induced to operate by the force of magic and of ritual. Worship in the true sense begins where the idea of God begins; and that is at the point where it is first possible to identify the universal principle of Being with the power that guarantees man's life" (Bowman 1958:28).

African independent churches seem to exemplify this argument, whereas mainstream church theologians are caught in methodological propositions for accommodating a composite Deus Christianorum. Here is a possible genealogical representation of prophetic imaginations:

Divine Sign	(Moses') Succession
Discontinuity in Human Order	Continuity of Message
Regional Churches	Universal Eschatology

We can measure the capacity of prophetic imaginations at three different levels of coherence: the level of enunciation, at which a symbolic sign expresses a confrontation between nature and supernature and presents to the prophet God's desiderata and interest in the human condition; the level of prophetic performance, which validates the founding inspiration and deduces a new orthodoxy within the geography of the Word and its incarnation; and the level of significance, which organizes governing policies and guarantees both God's sovereignty and the new Christian community's salvation.

The prophetic imagination establishes at its own source the evidence of specific signs, projecting visible messages. Let us look at a time frame: 1910–1919. Three major events powerfully marked some consciousnesses: a great influenza epidemic, the difficult post–World War I period, and a "mysterious" star which appeared in the sky—Halley's Comet. The actual sequence was the reverse: comet, war, flu. A Kimbanguist catechism makes these signs speak: "What do we know happened in that year [1918]? Large numbers of people died and not by the will of God" (Janzen and MacGaffey 1974:125, 156 n 40). The general context is directly linked with Simon Kimbangu's call to prophetism and his first miracles. At the other extreme of the continent, in South Africa, the vagaries of the comet also bore God's secret injunctions: "In the sky over the mountain a star approached, a very strange and different star—with a tail. The rational Whites called this strange celestial body Halley's Comet; but to Timothy [Cekwane] it was a messenger from God Himself. It moved slowly, yet approached so close; it almost touched that majestic mountain on which Timothy and his people were assembled. They felt the Spirit coming over them like a mighty wind" (Sundkler 1976:109).

Physical events, thus, become emulations and communicate providential messages. They seem, however, neither to dictate directly the order of a vocation nor to provide the totality of a mission (see Roberts 1982). Perceived as signs of God's will about his chosen prophet, they rather confirm a fate and a mission. Simon Kimbangu already faced his divine call in the "blessedness and origin" of his own life (*lusambulu ye tuku*), the symbol of his name which means witness (*mbangi*). According to a Kimbanguist catechism, this is also evident in his 1918 dialogue with Jesus, who allegedly told him: "Do not be afraid, I shall be with you" (Janzen and MacGaffey 1974:124–28). In the same manner, Timothy Cekwane's conception is sacred: in 1873, "God inserted a drop of blood into Cekwane's wife—the mother of the prophet—and she became pregnant" (Sundkler 1976:108). Similarly, in the same area, Job S. Mtanti, the precursor of the prophet G. Khambule, claimed that the Holy Spirit descended on him in 1910, and later on "he formed his church, the Zion Free Church Impumalanga Gospel of South Africa, as a response to the vagaries of Halley's Comet" (Sundkler 1976).

The prophet's imagination draws together marks and signatures in which similitudes open up as guidelines to God's project. Following the prescription of "the Spirit of the Holy Ghost" in 1917, Paulo Nzuza (1896–1959) professed to complete the genealogy which goes from Moses to Simon Peter and is known as the "Church of the Jews." He withdrew himself from the Esau–Saint Paul line, called the "Church of the Gentiles," and proclaimed a new horizon of salvation, the spiritual continuity of Canaanites in the "Church of the Spirit" (Sundkler 1976:99–100). In a similar way, the Central African prophet and healer Simon Kimbangu, "the next vessel of the Spirit" after Moses (Janzen and MacGaffey 1974:40), claimed to follow a divine order: according to the catechism of the church, "He was told by the Lord Jesus to go to Ngombe Kinsuka to heal someone seriously ill there" (Janzen and MacGaffey 1974:125).

The prophetic performances individualize the inspiration and, at the same time, formulate the texture of the message and its social impact. It is striking that the biblical referential generally constitutes the most manifest sign' of continuity and, thus, of the new doctrines' integration into the field of Christianity. In contrast, the social propositions, even when they place themselves in accordance with localized traditions (like the tradition of renewal among Kongo; see Janzen 1977), are often brought into play from truly "schizophrenic" perspectives and do intend social reorganization. For example, Paulo Nzuza's spiritual lines of redemption parallel Simon Kimbangu's racial and nationalist formulations of his mission. Religious discourse imposes itself at this level as a possible path to social transformation.

It is at the third level, the level of significance, that the contradictions of affirmations and interacting principles reveal themselves most clearly. The initial prophetic inspiration faces concrete accounts and conflicts brought about by its empirical irruption in social life. Can the privileges of a new grammar of Christian eschatology, conceived in a metaphorical inspiration, be articulated in institutional churches? In any case, projects toward a new geography of power are organized by the challenge of constituting regional loci for institutionalizing God's statements and laws. Kimbangu seems to have succeeded (see Asch 1983; MacGaffey 1983), while Mtanti and Khambule have clearly failed (Sundkler 1976:119).

The success represents a social respectability. It achieves the socialization of a utopia and thus indicates the degree of its banalization. Due to contradictions of social class, what was political excess of a religious nature integrates itself into the official organization of power. In the specific case of Kimbanguism, the transformation meant two important conversions. First, Kimbanguism shifted from a political marginality to an institutional status, a shift which was homologous to the passage from colonial rule to independence. The second conversion consisted of the institutionalization of procedures for guaranteeing an orthodoxy, thus closing the prophetic era.

Structurally, the most significant aspects of such a conversion from a prophetic to an institutional church can be seen at two levels: the administrative and the theological. The first duplicated the hierarchical model of mainstream churches on the basis of the classical opposition between the clerics and the faithful which, by its nature, organizes a structural distribution of competence. The theological level revised the challenging racial and utopian arguments of the genesis of the movement in formulating a new doctrine. A major ideological claim had been that Kimbanguism was a *Kirche ohne Weisse* (see Martin 1971). "Kimbanguism is conscious of being at the heart of Africa, the religion which integrates Jesus Christ's revelation and protects the best of what is inherited by Negro-African culture" (Dubois 1981:125). Yet the transformation of the church expresses a domestication of the prophetic imagination, a rewesternization of biblical inspiration in the name of universality, and a promotion of the traditional concept of "Christian essence." This was made on the basis of a canon proclaiming the truth of one God in three persons; the faith in Jesus Christ, his death and resurrection, as sign and condition of salvation; and, finally, the institution of four major sacraments: baptism, marriage, priesthood, and communion (whose sole originality resides in its formula: the use of honey—John the Baptist's food—for the Blood of Christ and a cake of potatoes, plantains, and eggs as the Body of Christ) (see Dubois 1981). The liturgical processions, chants, and sermons are now Protestant-marked performances in the pure Baptist style. This price paid by Kimbanguism to "the universality of Christianity" allowed it to become a full member of the World Council of Churches.

It is interesting to observe that, contrary to the Kimbanguist orientation, practices and researches in African Roman Catholicism have tended, so far, in the opposite direction, that is, toward experiencing the solidity of regional symbolisms and categories. Against the overestimation of universal axes in Kimbanguism, Roman Catholic thinkers put the emphasis on valorizing local meanings for thinking and celebrating revelation and salvation. The liturgy of the Mass in its post–Vatican II structure can be used as an illustration of the liberation of religious imaginations. Vatican II promulgations transformed the Roman rite of commemorating the Last Supper by establishing important alterations. First, there are spatial alterations represented by the complete turn of the celebrant, who faces the participants, and the displacement of the altar from the *ikonostasis* to the center, or the *naos,* of the church. The alterations, in fact, also erased the separation between the priestly or inaccessible space of the rite and the field of the nave. Second, morphologically and semantically, the new liturgy means a shift from the symbolic discourse of the Missa Major, centered around the mystery of transubstantiation, to a socialized Missa *privata*. This is a performance whose necessary and sufficient elements are a basic altar or table, a celebrant, some wine, and a piece of bread. It fully takes up its meaning when performed in public as a commemoration of Christ's death and resurrection. Finally, the use of the local language, by introducing a new syntax and thus a new semantic dimension, completes the transformation (see Williams 1978).

The change was rightly perceived as an opening up of two hermetically closed spaces: the *terribilis locus* of the ritual celebration and that of sacred closures represented by centuries of fixed connections in the semantics of the *mysterium fidei* (the mystery of faith) and its linguistic means of performance, the Latin language. Quite naturally African Catholics reorganized both spaces into what some observers have ambiguously called "tribal Mass." Here are some traits which can be observed here or there, although all of them are rarely found in the same place (Mveng 1964; Mpongo 1981).

1. A dramatization of the performance which extends the canonical frame of the liturgy of the Mass and incorporates processions, litanies, acclamation of the Cross, and happenings such as dialogues between the celebrant and participants.
2. A theatricalization of the oral proclamation of the Gospel.
3. A metaphorization of the euchological texts when stylistically submitted to procedures of African traditional models of prayers.
4. The use of stylized dancing during the celebration, very often during the Offertorium, and the presence of traditional paraphernalia.
5. Propositions for or experimentation with an African symbolism for the liturgical colors. "The black color, symbol of hope, is defined as the sign of eschatological victory and is or should be employed for ordinary masses; the red, symbol of the dialectic of blood and life, is used as the sign for the celebration of Christ's and his saints' passion; white, the symbol of death and the representation of the ancestors is used as the color for funeral masses; the yellow and the green, indecisive colors, are or should be used for ceremonies of anniversary of those departed" (Mpongo 1981).

One could note here that these propositions concerning the symbolism of colors do not really reflect the tradition they claim to represent (see, e.g., de Heusch 1985). They constitute in fact an interpretation. But that is a different problem. These traits, and others experimented with (Mpongo 1981), give the Roman Catholic liturgies an apparent authority within local cultures. As efforts, they constitute the other side of intellectual reflexes which, in theology, interrogate revelation from the awareness of the unsaid deviation of God's speech.

To go back to my point, we may now accept that the experience of independent churches tends to establish as a universal category the Deus Christianorum, at least in his genealogical depths, whereas mainstream churches, such as African Roman Catholicism, supposedly exploit local constructions to the point of somehow orienting toward the Deus Absconditus of the Scriptures (Acts 18:22–23). In the first case, the political performance of actualizing Christianity universalizes its claim on God's speech and revelation by going from a well-determined cultural context of heterodoxy to the very classical paradigms of the Old Testament and, sometimes, of the *traditio Christiana*. Kimbanguism seems to be one of the rare examples of a movement that completely achieved this evolution.

In the second case, on the contrary, the universal paradigms are called to witness to the local variety of God's speech and inspiration. In both cases, one could say that the religious systems and their interpretations present themselves as both hermeneutical elucidation and political performance.

I seriously suspect some mainstream church theologians of being only politically motivated. On the other hand, I would rather believe that most founding prophets' claims about their inspiration and God's manifestations are quite nonsensical. Their inspiration may be less than divine and more like astute correlations of fantasies with a psychological urge for power. At any rate, the deployment of their bewildering discourses, along with the interpretations of mainstream church theologians, both of which spring from beneath the surface of the orthodox discursivity of the Christian message, show the ambivalent valence of what they comment upon and clarify: revelation is fundamentally a political performance. And, naturally, African spirits begin to speak in the name of the Deus Christianorum but, often, with the voice of a Deus Absconditus.

2
Philosophy and Theology as Political Practices

Context and Texts: The Question of an African Philosophy

The notion of African philosophy is a recent paradigm. In most ethnographic or anthropological texts penned at the beginning of the century, one comes across expressions such as "primitive philosophy" or "philosophy of the savages" when the authors refer to what nowadays are commonly called local or indigenous systems of thought. Today it is clear that the scientific discourse on Africa was then made up of preconceptions and speculations on the history and the nature of the Great Chain of Being, which contained unproven evolutionary assumptions about cultures and human beings, as well as political considerations grounding the right to colonize. Within this intellectual mixture, African behavior, thinking, and *Weltanschauung* were qualified as a preliminary step toward a more progressive human capacity. With a *bel ensemble,* missionaries, anthropologists, and colonizers expounded means and techniques of changing the African context and transforming it according to both Western and Christian standards. An excellent indication of this period is the work of the Central African Roman Catholic priest Stephano Kaoze. Between 1907 and 1911, when he was still a seminarian, Kaoze published a long article on Bantu psychology in which he opposed the weaknesses of his own traditional system to the conquering force of Western philosophy and *Weltanschauung.*

The notion of African philosophy has been ambiguous since it was first used in the 1910s. The pervasiveness of primitivist ideologies marks the conditions of its possibility and implies references to prelogism in thinking, paganism in belief, and primitiveness with regard to the *Weltanschauung.* Furthermore, there is a more general reason for this ambiguity,

32

and it depends on the particular status of philosophy and its meanings. As a discipline, philosophy defines itself as essentially a critical, explicit, autocritical discourse focusing on human experience, its signs and symbols. Indeed, one can also understand philosophy in a wider sense and consider commentaries on a way of life and even the way of life itself as a philosophy. In everyday life there is no problem of speaking about the philosophy of American businessmen, French policemen, Italian singers, or African musicians as long as one suspends any consideration of confusing implied particular modalities of behaving with philosophy as a critical and explicit discourse. The expression "African philosophy" often assumes this wide understanding. As such it covers and designates the particularity of a *Weltanschauung* and commentaries bearing upon it. On the other hand, it seems clear that this wide usage of the notion of philosophy cannot be confused with the critical works of African professionals of philosophy.

I would like here to mark the limits existing between the two understandings of philosophy in Francophone Africa and to indicate, from a critical perspective, the points of their complementarity. I choose to deal exclusively with explicit commentaries and discourses on philosophy and not with either things or social formations and their sets of values. Yet I have every reason to believe that explicit discourses as well as practical wisdom and traditional sets of values might, under some conditions, participate in a philosophical effort. On the other hand, in speaking of African philosophy, I am aware of the discreet insistence of metaphors and epistemological traces called upon, as in the case of less controverted signs such as African astronomy, African geology, or even African philology, which for everybody simply means the rigorous practice of a discipline within a geographical framework that is African accidentally. When one runs through the chronological repertoire of works of African philosophy (Smet 1978b; Mudimbe 1982a), one fact strikes the eye immediately: the large number of books of philosophy published in Central Africa, mainly in Zaire. This quantity of publication is due to the influence of Catholic missionaries during the colonial era.

According to the terms of the 1906 convention between the Holy See and the Congo Free State, an elaborate structure of religious education was developed, leading to major seminaries where candidates for the priesthood were introduced to Thomist philosophy before they undertook studies in theology. As a consequence, the first Africans in this century to publish works claiming to be philosophical were churchmen: Alexis Kagame, André Makarakiza, François-Marie Lufuluabo, and Vincent Mulago. Spiritually they are disciples of Placide F. Tempels. They generally refer to and use his *Bantu Philosophy,* first published as *La Philosophie bantoue* (1945). Their status and the special order of their mission have prepared them to receive sympathetically the basic hypotheses of Tempels. This submission to a perspective has, however, never meant a mere repetition of Tempels' ideas, as shown by Kagame's reservation and the widening of his investigation from *La Philosophie bantu-rwandaise de l'être* (1956) to *La Philosophie bantu comparée* (1976).

Placide F. Tempels, a Belgian missionary in Central Africa from 1933 to 1962, offered his *Bantu Philosophy* to colonialists of good faith as a possible aid to the building of a Christian Bantu civilization. When he decided to publish his experience, Tempels had lived more than ten years among the Luba-Katanga people, sharing their language and culture. His *Bantu Philosophy* may be understood as the expression of doubt concerning the supposed backwardness of Africans, as well as a political manifesto for a new policy.

It must be remembered that Bantu philosophy is based on very simple premises. First, as in all cultures, life and death determine human behavior; or, presented differently, all human behavior depends on a system of general principles. Second, if Bantu are human beings, then there is reason to seek the fundamentals of their beliefs and behavior or their basic philosophical system. From this position, Tempels, according to E. Possoz, attempts "a true estimate of indigenous peoples," rejecting "the misunderstanding and fanaticism of the ethnology of the past and of the former attitude of aversion entertained with regard to them" (Possoz 1959:14). This "discovery" of Bantu philosophy, wrote Tempels, "is so disconcerting a revelation that we are tempted at first sight to believe that we are looking at a mirage. In fact, the universally accepted picture of primitive man, of the savage, of the proto-man living before the full blossoming of intelligence, vanishes beyond hope of recovery before this testimony" (Tempels 1959:167–68).

The polemical argument which arose from this perspective tended to redefine the European Christian mission toward Africa. Taking upon himself the responsibility of reinterpreting the highest European conscience, Tempels could defy the then ongoing policies of Christianization and colonization in a chapter significantly entitled "Bantu Philosophy and Our Mission to Civilize."

This is the result of a complex intellectual change. During the 1930s, the fundamental assumptions of colonization and Christian conversion had not yet been questioned. But some trends in French and German anthropology associated with scholars like Marcel Griaule and W. Schmidt were beginning to develop more sophisticated cultural taxonomies. With them, there emerges a new type of discourse which, apart from following Leo Frobenius and Maurice Delafosse's form of curiosity, insists on the originality of different cultures, thus, methodologically, implying the possibility of a typology of otherness (Frobenius 1899; Griaule 1948, 1952).

The most surprising fact is that an epistemological split had appeared within the anthropological field. This revolution has, until now, hardly been analyzed. Despite changes in methodology associated with the culturalist and the functionalist schools, professional anthropology continued to maintain an evolutionary perspective with all its implications. On the other side, we have a new orientation of what I would like to call missionary anthropology. During Schmidt's time, with the foundation of the Vienna school, the new development was an original trend within the professional field. Rapidly, however, contributions from missionaries at work in Africa shifted from anthropological postulates to strictly philosophical considerations. This shift is, for instance, already discernible in *La Religion des primitifs* (1909) by A. Le Roy as well as in P. Colle's study of the Baluba (1913), despite these authors' clear reliance on anthropological grids of their time. During the 1930s and 1940s the shift is widely observable in almost all missionary studies on African religions and traditions. N. De Claene, A. De Clercq, G. Hulstaert, P. Schumascher, G. Van Bulck, G. Van den Bosch, R. F. Van den Eynde, J. Van Wing, and B. Zuure, among others, represent the new trend.

Contrary to the evaluations often made by modern anthropologists and philosophers, even the best like Hountondji, the works of these writers are, in general, valuable and interesting ethnography. Most of them tend to follow the norms of the Vienna school, the German or the French traditions in anthropology. As a rule, missionaries' scholarly contributions carefully describe a given African group taken as a totality. Some of them, sharing or following the philosophy of *Anthropos* and, particularly, the aims of P. W. Schmidt's *Ursprung der Gottesidee* (1933–49), are inclined to arrive at synthetic conclusions from data provided by limited studies, for example P. Schebesta's analysis in "Die religiose Anschauungen Süd-Afrikas" (1923) or C. Tastevin's generalizations in "Les Idées religieuses des Africains" (1934).

The revolution represented by this current rests, first, on its heuristic procedures and, second, on its apologetic objectives. As in Schmidt's enterprise, the aim is not only the scientific practice of ethnography per se. Instead, ethnography is regarded as a means for the careful and patient study of a multitude of cultural particularities. Subsequently, the ethnographic method is supposed to allow us to discern a universal system which, if correctly described, would, in turn, account for all cultural particularities. From this viewpoint, even the smallest element may help, on the first level, in the description and understanding of the originality, the "soul," of a culture. Moreover, on the second level, it could contribute to a pancultural system, reflecting a universal theory. Thus, one of the major assumptions of the method is the existence of a universal theory or "philosophy" that each human community expresses in its own way and according to its own needs. This philosophy would be always and everywhere particular in its cultural and historical manifestations, but universal in its essence. Its presence marks the difference between human societies and animal communities.

Many missionary contributions on African religions published between the 1930s and World War II are largely supported by the above assumptions. During these years, the missionary viewpoint in anthropology encountered French cultural relativism, itself a product of what Léopold Sédar Senghor nicely described as the "German crisis of French thought," meaning the revolution which, in philosophy as well as in social sciences, followed the impact of Friederich Nietzsche, Karl Marx, and Sigmund Freud on French scholarship. In any case, it became acceptable to recognize some wisdom in Africans, and it was no longer considered absurd to write about African "morality," "philosophy," or "knowledge," as did, for instance, R. Allier in *The Mind of the Savage* (1929), V. Brelsford in *Primitive Philosophy* (1935) and, with particular brilliance, the French team working on Bambara and Dogon traditions: Suzanne de Ganay, Germaine Dieterlen, Marcel Griaule, and Michel Leiris. With his *Bantu Philosophy*, Tempels appears as one of the most remarkable among the theorists of this trend. His use of Thomist philosophical categories in order to clarify ethnographic data might seem today debatable, but at the time, it represented a sound answer to unsolved questions in the interpretation of African cultures and their future.

Kagame drew out all the consequences of Tempels' method. Using Aristotelian concepts, he tried, with his *La Philosophie bantu-rwandaise de l'être* (1956), to demonstrate that Bantu philosophy simultaneously reflects a perennial and universal philosophy and is the vital expression of the soul of a community. From this viewpoint, he adds, "The term philosophy could have been replaced by that of metaphysics so that we could have used 'The Bantu Metaphysics of Being' as the title" (Kagame 1956:8). This statement is important, since it explicitly indicates the significance of the epistemological revolution discussed above: philosophy is to be understood as metaphysics, and the discipline serves to describe an African theodicy considered as a reflected image of a universal theodicy. And it becomes clear that theodicy is simply another name for natural religion.

Kagame's *La Philosophie bantu-rwandaise de l'être* (1956) is both a critical response to Tempels' interpretation of Bantu culture and a sustained attempt to organize in a precise framework the philosophy of a "pagan culture." For the classical philosophical question What is, he substituted another one related to vital force. Following Aristotle, he distinguished, more rigorously than Tempels, four categories of being: *umuntu*, "the human being"; *ikintu*, "a thing"; *ahantu*, "somewhere"; and *ukuntu*, "the manner." This fourth includes seven of Aristotle's categories (quantity, quality, relation, action, emotion, position, possession) instrumental for his hierarchy of vital forces. The same process of transplanting Kinyarwanda categories into Aristotelian concepts—about the notions of existence, knowledge, and will, for instance—allowed him to describe the Bantu-Rwandese ontology, criteriology, psychology, cosmology, and ethics.

Most of Tempels' African disciples were more concerned about making philosophy agree with theology in order to promote a cultural integration of African thought with Christianity. Thus we have, for example, Jean Calvin Bahoken's *Clairières métaphysiques africaines* (1967), François-Marie Lufuluabo's *Perspective théologique bantoue et théologie scholastique* (1966), and Vincent Mulago's *Un Visage africain du christianisme* (1965). Until the 1960s their major guides were still the Roman pontiffs' teachings (Benedict XV's *Maximum illud* [1919], Pius XI's *Rerum ecclesiae* [1926], Pius XII's *Evangelii praecones* [1951]), which were based on the postulates that, in order to save Africans "sitting in the darkness and in the shadow of death," it was necessary to establish an adapted Christianity, that is, to naturalize the church and indigenize its teaching and liturgy. Gradually the policy shifted from this adaptation perspective insisting on the Africanization of external aspects of Christianity—for instance, the type of music and hymns used in liturgy—to a questioning of the content of Christianity. The new approach, the stepping-stone method, was based upon new premises. A major supposition would be that African traditions and cultures contain facts and beliefs, signs and symbols, which are already a *praeparatio evangelica*, that is to say, an awaiting of the Gospels. Thus, the Good News might be preached on this basis, and Christianity would automatically take on a new form.

The implications of these schools are obvious in their vocabulary. The first uses an agricultural terminology (plant, transplant, sow the African field, bring the good seed, spread the good seed) which implies a tabula rasa or, at least, a wasteland. The second approach seems to set a high value on vocabulary of construction (establish, implement, build, construct the church), implying that its aim is a new organization of an existing system of beliefs. All the African thinkers mentioned above use both approaches, sometimes emphasizing one, at other times combining both in a new perspective. Divorced, at least theoretically, from an organic relationship with colonial Christianity, they contribute to a philosophy and a theology of the implantation of the church, which is critical to the dominant and pervasive theology of mission. The latter orientation, as already noted, was expressed in a dichotomy implying an evolution from paganism to Christianity and involving binary oppositions like Satan versus God, and African primitiveness versus Western civilization. Hence, missionary objectives grew as a means of necessary metamorphoses: to substitute the health of Christian civilization for the illness of the African universe.

The new "discourse of method" promoted by Lufuluabo, Mulago, and others lists nationalist perspectives as indicating a reevaluation of pagan traditions and the generative possibilities of autonomous values. At first sight, it might appear as essentially a semantic revolution. The concept of pagan culture or, in current usage, traditional culture tends to replace that of primitiveness used by anthropologists. In an aggressive book, *Des prêtres noirs s'interrogent* (1956), young black theologians put forward new sets of symbols and evaluated classical mediators. One year later, in 1957, the papal encyclical, Pius XII's *Fidei donum,* seemed to approve of their primary desires: indigenization of the missionary philosophy of Christianization.

This religious commitment has created problems, either because one sees nostalgia for philosophical ethnocentrism based on platonico-aristotelico-thomism or Scotism, or because the usage these thinkers make of the term *philosophy* takes on a vulgar meaning, or because some critics have decided that these investigations depended on missiology and that the latter has nothing really to do with philosophy (Tshiamalenga 1977a). These critics tend to forget that the epistemological perspective of theological research and of the semantic or hermeneutic questions it raises belongs to a philosophical view. Pushed further, the debate, if it is to be critical, should take up once again the preliminary question: What is African philosophy? And this presupposes other questions: on the one hand, the defining of philosophy and theology; on the other, the norms of possible cooperation between the disciplines.

Alongside the promoters of the concept of a philosophy helping in the acculturation of Christianity, other thinkers, such as Tharcisse Tshibangu, without pushing their Africanness as an absolute criterion, pose a question about the status of theology as a science or, at the crossroads of historical, philosophical, philological, and theological methods, produce works of exegesis at a high level. Such works include the investigations of Joseph Ntedika's on the evolution of the doctrine of St. Augustine's purgatory and on the Latin patristic heritage; the book of Jean Kinyongo's on the origin of the meaning of the name of Yahweh; the analysis, provided by Dosithée Atal, of the structures of the Johannic hymn; and the study by Laurent P. Monsengwo on the notion of *nomos* in the Pentateuch. Several more recent books are very close to the usual idea and technique of philosophical work: for example, Alphonse Pene Elungu's on Nicholas de Malebranche, Alphonse M. Ngindu's on Lucien Laberthonière, and Octave Ugirashebuja's on Martin Heidegger.

When the Central African debate on African philosophy was intensifying, precisely between 1956 (the date of the publication of Kagame's first philosophical text) and 1965 (the date of Franz Crahay's article in *Diogenes* in which the conditions for the existence of a Bantu philosophy are put forward), the dominant trend in West Africa was in the traditional vein, except for the works of Senghor and the writings properly called Marxist. Works of a philosophical nature are limited in number. Moreover, these are, in general, articles. Before 1965, we could hardly count ten significant works with an explicit philosophical ambition. They included Ferdinand N'Sougan Agblemagnon's stimulating work on time in Ewe culture, his analysis of the concept of person, tradition, and culture in Africa, and his research on metaphysics and ethics in the evolution of Black Africa (1960, 1962); Meinrad Hebga's defense of African logic, which inadvisedly implies that the relativity of modes of thinking can be founded on the basis of philosophical implications from the existence of non-Euclidean geometries (1958); H. Memel-Fote's report on animist civilization prepared for a 1962 colloquium on religions held in Paris and his 1965 article on perpetual peace in the practical philosophy of Africans (1962); and, finally, Engelbert Mveng's *L'Art d'Afrique noire* (1964), an essay in religious aesthetics.

Suddenly, from 1968 on, vigorous texts appear in West Africa, proposing a rigorous usage of the concept and practice of philosophy. A critical school begins with the publication, in a 1968 issue of *Présence africaine,* of Fabien Eboussi-Boulaga's essay against Tempels' *Bantu Philosophy.* The works of the school's members, like Paulin Hountondji's and Marcien Towa's, overlap very widely or join the path marked out by Franz Crahay's position. These thinkers give the name *ethnophilosophy* to the investigation which, after Tempels and Kagame, speaks of describing and restoring traditional African philosophies. The impact and significance of this criticism modify philosophy considerably from the 1970s onward. External events indicate this clearly: first, the center of African philosophical thought shifts from Central Africa to West Africa. Then, methodologically exacting investigations and essays begin to come from Benin, Cameroon,

Ivory Coast, and Senegal, and philosophical reflection tends to take on a resolutely secular outlook. Another noteworthy fact is the eviction, albeit temporary, of churchmen. In fact, starting in 1970, the Faculté de Théologie Catholique in Kinshasa takes a new breath of life and seems now one of the most lively and dynamic centers of research in African philosophy and theology. It publishes three regular journals (*Les Cahiers de religions africaines, La Revue africaine de théologie,* and the *Bulletin of African Theology* of the Ecumenical Association of African Theologians). It has also launched three series of publications (Les Recherches Philsophiques Africaines, Les Recherches Théologiques Africaines, and the Bibliothèque du Centre d'Etudes des Religions Africaines) and organizes each year two international seminars, one in theology and the other in philosophy.

In their panorama of contemporary African philosophy, Oleko Nkombe and Alfons J. Smet, two members of the Kinshasa school, have produced a classification of African philosophers (1978). They describe the internal structure of African philosophy in the form of a totality with vertices formed by the following orientations:

1. The ideological current: reaction to theories and prejudices which, in the past, supported the slave trade and later justified colonization
2. The trend recognizing traditional African philosophy: reaction to the myth of the "primitive mentality" of Africans which, through hermeneutical restoration, speaks of asserting the existence, solidity, and coherence of traditional African philosophies
3. The critical school: reaction to theses or projects of the two preceding trends; it questions their validity and philosophical relevance
4. The synthetic current: the assumption of preceding trends and the orientation of the data collected toward a hermeneutical, functional philosophy or a search for new problematics.

As operative as it may appear at first sight, this classification remains perplexing: it elevates a working hypothesis to a thesis. In fact, on the level of external structure, African philosophy is defined as implying two kinds of knowledge—Western and African—these being in a relationship of subcontrariety, without one knowing exactly and clearly what is designated. At any rate the value of this manner of inclusive disjunction seems questionable.

In the elementary logic of propositions, in the immediate inferences or reasoning which are supported by a single premise and lead immediately to a conclusion, a relation of subcontrariety exists when two propositions can both be true at the same time but may not be false at the same time. Hence, there are three possible inferences: if the premise or first proposition is false, then the conclusion can only be true; if, on the contrary, the premise is true, then the conclusion is uncertain, since it could be true or false.

For example, in each of the following three types of reasoning, propositions are in a relation of subcontrariety.

1. This inference was dear to certain anthropologists at the beginning of this century:

    Some Africans are not human beings. (False)

    Some Africans are human beings. (True)

2. A geometry teacher could harass or amuse students by playing on the following reasoning:

    Some quadrilaterals do not have five sides. (True)

    Some quadrilaterals have five sides. (False)

3. A father, sooner or later, introduces his children to the following evidence:

    Some people are black. (True)

    Some people are not black. (True)

In order to fully understand the relationship of subcontrariety in the model presented to us, we must note two things. First, the authors set an implication between, on the one hand, African wisdom and European knowledge and, on the other, European knowledge and African wisdom. In other words, they establish the fact that African thinkers and Africanists draw from European knowledge their models of analysis, interpretation, and speculation. On the basis of this observation they conclude that "it is inconceivable to understand African philosophy today, outside the relationship which unites it to European knowledge (Nkombe and Smet 1978:264). From the point of view of content, however, they believe that all African philosophical currents preoccupy themselves with the problems which concern the Africa of today. Between European knowledge and African wisdom would therefore exist, according to the authors, a relationship of subcontrariety, because such categories are compatible with each other. Nkombe and Smet write, "We think that in spite of the differences existing between African wisdom and European knowledge, a common denominator can be found" (1978:266).

The second point is that the authors state the resemblance between this relationship and inclusive disjunction. It is a two-argument operation which produces a true result in three cases: when the two arguments are both true and when either argument is true. This is all fine, and even extremely provocative. But this very abstract model poses some problems of which the most immediate and perhaps the most important are contained in the arguments themselves: What are they and what exactly do they mean? I fear in fact that, in spite of their apparent clarity, European knowledge and African wisdom are, as expressions, opaque and thus insufficient to demonstrate support for a process of computation of propositions and analysis of propositional variables. Moreover, Nkombe and Smet insist on certain intellectual filiations. For example, they note the influence of Aristotle and the scholastics on Tempels and Kagame, that of Hegel on Eboussi-Boulaga and Towa, and that of Karl Marx and Louis Althusser on Stanislas Adotevi and Paulin Hountondji. One could agree that it is one thing to observe and analyze intellectual or spiritual genealogies and quite a different thing to generalize and speak of inclusive disjunction between European knowledge and African wisdom.

Whatever the case may be, if one accepts that, internally, African philosophy could be represented as a lozenge of subcontrariety with the four trends as its vertices, one may assume that tension would be identical between vertices and would allow the latter, and hence the form of the lozenge, to be maintained. But is this obvious? Doesn't the trend toward the recognition of an African philosophy tend to be reconciled with the ideological school, while the synthetic tends to fuse with the critical? One could graphically represent the result as a wavy line, like a snake with the tail representing the first two trends and the head the remaining two. In case the image of the tail might appear pejorative, let us suggest the image of a snake with two heads. This might express better the tensions between the principal orientations of African philosophy. On the one side, there are investigations of cosmologies and mores—Tempels and his disciples' perspective—on the other, there are the more modern trends that emphasize the critical virtues of philosophy.

To be clearer, it seems to me that investigations to restore traditional African philosophy (the second trend) are complementary to the ideological school—eminently theoretical—of which they are concrete expressions. Nevertheless, the critical trend—the third school—should be considered as an indispensable stepping-stone or, more precisely, as the first essential thing without which the fourth orientation—the question for syntheses, for hermeneutic or functional philosophy—would have no meaning, at least as a rigorous project.

Let us therefore propose a representation which is at the same time less complex and more eloquent, one which symbolizes the unity of African philosophy. Let A and B (Fig. 1) be two groups in proportion to partial inclusion: the first would unite the works with a strong ideological bias (in the widest sense of the qualifier), that is, it would take up Nkombe and Smet's ideological trend and the school promoting a traditional African philosophy; the second would comprise productions with a philosophical

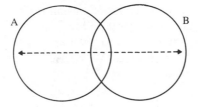

Figure 1

bent in the strict sense, that is, works coming from critical perspectives. And let us admit, by virtue of hypothesis, that at the intersection of the groups, there exist African works which, by their aim or because they possess certain characteristics, can be considered as belonging to either of the two groups. For the second phase, in each of the two groups, it would, in principle, be possible equally to raise some smaller groups in proportion to partial inclusion. Thus, for purely schematic reasons, we will have the following representation: in A, A1 and A2; in B, B1 and B2 (Fig. 2).

Now, if we trace a theoretical line (Fig. 1) which, from the center of the intersection of A and B, would run horizontally to the left and to the right, I propose that, on the left, the line indicates a decreasing application of philosophical principles and, on the right, an increasing application of the same. In other words, I shall say: on the left, the further one gets from the intersection of A and B, the more the works can be qualified as philosophical in only the broadest sense. In the other direction, the more the line penetrates into B, the more it involves philosophical works in the strict sense, approaching more or less the philosophical ideal—to refer to the definition proposed by F. Crahay—an analytical explicit, critical, and autocritical reflection (1965).

This representation could, in theory, be applied to the corpus of any non-African cultural tradition. In any case, it solves, in a simple way, the question of the definition of African philosophy. In order to establish a wide acceptance, Marcel Tshiamalenga invoked realism against Crahay,

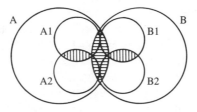

Figure 2

Hountondji, and Towa in his definition of philosophy (1977a, b). And, in view of relativizing the rigor of the ideal concept of the discipline, he asked, subversively, if Immanuel Kant were radically critical and autocritical? What was autocritical in G. W. F. Hegle, Arthur Schopenhauer, Søren Aabye Kierkegaard, Albert Camus, Gabriel Marcel? Finally, he asked, What was analytical in the pre-Socratic philosophers? Such questions are not easily answered. Our diagram simply indicates that one must openly understand and accept African philosophy as being a corpus of texts and discourses with a philosophical bent, in the strict and wide sense. One can, if necessary, occasionally circumscribe a more restrained field of philosophical exercise in the strict sense, in view of precise objectives.

How can one illustrate this diagram in a concrete way? Let us follow the process of the increasing complexity of philosophical practice in African thought by considering the contents of groups A and B. In Group A, let us characterize two subgroups. The first comprises works arising from the need to express and to render faithfully the unity and the coherence of traditional African systems (*Weltanschauungen*) supposedly neither marked nor influenced by Western contributions. The second unites the works qualified by an explicit intention to separate and to analyze present constraints of African society, marking the present and future situation while remaining true to African ideals. In the first subgroup, the text produced could be called ethnophilosophical; in the second, ideologico-philosophical. Let it be understood that the two qualifiers are not, in any way, pejorative; they must be understood simply as classifying devices, allowing a differentiation by class in terms of the content of the works, of their methods and aims.

In the ethnophilosophical subgroup, three classes may be clearly distinguished. The first is that of ethnographic description and ethnological exegesis. Of this, Western Africanists have provided numerous models, either strictly descriptive or in the form of anthropological analysis and interpretation. As an example of this class, we will cite two cases, namely, the works of Delafosse and Griaule. Numerous Africans have written works which belong to this group: essay writers like A. Diagne and M. Sibide, both of whom published in the *Bulletin du Comité d'Etudes Historiques et Scientifiques de l'AOF* (1916–38); Paul Hazoume, who produced *Doguicimi* in 1935; or, to go back to the 1910s, S. Kaoze, who wrote an article on the psychology of the Bantu. One may wonder whether or not this kind of work should be excluded from a classification of philosophical works and instead be relegated to the field of anthropology. Reasons for doing this are not wanting. But perhaps these works should be held provisionally in abeyance until the field of African philosophy is clarified. In fact, how can one understand the purpose of Ahmadou H. Ba's investigations (1972) or those of A. Fu-Kiau (1969) if one takes away their explicit philosophical ambition? They proclaim the reality of an African tradition as a canon of truth and knowledge. They believe that there is an African tradition in itself and consider themselves as the interpreters of this particular experience (see Hama 1969, 1972). Yet in stating that Africans have their own distinct mode of being, they insist that this singularity is the condition of universality: if there were no particular individuals and traditions, there could not be real universals. This same orientation is true of Boubou Hama's reflection on the encounter of Africa and Europe. His aim is to account for the African originative experience vis-à-vis Western interpretive systems (1972). And a book like Tulu Kia Mpasu Buakasa's on sorcery and witchcraft in the Kongo country (1973) is also affirmed as explicitly revealing a trait of an unthought element of an African tradition.

Two other classes of ethnophilosophical works are made up of those in which the authors attempt to restore the dignity of African culture either ontologically or hermeneutically. Ontological restitution, as Tshiamalenga calls it, is undertaken by some of Tempels' successors, such as Kagame and Lufuluabo, who construct an African philosophy by finding in African cultures the equivalents of Aristotelian or Thomist categories, thanks to which they claim they can reveal implicit African systems of thought. The third class is characterized by efforts toward hermeneutical restitution. The authors identify a structured philosophy by sorting through the contents of extant ethnographic studies and collections of myths, stories, prayers, and ritual formulas. An example is provided by E. N. C. Mujynya's analysis of the status of man in the Bantu universe (1972). Other examples include Mulago's study on Bantu religion and G. de Souza's on the concept of life among the Fon (1975). The problem of these restitutions lies in the value of the translation which is operated from a more or less implicit original to a speculative discourse and authorizes the latter to be presented as a faithful mirror of an implicit philosophy. The step taken would be perfectly philosophical if, first, it clearly started with a demonstration of an explicit character of the thought expressed by the traditional texts. These, it will be agreed, are neither completely silent nor chaotic (Kinyongo 1979:12–16). Then, relying heavily on them, the project would be fully philosophical if it offered a translation granted to the norms of hermeneutical readings. Alas, even when well started, this step often short-circuits the creative jump assumed by any translation and, satisfied by its initial movement, returns lazily to its point of departure to organize the supposed thought reflected by some fragments of initial texts.

It goes without saying that the distinctions established between the three classes of ethnophilosophical texts are theoretical. These classes do communicate, for the very reason that their intersections are inhabited. Hence, by way of illustration, J. C. Bahoken's study on the philosophy and religion of the Bantu of South Cameroon (1967) is linked at the same time to the hypotheses of ethnological exegesis and to the projects of ontologizing restitution. In another noteworthy case, Vincent Mulago, whose important study on the complementarity of Christianity and Africanity, *Un Visage africain du christianisme* (1965), situated in the wake of ontologizing restitution, has recently produced an investigation of traditional Bantu religion which could be perfectly inscribed in the trend of hermeneutical restitution (1973a).

The second subgroup unites works which are ideological in nature, the texts of which are defined as ideologico-philosophical. Ideology is to be understood here in its strict sense, as a body of ideas clearly structured and influential in the thinking and, possibly, the behavior of the members of a given community. It presents the values contained in expressions like ''a working-class ideology,'' ''a political ideology,'' or ''an ideology of commitment.'' The joining of the terms ideology and philosophy, however, poses a problem: the first, by definition, generally establishes itself as active, militant, and practical; the second, as essentially speculative and contemplative. In my opinion, this problem expresses the very ambiguity of this subgroup, of which certain works—if not all—are equivocal. In any case, the best-conceived and the most elaborate depend as much on the play of opposites customary to ideological militancy as on the efforts and abstract operations of philosophical speculation.

From then on, it would be superficial to dissociate clear and distinct classes. Let us be satisfied with noting prominent currents and then indicating rapidly the authors whose works are, in the main, philosophical. A common denominator in different trends would be Black African nationalism. This is found in the pan-Africanism illustrated in particular by Cheikh Anta Diop, Patrice Lumumba, and Kwame Nkrumah. The same passion for the continent characterized L. S. Senghor's or Julius Nyerere's African socialism. But contrary to its nonreligious origins, the socialist ideology in these projects has been spiritualistic and community-oriented.

The movement of negritude and African humanism put forward by Senghor is more speculative (Senghor 1964). Numerous commentators have explored it: sympathetically, as in the cases of Alioune Sene (1966) and Thomas Melone (1962), or with violence, as in Towa's 1971 critique of Senghor. In spite of the criticism to which it has been subjected, negritude still inspires the quest for an African personality and its cultural values either through contrasted reflections, as Jean-Marie Abanda Ndengue has tried to show in Cameroon (1970), or as a reflector, as in the book which I. Kimoni has devoted to Negro-African literature and the culture which brought it about (1975), or again as an exemplary place of fascinating norms. Thus, with Alfonse Nguvulu in his research on humanism and, unassumingly, in Kinyongo's meditation on "the evident Being" (1973), we are spellbound by its authenticity. The ideology of authenticity, despite the 1967 specifications of Mabika Kalanda, who wished to question all values, whether African or not, and despite Senghor's efforts to promote authenticity through negritude (1977), is nevertheless on its way out. Only with great difficulty can one put such a mystification side by side with Eboussi-Boulaga's investigations of African authenticity and philosophy. The Cameroonian philosopher has preferred serious reflection on the processes and conflicts of being an African today to easy ideological militancy (1977). Finally, we have the last trend in ideological investigation with, for example, Kwame Nkrumah's *Consciencism* (1964) and Marxist theorists who, promoting African development, militate for strict loyalty to Marxist rules.

Now that we have made a general survey of classes and trends of ethnophilosophical and ideologico-philosophical works, should we not recall that these systems are complementary? Or that there exists (to take up again the classification of groups used above) an intersection between these two subgroups? In effect, we have proposed from the beginning the following hypothesis: because of the aims of their contents, these works originate in the same context.

Two facts, one internal to the corpus and the other external, confirm this complementarity. On the internal side, the reflections on African humanisms and the ideologies of negritude all generally draw their material from an ethnographic context, and they are often inspired by anthropological exegeses. We could, for example, imagine Senghor without Frobenius or Delafosse. But negritude cannot be understood outside ethnological discourse, as Senghor himself confirms in his last book, *Ce que je crois* (1988). Another example of a different nature is that of pan-Africanist ideology. If this ideology cannot be confused with trends toward restoring traditional African philosophies, it nevertheless resembles them. Like them, it is motivated by negation. The projects of philosophical restitution deny the negation given to African culture until recently; pan-Africanism opposes the negation of African societies imposed first during the slave trade and later during the colonization and balkanization of the continent. That said, I do not believe that this would be the place to question the validity and the relevance of this compensatory negation.

Externally, it is interesting to note some syntheses of the ethnophilosophical and ideologico-philosophical elements. The virtuosity of J. Jahn's *Muntu* (1961) is well known. The book integrates the categories of Kagame's Bantu-Rwandese philosophy with Senghorian concepts in order to present a new African culture. According to Jahn, African tradition as well as neo-African culture is a matter of choice: Africans have "a perfect right to declare authentic, correct and true those components of their past which they believe to be so" (1961:17). The argument, which is close to that of African traditionalists, is interesting. It asserts that people invent their own versions of history or culture, and from this viewpoint history or culture is nothing more than a symbol (see Mudimbe 1988). Outside Catholic Church circles, little is known of Dominique Nothomb's undertaking (1965), which, inspired by the same sources, establishes African humanism with regard to indigenous stepping-stones toward Christianity. From a strictly philosophical point of view, one could, as Crahay did for Jahn, criticize these syntheses for being based on texts of uncertain philosophical status. That done, one can see that these syntheses attest to the skillful use of the complementarity existing between ethnophilosophical and ideologico-philosophical texts.

I must now note some ideologico-philosophical texts, most particularly the essays of Nkrumah and Senghor. They are different from other texts of the same group because of their explicit, autocritical, and rigorously organized discourse on specific languages and conditions. Let us take, for instance, *Nation et voie africaine du socialisme* (1961) or *Pour une relecture africaine de Marx et d'Engels* (1976) by Senghor. Both expand the philosophical dimensions of reading and of understanding the needs of the development of Black Africa. Both rely on an ideological horizon, but one can easily concede that the depth of patience and reflection which supports these texts, as well as their critical perspective, places them in a strictly philosophical field. If we refer to Figure 1, we might say that this space is in Group B, which consists of works of a strictly philosophical bent.

In Group B, the works tend to correspond or, more precisely, respond to Crahay's ideal definition of philosophy: "an explicit, analytical, radically critical and autocritical as well as systematic reflection, bearing on experience, on its human conditions and the meanings and values which it reveals" (Crahay 1965). It is, however, clear that all the texts of the group cannot, in the same way or to the same degree, manifest the conditions required by this ideal definition of philosophy. For a vivid illustration, let us take our horizontal line running across groups A and B from one end to the other. If the theoretical function of the full realization of all the philosophical conditions required by the definition is a given point on this horizontal line, then this point is found at the extreme right of the line. The field of philosophy in the strict sense would be on this line, between two limits: on the left, in A, on the border of the relation of partial inclusion existing between A and B; on the right, the extreme point of B, beyond which there can no longer be any elements which are members of B. The works of African philosophy, in the strict sense, would therefore be displayed along the line and would be included between the two limits noted. By the manner in which they realize the presuppositions of philosophical work, some texts would be close to the philosophical ideal, situated, as we have seen, at an extreme point on the border of B. In the other direction, some other works, because of their proximity to the ethnophilosophical and ideologico-philosophical productions, would be near the point limit in A: stated in a different way, they would be close to a place on the arc which, in A, demarcates the zone of inclusion of B. Nevertheless, realism would urge us to consider this border as not well defined. Instead of supposing a clear division, we would have to make provision for a relatively free zone to allow movement from the field of philosophy in the strict sense to that of philosophy in a wider sense. And, if one can accept comparisons, this intermediate region would be similar to the isoglossal zones which philologists recognize in the drawing of geographical borders separating two linguistic communities that are spatially close to each other.

How is African philosophy in the strict sense presented? As a new field, it is difficult to establish an organization for it as clear as that of the works of philosophy in the wider sense (Dieng 1983; Smet 1980). To begin with, because of the criterion of increasing complexity of philosophical needs, the easiest way would be to take note of its high points in chronological order: a philosophical reflection on the conditions of the possibility of African philosophy, a reflection on the significance of Western science, a reflection on philosophy as a critical auxiliary to the process of African development, and, finally, philosophical hermeneutics.

The first African text which seriously invites critical reflection on the foundation of an African philosophy is F. Eboussi-Boulaga's "Le Bantu Problématique" (1968). It is a long article published in *Présence Africaine* and built on two startling premises. The first is a comment by Albert Gérard concerning a statement made by the Congress of Black Writers and Artists held in Rome: "By declaring that the philosophical effort of traditional Africa has always been reflected through vital attitudes and has never had purely conceptual ends, the Committee on Philosophy created by the Congress of Rome recognizes in fact that African thinking has not gone beyond the preconceptual stage." The second involves a major problem with the schema of Tempels's *Bantu Philosophy:* the presupposition that an ontology can be derived from behavior and customs, not as a symbol of human language, but as a sort of observable being. From these two positions, Eboussi-Boulaga is going to hunt down the meaning, trace the limits, of "this beautiful argumentation from the outside" operated by

Tempels, and he ends with the need for a philosophical thinking of another kind. Towa expands the question by insisting that we go back to the analysis of ethnophilosophical assumptions and to the necessity of promoting an essentially critical step (1971b). He thinks that bringing to light a genuine Negro-African philosophy would securely establish the fact that our ancestors philosophized, without at the same time absolving us from philosophizing. It is surely Paulin Hountondji, however, who, with his book pointedly entitled *Sur la philosophie africaine* (1977), draws all the conclusions for a critical African philosophy. He pleads for an African philosophy which would be fully a philosophy; therefore, like any philosophy, in one sense, it is a metaphilosophy, evolving through thought and critical reflection on its own history and its own sociohistorical conditioning.

The second point, that of a critical reflection on the significance of Western science, derives from the criticism of anthropology and extends to the human sciences (e.g., Adotevi 1972). This reflection has recently been used with particular success in the field of psychopathology by Ibrâhîm D. Sow. His book on a dynamic African psychiatry (1977) seeks to define closely an African model that is psychopathological and culturally regional. Works of this type seem unduly critical to some and have been reproached for overcrowding the scientific horizon with reiterative challenges which merely show impotence and sterility of thought, rather than dynamic creativity. In actuality, up to now, criticism has tended to focus mainly on works discussing the possible conditions for African critical discourse. Often unfair, it too quickly discredited new currents aspiring to show, on the one hand, an exacting philosophical maturity and, on the other, a challenge to ideological complacency that promotes mystification in African studies. At least these discussions are good indications of the creative power of African self-criticism.

These trends favor the most prolific orientations in contemporary work: the search for a philosophy which could become a critical aid to development and for a philosophical hermeneutics. The first, illustrated by N. Atangana (1971), E. Njoh-Mouelle (1970a, 1970b, 1975), and A. P. Elungu (1973a), was well covered in two seminars organized by Zairean philosophers: one, at Lubumbashi University in 1976, on the theme "The Place of Philosophy in the Human and Cultural Development of Zaire and Africa"; the other, in Kinshasa in 1977, on "Philosophy and Liberation." With his book on the crisis of Muntu (1977), Eboussi-Boulaga elevated the debate to a higher level of complexity, especially by raising questions about the psychological maturity, the linguistic tools, and the usefulness of new critical outlooks. At the same time, in the

1970s, hermeneutical research was born. Avoiding the dead end into which works of restitution inspired by Tempels had led, the new generation was inspired by Hans Gadamer and Paul Ricoeur to read and interpret African "traditions"; Tshiamalenga, for example, conducted research on the Ntu vision of humanity and the philosophy of sin in the Luba tradition (1973, 1974). The same is true of such stimulating works as those by Prosper I. Laleye, Oleko Nkombe, and Oscar Bimwenyi.

In conclusion, we must once again note that some African thinkers philosophize quietly, far from the insistent arguments concerning Africanness and negritude. They brave the thought of Saint Augustine (Ntedika 1966), Malebranche (Elungu 1973b), Heidegger (Ugirashebuja 1977), and Laberthonière (Ngindu 1978).

This African philosophy (which is now thought, sought, defined, and affirmed by itself) is diverse and multiple. Limitations do exist to the outline I have proposed. First, African philosophy cannot yet be thought of in the past, as is, for example, the case with the German philosophy of the eighteenth century. Recent and new, African philosophy exists in the present and, rightly or wrongly, promises itself a fine future. Second, my presentation is only one possible view of this philosophy. One could very easily give another picture of it which, for example, might take into account three major variables: the type of philosophical reflectors, the objective of philosophical systems, and the meaning of the concept of philosophy. One example would be Tempels and Kagame versus Towa and Hountondji. On the one hand, Aristotle and Thomas Aquinas are reflectors of a philosophical practice; on the other, one finds Hegel, Marx, and Althusser. Tempels dreamed of an African Christian civilization; Hountondji believes that Africa's salvation should come from a Marxist lesson and at any rate that it is conditioned by the advocacy of science. Tempels thought that philosophy was a means of vital communication; according to Hountondji, philosophy can only be metaphilosophy. This incredible dialogue seems highly amusing as long as nobody introduces another variable: the possibility of challenging and questioning the epistemological field that allows it and accounts for its pertinence.

In any event, one might observe that the trends I have presented could also, from the viewpoint of their methodological presuppositions, be classified into three main groups: first, the domain of anthropological philosophy which, initiated by Tempels and his disciples, has developed into theories of cultural contrasts (Laleye, Mulago, and Sow) as well as into hermeneutics and linguistic philosophy (Kinyongo, Nkombe, Tshiamalenga, and in general the school of Kinshasa); second, the domain of speculative and critical philosophy, which in a radical manner opposes both the silent sectarianism of anthropology and the methodological laziness of ethnophilosophy, defining itself as a field of metaphilosophy and promoting questions on the being of African philosophy (Eboussi-Boulaga, Elungu, Hountondji, and Towa), while allowing strong debates on relationships existing between philosophy, cultures, and epistemological frameworks (Adotevi, Sow, and Pathe Diagne); and third, the domain of Marxist projects with its various charter programs, which emphasize the universality of Marxist methodology and specify intellectual, materialist practices as instruments for a political power that would organize African social formations according to a socialist rationality.

In this analysis, I have preferred to understand Kagame and Mulago as philosophers in the same way as are Hountondji and Eboussi-Boulaga, because, in my estimation, all of them are part of a history of African philosophy in the making. A historical process may well do without the distinctions on the strict or wide use of a discipline and may only retain corrections, complementary acts, and successive "goings beyond" in the image of the model offered by E. Fleischman in his Jewish criticism of Christianity (1970). And this criticism, let it be said in passing, was not, except in a few cases, made by professional philosophers. In my analysis, then, the distinction between philosophy in the strict sense and philosophy in the wider sense means that it allows a possible classification and a question: What is philosophy? More immediately, how can it be understood in Africa?

I have discussed some of the most representative works attempting to answer these questions. Answers are also given in a number of journals and good periodicals. Departments of philosophy in most French-speaking African universities (in Benin, Cameroon, Congo, Gabon, Ivory Coast, Senegal, Togo, Zaire) produce much ongoing research. Professional and scholarly associations are being formed, including L'Association des Professeurs de Philosophie (Ouagadougou), Le Conseil Inter-Africain de Philosophie (Cotonou), La Société Africaine de Philosophie (Dakar), and La Société Zaïroise de Philosophie (Lubumbashi). We must finally note the important role played by the journal *Présence africaine* and the African Society of Culture. They originally subdivided the areas of research in this domain and continue to provide outlets for African thought.

Recent Milestones in African Philosophy

1887: E. W. Blyden, *Christianity, Islam and the Negro Race*
1899: L. Frobenius, *Die Geschichte des afrikanischen Kultur*

1907–11: S. Kaoze, *La Psychologie des Bantus et quelques lettres*
1933–49: W. Schmidt, *Die Ursprung der Gottesidee*
1945: P. Tempels, *La Philosophie bantoue*
1948: M. Griaule, *Dieu d'eau: Entretiens avec Ogotemmeli*
         J. P. Sartre, "Orphée noir"
1954: C. A. Diop, *Nations nègres et culture*
1956: A. Kagame, *La Philosophie bantu-rwandaise de l'être*
1958: J. Jahn, *Muntu: Umrisse der neoafrikanschen Kultur*
1962: L. S. Senghor, *Pierre Teilhard de Chardin et la politique africaine*
1964: K. Nkrumah, *Consciencism*
1965: F. Crahay, "Le 'Décollage' conceptuel: Conditions d'une philosophie bantoue"
1968: F. Eboussi-Boulaga, "Le Bantu Problématique"
1975: A. J. Smet, ed., *Philosophie africaine*
1977: F. Eboussi-Boulaga, *La Crise du Muntu*
         P. Hountondji, *Sur la philosophie africaine*
1980: A. J. Smet, *Histoire de la philosophie africaine contemporaine*

Vincent Mulago and the Roman Catholic Theological Discourse

In 1966 Vincent Mulago organized a center for the study of African religions, Le Centre d'Etude des Religions Africaines. It was created within the School of Theology of Lovanium University. Mulago's objective was twofold: to promote analyses and interpretations of African traditional religions and to propose methods for integrating Christianity in Africa based on positive figures and values of African religions. The objective seems ambiguous, not least because it is fundamentally a straightforward ideological reversal of colonial anthropological and religious policies. It posits disciplines that it challenges—anthropology, history, and philosophy—as auxiliaries of the new enterprise but does not directly interrogate their incapacity to unveil the reality of traditional beliefs. In doing so, the new project defines its own credibility within the efficiency and the power of the very theological discourse which used to negate the pertinence of traditional religions. But here is the point of the matter: the newness of Mulago's project resides in its strategy for enlarging the theological discourse to the multiplicity of cultural experiences, namely to African propositions on God and human fate. The journal of the institute, *Cahiers des religions africaines,* specified its mission and that of the Centre: "to pursue research for a scientific understanding of African traditional religions, beliefs and customs, in order to give an object of reflection to theologians and African humanists'' (cover of the journal, 1966–69).

This prudent formulation is, in fact, an answer to criticisms which possibly could come from orthodox and colonial-minded theologians. In order to minimize what could appear as a controversial program—the founding of a discourse on God from a strictly African locus—Mulago insists on the modesty of the enterprise. He wants to establish a library of traditional religious data and offer it for evaluation to theologians who eventually might decide about the methods of integrating African elements into Christianity. In its prudence the project implies also something else: a discreet critique of anthropology. The first two issues of the journal (January and July 1967) are devoted to a bibliographic survey of principal Central African communities: Bakongo, Baluba, Banyarwanda, Bashi, and Mongo. The third and fourth issues (January and July 1968) present a critical bibliography introduced and commented on by an anthropologist, P. Van Leynseele, who notes that "the different chapters (of the bibliography) are arranged in such a way that specialists from various disciplines can easily find out what interests them" (3, no. 2:177).

The basic principles of the Centre and its journal were made explicit for the first time in the third issue of the journal. The editorial of the issue is, from beginning to end, made up of important quotations from pontifical texts: Paul VI's message *Africae terrarum,* his encyclic *Populorum progressio,* and a homily of his which comments on the meaning of "African traditional values." These references suggest the necessity of analyzing African values in terms of the Church's duty (*devoir d'Eglise*). Tharcisse Tshibangu, who in 1965 was a newly proclaimed "Maître en theologie" from Louvain University (the highest academic rank that can be obtained in theology and philosophy beyond the doctorate) and professor of fundamental theology, committed his authority and contributed an article in which he explicitly stated: "In the past, African religion and the thought that it implies were more lived and implicit than conceived as fully explicit reflexes. Today and for the future, we have to rediscover the soul of this religious thought, and analyze it critically, in order to integrate this thought into the new forms of present-day African cultures. That's our task for today and tomorrow to be done at many different levels and in many different ways" (2, no. 3:11–21). Agreeing with Mulago's general plan, Tshibangu contemplates going beyond the shelter of anthropological discourses which witness to implicit paradigms of life, and he proposes a dramatic search for a critical self-representation. Strictly speaking, he does not posit a confrontation between the Christian tradition and African beliefs, but rather a method for joining them in "new forms of African culture," that is, a new reading and an explicit apprehension of an implicit religious thought and its critical integration into present-day demands.

One needs only to look at the monolithic force of missionary Christianity, particularly Catholicism, in order to understand this prudence of pronouncement. It signifies a decisive period in an endeavor whose roots go back to Mulago's doctoral thesis on the Bantu's vital union presented in 1955 at the Roman Urbanian University. The dissertation was published as a book by Présence Africaine under the title *Un Visage africain du Christianisme* (1965). It claims to avoid the danger of bringing Catholic discourse into a heterogenous space in which Christian theology could be simply arrayed next to beliefs, experiences, and knowledge that it has always opposed. At the same time, its ambition seems to shake off the dividing line between pure and impure systems of religious beliefs and to express in new cultural terms the possibility of both a renewed theological and pastoral activity.

According to Mulago, African theology as a scientific discipline needs a universal reference in intellectual method and seeks the truth in a well-localized human experience about God. Moreover, it is from the body of orthodox Christianity and its representations that this new discipline establishes contact with African religious figures, fragments of local wisdom, and enduring manifestations of God. In fact, the new discourse engineers the triumph of Christianity in an original way. In contrast with most of missionary methods which tended to situate Christianization and westernization in a relationship of necessity, Mulago sees not only Christianity but also its theology as a possible locus of fulfillment and dialogue for diversified and various cultures. The position does not seem unorthodox, since it actualizes the teachings and invitations of such popes as Benedict XV, Pius XI, and Pius XII, known as missionary pontiffs. Intellectually, it pursues the pioneering openings made in the 1920s by the Belgian Jesuit Pierre Charles, who emphasized in his missiological books the theological pertinence of diversity in Church life and customs. Yet Mulago is considered a radical. His being black does not seem to have been very important, at least for Rome, which was then promoting the first black bishops. But Mulago is one of the first Central African priests to graduate from a pontifical university. He received a doctorate in theology from the Urbanian University in Rome in 1955, a B.A. in canon law from the Gregorian University in 1956, and in the same year a diploma in journalism from the Roman University of Social Sciences. Rightly, the colonial authority and the ecclesiastical hierarchy feared that others might follow his critical path. Unjustifiably, they punished him for what we would consider political perspicacity. The Belgian Congo governor Pétillon worried about the effect of Mulago's subversive ideas on African identity. After a talk Mulago gave to the mixed intelligentsia of Bukavu in 1956 in which he addressed the falsehood of Cham's curse as well as the political future of his country, the Church moved him from his position as associate pastor in Bukavu to the countryside as teacher in a high school for potential seminarians (see Ngindu 1981a:293–318).

What, precisely, are the revolutionary ideas of Mulago? Drawing heavily upon the contributions of Placide Tempels and Alexis Kagame, Mulago envisaged an agenda based on three paradigms: unconditional fidelity to the Catholic *magisterium* and Christian Credo, a real attentiveness to local cultures, and an expository analysis reconciling the best of African traditions with Christian dogmatic and moral prescriptions (Mulago 1959). Following official Christian teachings and the soundest theological propositions of the 1950s, Mulago decided to apply procedures of critical concordance to the exploration of African religious alterity. He called the most positive values in Central Africa (solidarity, hospitality, blood union, the sense of a living *communitas,* belief in one Creator and omnipotent God) *pierres d'attente du Christianisme,* that is, stepping-stones of Christianity, and defined them as natural and providential signs of God's benevolence, waiting for their fulfillment in Christian revelation (Mulago 1956a, 1956b, 1958, 1965a).

His first major publication, "L'Union vitale bantu . . . chez les Bashi, les Banyarwanda et les Barundi" (1956), distinguished him from the dominant missionary ideology. Although the fundamental assumptions of this thesis are of an anthropological nature, Mulago explores Tempels' philosophical theses on Bantu ontology and Kagame's extensions of the Belgian Franciscan's insights. His own acquaintance with the cultural milieu he analyzes shows that nothing blends so well as intellectual vigilance, anthropological knowledge, and existential participation in the studied area. Mulago's main point is that the East African pact of blood and pacts of friendship practiced in traditional communities could be usefully employed as symbolic schemata for a theology of communion and sacraments (Mulago 1957b, 1958). His position that cultural identity should be the highest legitimating factor in African theology was expressed in two theoretical articles: the first invited an adaptation of the missionary legacy (Mulago 1958); the second bore on the responsibility of African Christian theologians to subsume in an intelligent manner two apparently contradictory characteristics, those of being simultaneously an African and a Christian theologian (Mulago 1959).

In brief, a good understanding of the meanings expressed in African symbols and customs is regarded as essential for a solid anchorage in the most profound stratum of the known and the familiar. It should bring about a comprehensive representation of the local picture which unites nature, humans, and God (Mulago 1968a, 1972). But because of its intrinsic limitation, since it does not witness to the real revelation, this dialectic and its symbols should be purified and assumed by the Christian experience in *catholic* spirit (Greek *katholikos* means universal): "In the same faith nothing impedes a variety of customs of the Holy Church" (St. Gregory, in Mulago 1981:41). For instance, Mulago emphasizes the model of conversion that Gregory gave to Augustine for the conversion of Anglo-Saxons: to avoid a transplantation of Roman customs, even that of traditional forms of ecclesiastical life and liturgy, and systematically to use local customs, ceremonies, places of pagan sacrifices, and only progressively to transform them and orient them toward the celebration of the true God (Mulago 1981:9).

Christianity has thus been culturally marked by its integration into various European cultures, and those Christian customs and feasts which are genealogically linked to immemorial pagan traditions bear silent witness to this fact. Mulago bases his method on this prescription and its subsequent generalization as the Church's policy of conversion (*Conversio Gentium*) established in the 1659 Instruction of the *Sacra Congregatio de Propaganda Fide*. He notes the methodological necessity of distinguishing two steps. First, he insists on a careful observation and selection of African religious practices and beliefs in terms of their similitudes with Christian values. For him, this analysis should clearly distinguish fruitful and unfruitful institutions and symbols. The second step reinterprets African religious signs and explicates them within the spiritual economy of Christianity (Mulago 1957a, 1971b).

At this point, one might begin to understand that Mulago's theory for an adaptation theology refers to delicate issues concerning the differentiation of human cultures and of human consciousnesses. For him, the African has to confront Christianity, the unknown realm, from the solidity and authenticity of his or her known cultural experience. Thus, conversion becomes both a locus and a moment of mediation in which a symbolic apprehension transforms itself by uniting a cultural matrix and the *traditio Christiana* (Mulago 1956a, 1958, 1962, 1967b).

Mulago's genius resides in the subtle way he silently brings together the fact of the diversity of cultures and a theory of the differentiation of consciousness (Mulago 1976a, b). His readers readily accept the logical deductions of his premises. Yet some seem to feel that the self-evidence of conclusions may lead too far. Orthodox theologians, particularly Europeans, fear that Mulago might force them into the signs of otherness; these rapidly could become expressions of a negation of the tradition of the Church which, historically, has been isomorphic with the *traditio Christiana*. Other theologians, particularly Africans, would tend to oppose Mulago's order of Christianity, which, by positing the reduction of African experiences and symbols to a paradigmatic *traditio,* seems to postulate an identity between conversion to Christianity and allegiance to European history (e.g., Mveng 1981).

I do not think it a lapse into an easy generalization to state that Mulago symbolized the intellectual necessity of an era. Even those who, coming later, have challenged his method have found inspiration in his work of the early 1950s (see Mveng 1978). Kwesi Dickson, a theologian from Ghana, provides the best synthesis of Mulago's theological principles, as assumptions basic to African Christian churches (Dickson 1978:392).

1. The revelation of God given in His son Jesus Christ cannot be totally discontinuous with the African's traditional Knowledge of God; if God is the father of us all, as Christ taught, then He must be involved in the life and thought of all peoples.
2. In the early days of the Christian Church following the resurrection of Christ, being a Christian, for the Jew, did not necessarily involve the rejection of all the ancient marks of Jewishness.
3. The Biblical attitude to other religions is ambivalent. In both Old and New Testaments there is a tradition which rejects those of the non-Jewish faith, but this tradition exists side by side with the view that God accepts those of other faiths, though in two Biblical passages which express this view it is made clear that such should be in the right spiritual condition.
4. The Biblical evidence shows that God is interested in the totality of man, not only in the spiritual aspect of him. In other words, man is encouraged to come to God as he is, in the particularity of his cultural situation.

Mulago's writings are not strictly theological, nor anthropological in a classical sense. They are in between and integrate both disciplines. One of his books, *La Religion traditionnelle des Bantu et leur vision du monde* (1973) illustrates the general framework of his method. It is organized in four parts. The first is an analysis of the themes which in anthropological literature define the particularity of "primitive religions," namely magic, sorcery, divination. The second part focuses on specific rites and cults of ancestors as still performed today among the Kongo, Shi, Banyarwanda, Mongo, and Luba-Kasai. The third is an interpretation of both the representation and significance of relationships existing between God and humans according to the same ethnic groups. Finally, in the last part, Mulago indicates how certain traditional customs and beliefs fit into the Christian grid. It is conspicuous that in this process, anthropology as a whole becomes a simple key to the theological and pastoral programs of Africanizing Christianity. The first three parts of the book have no meaning independent from the last, which sets forth a major thesis: the Church and its truth should integrate and fulfill the best of local customs. "The Church, people of God by which this kingdom of Christ is incarnated, takes nothing from material riches of whatever culture. On the contrary, she serves and assumes all the positive faculties, resources and forms of life of those people. In assuming them, she purifies them, she reinforces them, and she promotes them" (Mulago 1973a:154).

The stepping-stones of Christianity in the African contexts should therefore, according to Mulago, serve as founding principles of an African Christianity. They are, precisely: the concept of unity of life which, in a Central African *communitas,* unites members in an "ontic" structure and a hierarchy of vital forces; the principle of vital communion which links all beings within an "ontological order" expressing itself as participation or rejection (all existing realms—mineral, vegetable, animal, human, ancestral, and divine—are interdependent and act upon each other); and the pervasive symbolism of themes of vital participation in both beliefs and everyday life (Mulago 1965a, 1968c, 1969b). In sum, Mulago legitimates Tempels' intuitions and observations about Luba-Shaba. And he insists that his conclusions come from both his reading of anthropological literature and his direct knowledge of all the communities he writes about (Mulago 1973a).

Since 1962 Mulago has been professor of African religions at the Faculté de Théologie Catholique in Kinshasa. His teachings as well as his publications are generally framed into the grid which produced his 1973 treatise on Bantu religion. Among his students were Alphonse Ngindu and Oscar Bimwenyi, who in the 1970s became the most ardent proponents of "incarnation theology," a radical critique of the *pierres d'attente* theology. For them, God directly speaks to all humans, and it is up to the Church to adapt to and integrate itself into local cultures and not the contrary, as expounded by Mulago.

At any rate, in the 1960s Mulago was still a kind of ambiguous prophet. Dominique Nothomb's book on Rwandese humanism (1965) makes both Kagame's claim about the existence of a Bantu-Rwandese philosophy and Mulago's theology of *pierres d'attente* acceptable and credible by sorting out "harmonies" existing between Christian paradigms and Rwandese beliefs and attitudes. African theology was no longer a secondary subject. African countries were becoming independent, and the future of Christianity seemed at stake. Indeed, by then, the Church was officially seeking methods of differentiating itself from colonialism and its implications. The leadership of the Church was increasingly becoming African. Meetings of experts multiplied all over Central and West Africa, and they could hardly conceal their ideological search for a means to legitimize Christianity as universal experience. New institutions of pastoral research conducted experiments, particularly in liturgy, on ways of reconciling Christian message and African heritage. More important, one observes that the spirit of the then ongoing Vatican II Council explicitly legitimated and strengthened the most dramatic moment: its official consecration came in 1967, when Paul VI in *Africae terrarum* qualified the search for an adapted theology as the Church's duty (Mulago 1981:34–55).

Within this context, Mulago rapidly gained the status of an institution. He foresaw, ten years in advance, what was ten years happening. In the 1960s his Centre d'Etude des Religions Africaines was perceived with fear and hope as a laboratory which could produce either a beautiful catastrophe or a new starting point in theology. Soon he was elected vice dean of the Faculté de Théologie Catholique, asked to serve in Rome as consultant on the Committee for Non-Christians, and named a full member of Pope Paul VI's International Committee on Theology. Despite these honors, the man remained committed to his local project and devoted himself to three main tasks: the stabilization of his Centre within the Faculté de Théologie and the internationalization of its advisory bodies, the promotion of essential texts of Christianity, and the building up of a new spirituality and liturgy to be based on a solid footing. His aim was to implement a research policy embracing the complementary aspects of theology and African studies rather than their conflicting models. He reinforced the scientific credibility of the Kinshasa school by including many respected scholars on his committees, such as F. Bontinck (Zaire), A. Kagame (Rwanda), E. Mveng (Cameroon), C. Nyamiti (Tanzania), L. V. Thomas (France), T. Tshibangu (Zaire), and J. Vansina (United States). Mulago personally directed a team which translated the New Testament into his native language (Mulago 1973b). Using his concordist method, Mulago extensively published on marriage, sacraments, and religious symbolism. In collaboration with Théodore Theuws (1960) he even tried to bring back to an orthodox line the spiritual experience of the controverted Jamaa movement created by Tempels.

Mulago was soon no longer alone in the intellectual process of adapting Christianity to the African context. In fact, he has never been completely alone, but merely the most resolute and systematic in carrying out his ideas, and thus the most visible. A number of other theologians, most of them educated at Roman universities, also participated in the emergence of adaptation theology. The Franciscan François-Marie Lufuluabo, one of the most active, between 1962 and 1970 published four booklets on the topic. His *Vers une théodicéé bantoue* (1962) is a good introduction to the Bantu conception of divinity. *La Notion luba-bantoue de l'être* (1964) presents the concept of being in Luba culture on the basis of a careful linguistic analysis. *Perspective théologique bantoue et théologie scholastique* (1966) is the closest approach to Mulago's concordism and defines theological tasks in Africa as a derivation of the Scholastic method. Within this same perspective one would situate two illustrative studies written by African members of the religious community of Scheut: *Pour une anthropologie chrétienne du mariage au Congo* (1968) by L. Mpongo proposes the practicality of using some rites of the Ntombe N'jale community for the celebration of the sacrament of marriage; and *Initiation africaine et initiation chrétienne* (1966) by Célestin Mubengayi Lwakale offers advice and specific ways of transforming some procedures of traditional initiation into Christian liturgy.

Let us be more specific and refer to concrete projects. The best illustration of the adaptation policy might be John Mbiti's *New Testament Eschatology in an African Background* (1971), which presents a "process of proclaiming the Gospel and establishing the Church in an African tribal setting": the Akamba. Its method is quite simple. Mbiti presents and analyzes Akamba traditional concepts related to Christian eschatology; then, from this background he proposes a new reading of the Gospel's eschatological message which could help its being taught to the Akamba peoples. For instance, the Kikamba word for heaven is *itu;* its plural, *matu,* means the space overhanging the earth. But according to Mbiti, if the Akamba believe that God dwells in heaven, a careful analysis of their tradition indicates that God dwells beyond the *matu* and also that the departed do not live there but rather somewhere on or in the earth. Thus, a specific cultural articulation simultaneously opposes and unites earthly objects associated with the departed and heavenly objects related to God. Consequently, in order to reconcile this African cultural feature with Christian theology, Mbiti emphasizes the metaphorical meaning of the New Testament *heaven:* it does not designate a geographical location. "Heaven is not heavenly, has no independent reality as such. The New Testament emphasizes Jesus as the one through whom and in whom life is given, life is heavenly" (Mbiti 1971). John Mbiti is harsh on Tempels and his disciples. Yet his method is probably the best illustration of their dreams.

Closer intellectually to Mulago is Henri Maurier, whose *La Philosophie de l'Afrique noire* (1975) exemplifies philosophically Kagame's and Mulago's belief and concordist method. Henri Maurier, a White Father, is a longtime student of African cultures. He began his career in the 1950s as professor of philosophy in major seminaries in France and in Upper Volta. From 1970 to 1977 he was in charge of the African seminar at *Lumen Vitae* Institute in Brussels. Since 1978 he has taught evangelization and civilizations at L'Institut Catholique de Paris. In his book, he attempts to found a discourse on African *Weltanschauungen* from a philosophical viewpoint and formulates two preconditions. Maurier first asserts the usefulness of a dialogue between Europe and Africa, for "the West (to only speak of it) is therefore a willing or undesirable accomplice, though an inevitable patron. In the face of an Africa defining itself, there is a West that continues to have its own idea about Africa" (1975:12). Second, he chooses an explicitly rationalist perspective which, according to him, very well accounts for the present-day consciousness and the demands of modernity. Moreover, as he put it, "the way toward modernity, in which Africa is irresistibly engaged, demands that one define himself very critically and according to rationality" (1975:13).

Philosophy, notes Maurier, is and should be understood as reflexive, rational, critical, and systematic thinking. Yet his project is not strictly about the derivation of this practice and its African acclimatization but rather about the possibility of a critical reading of African "traditions" as philosophical experiences. This leads him to suggest and insist on the concept of a plurality of philosophy. I think Maurier conforms to *l'air du temps*. No one believes any longer that there is such a thing as an already found and definitely constituted truth. If contemporary theories and orientations teach us anything, it is that, as Mulago indicates (1965a), all civilizations are options in which one finds a variety of discursive practices about truth. Maurier is quite right when he thinks that the diversity of *Weltanschauungen* cannot be expressed in terms of more or less advanced human experience but should be qualified on the basis of differences existing in human options. In fact, in terms of method, Maurier integrates in a stimulating move the ethnophilosophical project of Placide Tempels, Alexis Kagame, and Vincent Mulago (who believed that they could translate in an explicit language the implicit philosophy of the Bantu) with Franz Crahay's and Paulin Hountondji's evaluations of the shortcomings of this argument.

My only reservation is about Maurier's conceptual hesitations. He clearly demonstrates that one can derive a philosophical theory from African *Weltanschauungen* and succeeds in demonstrating what can be called a theory of the African subject. Yet his claim (which accounts for the title of the book) that these *Weltanschauungen* themselves are philosophies seems like an ethnophilosophical thesis and, at any rate, is subject to debate.

The book expounds three main themes: the form of African thought and its categories; the dynamic or economy of African social relationships and their symbolism; and ritual and sacrifice and their meanings. The first theme derives from a major postulation: the relative autonomy of the African *forme de pensée,* cognitively and affectively dependent upon the lifeways of a culture. This "form" is, according to the author, characterized by three factors. First, an anthropocentrism affirms the centrality of the human, while defining everything else in terms of this human locus. Second, this anthropocentrism would be community-oriented insofar as the African individual is always perceived as a member of a specific community, that is to say, his or her being-for-itself can only be linked to his or her being-with-others. Thus, a third factor: this individual is essentially a relational being who gets significance and pertinence by his or her integration in a given human community. Maurier thinks one could deduce that the form of thinking in Africa is relational. On the level of ideas, this seems to confirm Mulago's findings. But Maurier furthers his analysis and observes that this African way is the reversal of the Western tradition. Against the ancient Greek cosmocentrism in which the human is a simple element in the cosmos, the African anthropocentrism reduces the universe by defining it from the human (see Mulago 1956a). In the same vein, against the Cartesian cogito which posits the individual's consciousness as the sole point of certainty and an absolute beginning of knowledge, African paradigms would promote a preindividualist awareness, emphasizing integration in a preexisting social order (see Mulago 1965a). In fact, Maurier confirms Senghor's remarkable metaphor about the opposition of the European *raison-oeil* and the African *raison-étreinte.* It is from this epistemological background that Maurier specifies what he considers to be the basic categories of the philosophy of Black Africa, namely the notions of relation, subjectivity, corporality, manipulation (in terms of relations) and, finally, the irreducible or *l'Au-delà de la relation normale* (see Mulago 1956b, 1957b).

The analysis of the economy of social relationships actualizes a philosophical meditation which tries to go beyond the conclusions offered by Tempels' *Bantu Philosophy,* for example. Maurier has read good anthropological works and believes that there is an African model (*un schéma d'ensemble*) which should account for the dynamics of social relations (see Mulago 1979c). This *schéma d'ensemble* is a dialectical progression in three stages. From stage zero to stage one, the movement jumps and blasts as differentiation. One naturally thinks of objective separations: men vs. women, dead vs. living, exogamy vs. endogamy, opposition of age-class and opposition between family relations, etc. These tensions would indicate a social hierarchy which is both an expression and a consequence of a cumulation of unequal relations. What is striking in Africa, writes Maurier, is "the last of a somewhat ritualized and institutionalized tension" (1975:120). The second moment would represent another point, an extreme one: "The relational life, therefore, is not realized without some moments of tension-separation" (1975:120). The third and last moment would represent a unifying synthesis exemplified by reciprocity in gifts and exchanges.

The last part of Maurier's study focuses on rites and sacrifices considered as vivifying signs of social relations. The core is surely his theory of sacrifice, in which he distinguishes the mechanism of a sacrifice (the sacrifice itself) from its effect: the possible resolution of any tension created by a socially dangerous unanimity. In fact, Maurier integrates Réne Girard's thesis about the "mécanisme de la victime émissaire" (1975:252). Indeed, after Luc de Heusch's masterful study on African sacrifice, we may wonder whether Girard's hypothesis, and thus Maurier's interpretation, still makes sense. I personally think that they do not. Maurier knows more about Africa than Girard. By analyzing concrete examples of sacrifice, he could have checked Girard's generalizations. He might have resolved some of the issues with which de Heusch is still struggling, or confronted Mulago's propositions on blood pact (1957b), symbolism (1979c), and the very concept of a dialogue between Christianity, philosophy, and African practices.

How, then, should we globally evaluate adaptation theology? In the 1970s Mulago's students and many others faced two new problems. It was clear that the major argument of the method required an ideological presupposition, that of otherness, and its manifest sign, the right to cultural alterity. How could one reconcile this with Christianity if one postulates that there is a universal dimension to it? Conversely, looked at carefully, the adaptation program as an event for a possible dialogue does not really seem to constitute a mutation of missionary Christianity. It only adapts some external signs of experiencing and expressing Christian faith and maintains, as an absolute rule, the being of Christianity as signified and historically actualized in the Western experience. If Christianity were really universal, then it should be capable of *incarnating* itself within the complexity and alterity of all human cultures. In sum, to use a somewhat frivolous metaphor, the African Christianity of adaptation theology is similar to "tropicalized" cars or refrigerators. Some particular and special pieces are modified in the body of the object in order to make it capable of adapting itself to the tropical milieu, but the structure of the object and the copyright attached to it witness to its builders and the institutional context which made it possible.

What should we make of all this? I have heard righteous Westerners insisting that Africans have simply to accept the being and usefulness of Christianity in exactly the same manner as they accept the practicality of technological goods and knowledge imported from the Occident. At the other side, some Africans affirm that the project of Africanizing Christianity does not make sense, since one can more productively choose to promote or adapt one's own religion and tradition. In between, some Christians from both Africa and Europe emphasize, as Mulago has been doing since 1955, the universality of the Christian message and the mission of incarnating it in all cultures; in brief, the demand of pluralism in the practice of Christian theology.

"We must reject as absolutely false, the concept of one universal theology," writes Alphonse M. Ngindu (1974). A former student of Mulago's, he served as his closest collaborator in the management of both the Centre and the *Cahiers des religions africaines*. But his statement can be traced back to the dialogue which, in 1959, brought together Canon A. Vanneste, dean of the Faculté de Théologie, and one of his students, Tharcisse Tshibangu, who later became the president of the university and the auxiliary bishop of Kinshasa. Tshibangu invoked the possibility of an African theology which could be, metaphorically, an analogical reflection of the diversity of humankind's richness as manifested by the multiplicity of languages and systems of thought. The particularity of this theological discourse would reside in the truth and the originality of its cultural space and specifically in its local sources of metaphors and "theological stepping-stones." Canon Vanneste's answer focused on the concept of Christian theology as unitary and universal, and on international norms for the practice of the discipline. He insisted that "African theologians" have nothing to gain by retiring within themselves. "They might in so doing condemn themselves to remain second zone theologians" (Tshibangu and Vanneste 1960:333–52).

The dialogue rapidly became an international debate in which J. Danielou, H. Maurier, and G. Thils, among others, intervened (Actes 1969). Most of the scholars bore witness to the privilege of theology as a discourse which in its being and by its very vocation should subsume all of God's manifestations and the varieties and modalities of expressing his signs. It was a bewildering debate. In fact, African theologians rejoiced. A Catholic theologian from India entered into the discussion, claiming that the raison d'être of Christianity is to integrate all human experiences in the eternal body of Christ. From Japan, another theologian said exactly the contrary and insisted on the providential spiritual and intellectual continuity which links the Western experience of God's revelation to the vocation of Israel, the chosen people. Some African interventions in the debate completely missed the point by alluding to Vanneste's unconscious or conscious ethnocentrism. In fact, Vanneste's text is subtler than one would believe at first reading. For excellent reasons, it insists on the necessity of a sound and rigorous method in the interpretation of the Gospel's message. Unfortunately papers on adaptation theology are not always examples of intellectual rigor.

There is, however, a discreet problem in Vanneste's intervention that nobody has, so far, addressed. Canon Vanneste does not reject en bloc African theology. He believes in the feasibility of, and wishes for, a rigorous scientific theology in Africa. This is only possible, according to him, on the condition that the classical rules of the discipline be respected. One understands that the condition, in fact, implies a silent comparison between, on the one hand, the scientific dignity of historical, exegetical, and philosophical methods which traditionally have been the faithful auxiliary sciences of the Western practice of theology and, on the other hand, the vague and shifting methodological principles of anthropological knowledge invoked by African theologians. It would be, I am afraid, unwise to challenge Vanneste on this point, since, in its intention as well as in its program, adaptation theology has itself proclaimed anthropology's methodological weaknesses, its prevailing misunderstandings and errors. Mulago indicated the generality of this suspicion by insisting on the usefulness of fieldwork conducted by African scholars among Africans in order to check and correct anthropologists' generalizations and interpretations (see Mulago 1956a, 1968a, 1973a). The major question coming out of Canon Vanneste's proposition concerns the dignity and credibility of anthropology as a scientific auxiliary of theology but does not challenge the intrinsic value of African theology per se.

Nevertheless, Tshibangu's pronouncement was sound. As linguistic, social, and cultural structures vary, so necessarily do intellectual and cosmological schemata. Every society has its own spiritual configuration and systems of perceiving and incarnating God's message. In saying this, Tshibangu was, in fact, following Mulago and expressing in a more sophisticated epistemological framework what Mulago had been expounding since 1955–56, namely that theological discourse cannot but reflect the contingency of contextual determinations and particular sociocultural representations. It is noteworthy that, years later, Tshibangu wrote that only afterward did he fully perceive the pertinence of his relativistic intuition about Christian authenticity, precisely in 1964, when at Louvain University he was finishing his doctoral dissertation on the theology of the sixteenth-century Spaniard Melchior Cano. In 1965 he published his magnum opus, the most ambitious book ever written by an African theologian, according to Hastings, in which he critically analyzes the variations of Western theological discourses in both speculative and positive theologies. This book was followed by a number of remarkable exegetical and philological studies which make the same point. Among the most important, let us rapidly mention Jean Kinyongo's book on the origin and signification of the sacred name of Yahweh (1970), Joseph Ntedika's imposing work on the evolution of the Latin liturgy for the departed (1971), Dosithée Atal's analysis and interpretation of the beginning of the Johannic hymn (1972), Laurent P. Monsengwo's semantic study of the Hebrew notion of *nomos* in the Pentateuch (1973), and Alphonse M. Ngindu's dissertation on Laberthonière's religious philosophy (1978), one of the best works to date on the topic, according to the French philosopher J. Lacroix.

These theologians were consciously or unconsciously displacing questions about the pertinence and validity of African theology. Interrogating the Western tradition of Christianity in its own terms and with the most scrupulous and canonical methods, they could not but conclude that the endeavor of African theology did indeed make sense. Theological discourses or commentaries on God are always culturally contextual, and the Gospel's message is significant only in the way it incarnates itself within given and specific cultures. In 1977 at the University of Strasbourg, France, where he was receiving an honorary degree, Bishop Tshibangu could state: ''The discussion on problems of principles and foundations of an African theology is over. What we need now are specialized studies which will demonstrate the originality of African theology.''

A new era began, that of a theology of incarnation dominated by the notion of the uniqueness of each human experience. One of its most significant events was the organization in 1979 by Vincent Mulago of an international colloquium on African religion and Christianity. The conference had encouragements from Rome and the highest ecclesiastical authorities and brought together some of the best students of the subject. At the end of the conference, evaluating the work, Mulago stated:

> With lucidity and firmness, [the Conference] has asserted the necessity of a frank dialogue between the African religious genius and the Gospel, a dialogue favorable in every aspect to the blossoming and the rise of an African theology. A theology which will not simply be an echo of the missionaries who have brought the Gospel to us but a theology which must show itself capable of assuming, of taking charge of the real life of the Africans. It will

be a theology fully informed by life itself, a theology open to life and all its dimensions and susceptible to found an ethical system, a social practice, a specific spirituality so as to integrate in its bosom the religious sensibility peculiar to the Africans.

In the general euphoria of the meeting, a former student of Vincent Mulago's who by then was his colleague, Alphonse M. Ngindu, became the editorial secretary of the *Bulletin of African Theology,* the organ of the Ecumenical Association of African Theology; Mulago serves as a member of the editorial board. Mulago also serves in a more ambiguous position on the board of the *Revue africaine de théologie,* created in 1977 by the Kinshasa school (to which he has belonged since 1962) in order to counterbalance the influence of his *Cahiers de religions africaines.* In 1977 Mulago celebrated his twenty-fifth anniversary in the Roman Catholic priesthood and the fifteenth anniversary of his Centre d'Etude des Religions Africaines. Alphonse M. Ngindu, his deputy director, asked some of Mulago's friends in the world, colleagues at the Catholic school in Kinshasa, and former students to participate in the publication of a festschrift to honor him (Ngindu 1981a). Most of them declined the invitation. Mulago was still perceived as too radical and, despite the Vatican's blessings and honors, too controversial.

3
What Is the Real Thing?

The Past as Doxology

Tu autem in nobis es, et nomen sanctum tuum invocatum est super nos.

Breviarum Romanum

The primitive, the barbarian, and the civilized — the last of these three concepts, as a concept as well as a moment, seems always to imply a past in which the two preceding ones actualize themselves as its imperfect signs or, to put it in a more positive light, as its antecedents. Even Marxism sets itself the task of understanding and commenting upon the dialectical dynamism of a progressive transformation of modes of production through stages and discontinuities which reflect these concepts. Freud, in *Civilization and its Discontents* (1953–74, vol. 21: 59), neatly dissociates and opposes the primitive to the civilized pole, in a clear diachronic tempo. Anthropologists and psychoanalysts, since the debate between Jones and Malinowski, have been expounding contradictory interpretations about the universality of Oedipus in history and in space.

In this chapter, I shall address two linked issues: the fatality of a universal tempo of progression and its relation to the figure or structure of Oedipus and Electra. I have chosen to proceed from a brief synthesis of Deleuze and Guattari's proposition on the "primitive machines" (1977) to a simple but critically synthetic reading of Luc de Heusch's magnificent analysis of the origin of the state (1982) by focusing on Oedipus' or Electra's images and subtle duplications in mythical narratives.

Sive Autem Tribulamur

Let us begin by locating a question. The radical "meaning of it all" as well as the very "sense of it all," as proposed in G. Deleuze and F. Guattari's

Anti-Oedipus (1977), springs from a majestic order of explanation: a history of philosophy and a philosophy of history which posit a rational line of succession of events and stages in the organization and administration of societies. In fact, one might call it the evidence of a universal history. Deleuze and Guattari say, "First of all, universal history is the history of contingencies, and not the history of necessity. Ruptures and limits, and not continuity" (1977:140). More specifically, to use a paradigm which could, *a posteriori,* account for the fact that there is such a thing as a universal history, they propose a thesis: "in a sense, capitalism has haunted all forms of society, but it haunts them as their terrifying nightmare, it is the dread they feel of a flow that would elude their codes. Then again, if we say that capitalism determines the conditions and the possibility of a universal history, this is true only insofar as capitalism has to deal essentially with its own limit, its own destruction—as Marx says, insofar as it is capable of self-criticism [at least to a certain point: the point where the limit appears, in the very movement that counteracts the tendency]" (Deleuze and Guattari 1977:140).

In sum, this statement means that the Marxist theorist or practitioner is looking for the "sense of it all" because he or she has already found it. Conversely, it is in the materiality of this found logic that a history of contingencies seen and analyzed from capitalism as a concrete experience (or as an object of desire) transmutes itself into a universal history and unveils the logic of ruptures and discontinuities in the active progression of modes of production. The "primitive territorial machines," for which "filiation is administrative and hierarchical, but alliance is political and economic, and expresses power insofar as it is not fused with the hierarchy and cannot be deduced from it, and the economy insofar as it is not identical with administration" (Deleuze and Guattari 1977:148), can only precede the "barbarian despotic machine" and its imperial representation: "Exogamy must result in the position of men outside the tribe who for their part are entitled to an endogamous marriage and are able, by virtue of this formidable right, to serve as initiators to exogamous subjects of both sexes: the sacred 'deflowerer,' the 'ritual initiator' on the mountain or across the waters" (1977:200). The third and last moment of the "evolution" is represented in the "civilized capitalist machine." It localizes itself in the meeting of two constituents: "On one side, the deterritorialized *Worker* who has become free and naked, having to sell his labor capacity; and on the other, decoded money that has become capital and is capable of buying it" (1977:225). In terms of representation, according to Deleuze and Guattari, the capitalist locus is a product of a maximalized process of "the decoding and the deterritorialization of flows in production" (1977:244).

Capitalism would have internalized alliances and filiation and would have privatized the family. This latter can no longer shape the social grids of economic reproduction. Situated outside the social field, the family is now a simple reflection of symbolizing images such as "Mister Capital," "Madame Earth," or "working child," whose "alliances and filiations no longer pass through people but through money; so the family becomes a microcosm, suited to expressing what it no longer dominates" (1977:264). For our authors, in these processes as well as in the flows it allows,

> [Capitalism] produces schizos the same way it produces Prell shampoo or Ford cars, the only difference being that the schizos are not salable. How then does one explain the fact that capitalist production is constantly arresting the schizophrenic process and transforming the subject of the process into a confined clinical entity as though it saw in this process the image of its own death coming from within? Why does it make the schizophrenic into a sick person—not only nominally but in reality? Why does it confine its madmen and madwomen instead of seeing in them its own heros and heroines, its own fulfillment? (1977:245)

We are now able to ask a question: what is this universal history which can be but a history of contingencies whose fulfillment is the capitalist or the socialist experience? It would be easy bad faith to use Mably's pessimistic evaluation of history as "an almost unbroken succession of miseries, disasters, and calamities" (quoted in Furet 1984:125–39). A more correct interpretation would note the Marxist assumption of Deleuze and Guattari's *Anti-Oedipus,* which explicates that history coincides with a tale about objective transformations, discontinuities of modes of production and their ideological representations. One could still question this definition and the thesis it carries. What is puzzling is that Deleuze and Guattari would agree. They even refer to, and accept as obvious, the strongest critique against the imperialism of a history which traditionally has entertained the idea that primitive societies have no history: "The presence of history in every social machine plainly appears in the disharmonies that, as Lévi-Strauss says, bear the unmistakable stamp of time elapsed" (Deleuze and Guattari 1977:150–51). Yet immediately thereafter, they make a move toward a possible universal historicization of individualities by distinguishing types of interpretation of socioeconomic disharmonies. In effect, as they propose, these may be perceived and understood in several ways: ideally, through "the gap between the real institution and the assumed ideal model"; morally, "by invoking a structural bond between law and transgression"; and physically, as "a question of attrition" for the "social machine" (Deleuze and Guattari 1977:151).

The being of a so-called primitive socius is a historical way of being. For to be a living human being is to witness a natural history as a permanent and progressive achievement genetically coded. On the other hand, the individuality of the being is given by and, at the same time, defines itself from a sociocultural context marked by a dialectic of conventions and inventions which animates its institutions, language, systems of beliefs, and symbols (see Wagner 1981). Deleuze and Guattari claim that the "primitive socius was indeed the only territorial machine in the strict sense of the term. The functioning of such a machine consists in the following: *the declension of alliance and filiation* declining the lineages on the body of the earth, before there is a State" (1977:146). This arrangement fixes two memories: on one side, the alliance or the memory of words and agreements that keep vivid facts concerning a circulating capital and the system of debts; on the other side, the filiation or the memory of blood which maintains a fixed capital and the filiative stock. Deleuze and Guattari can thus state that this primal "machine is *segmentary* because through its double apparatus of tribe and lineage, it cuts up segments of varying lengths: genealogical filiative units of major, minor and minimal lineages, with their hierarchy, their respective chiefs, their elders who guard the stocks and organize marriages; territorial tribal units of primary, secondary, and tertiary sections, also having their dominant roles and their alliances" (1977:152).

What about Oedipus? One may repeat here the arguments which opposed Malinowski to Jones, Kardiner and Fromm to Geza Roheim. The question remains, simple and obvious: Do cultural grammars of social formations constituted by different modes of production invent Oedipus and Electra in some cases and not in others? Deleuze and Guattari believe that "it is correct to question all social formations starting from Oedipus. But not because Oedipus might be a truth of the unconscious that is especially visible where *we are concerned;* on the contrary, because it is a mystification of the unconscious that has only succeeded with us by assembling the parts and wheels of its apparatus from elements of the previous social formations. It is universal in that sense. Thus it is indeed within capitalist society that the critique of Oedipus must always resume its point of departure and find again its point of arrival" (my emphasis, 1977:17).

Here is, then, the paradox. The universality of Oedipus is postulated in the necessity of a history fulfilling itself today in the capitalist experience. This very history itself, however, carries on this universal necessity of Oedipus insofar as it alone seems to have the power of referring back, even to the absolute beginnings, in which Oedipus is mythologized silently.

The Original Sin as Historical Myth

Pro Vestra Exhortatione

Julia Kristeva writes: "Now, among the Bemba, power is in the hands of men, but filiation is matrilineal and residence, after marriage, is matrilocal. There is a great contradiction between male rule and matrilineal residence; the young bridegroom is subjected to the authority of the bride's family, and he must override it through personal excellence during his maturity. He remains nevertheless, because of matrilineality, in conflict with the maternal uncle who is the legal guardian of the children especially when they are growing up" (1982:78). The Bemba, let us put it clearly, are part of a vast cultural complex which, according to both their own founding myths and historical evidence, include the Luba and the Lunda. Luc de Heusch proposed the following genealogical reconstruction (1982:20), carefully integrating Jan Vansina's contribution: "The history of the peoples in the savanna in the five centuries preceding 1900 is the history of the development of a Luba-Lunda civilization in the East and of a Kongo and colonial Portuguese civilization in the West" (de Heusch 1982:10–11).

Mbidi Kiluwe
↓
Kalala Ilunga
  (Founder of the Luba Kingdom)
↓
Ilunga Walefu → Chibinda Ilunga   → Chitimukulu
                   (Founder of the   (Founder of the
                   Lunda Kingdom)   Bemba Kingdom)

From Luba founding myths to Lunda and Bemba, one finds a regular pattern which unfolds linkages between incest and regicide and also marks or suggests a transition from strict patrilineality to strict matrilineality.

The narratives I am referring to are not, strictly speaking, historical. In effect, they do not claim to offer a reenactment of the past even when they comment on and narrate historical beginnings. One could say that these narratives simply constitute a discourse on and an interpretation of the past. As such they are different in nature from, say, the historical genre insofar as in the latter the historian's critical consciousness is said to prove that "history is the account of events happening to a nation" (Veyne 1984:81). Both the historian and the anonymous authors of mythical narratives know that "the knowledge of the past has always fed curiosity and ideological sophisms; men have always known that humanity is in a state of becoming and that their collective life is made up of their actions and their passions" (Veyne 1984:78). The major difference resides in the fact that the mythical narrative explicitly speaks from a collective memory or a totalizing auto-biography, whereas the historian's narration claims to describe "what is true, what is concrete, experienced, sublunary" (Veyne 1984:166) in order to contribute to the constitution of a collective memory. Thus, on one side, we have an autobiographical narrative and its variations on beginnings: the original authenticity, and its progressive transformations; and, on the other, the belief in a theme: a technique of narration or history should translate a given plot, its causalities and its becoming, into a coherent and intelligible grid. In this framework, one understands how it is possible to postulate that myth speaks about history, and history about myth. For "all knowledge supposes a horizon reference beyond which all examination is impossible, and this framework is not supported by reasoning, since it is the condition of all reasoning. Thus, history sees equally legitimate *weltanschauungs* follow each other, and their appearance remains inexplicable; they follow each other only by the breaking and changing of frameworks, reasoning that would be irrefutable if it did not consist of reifying abstractions" (Veyne 1984:115). Mythical as well as ritual narratives also do exactly that (see Turner 1967, 1968a, 1969). There is no amnesiac society, and every-one speaks from a somewhere which always indicates a historicity, a becoming, and their questions.

An analysis of sources utilized by Luc de Heusch confirms this inter-pretation. A basic grid in Luba myths and traditions unites and opposes simultaneously endogamy and exogamy in the body of the king. In the myths, two opposing founding fathers, Nkongolo and Mbidi Kiluwe, face each other. The first is cruel and wicked and has incestuous relations with his two sisters: "Because he is suspicious of the power of women, he decided to avoid marrying outside his own family" (de Heusch 1982:15). The second is civilized, discreet, and married to a foreigner. What all the versions of the myth of the foundation of the Luba kingdom show is an opposition between a "primitive" royalty and a "civilized" kingship. The first is marked by incest and symbolized in sterility; the second character-izes itself by hyperexogamy and in symbols of procreation. But, as de Heusch notes, "A surprise awaits us when we compare the myth with the royal installation ceremonies which it legitimizes. For while the myth celebrates the abolition of incest, the ceremony incorporates the shameful legacy of Nkongolo. A new sovereign has ritual relations with his mother and his sisters at the time of his investiture; his daughters and his brother's daughters become his wives'' (1982:31). A similar ritual can be observed for the installation of the king of Yeke and Sanga in Bunkeya.

The body of the king incarnates the paradoxical encounter of endogamy and exogamy. It denounces itself as a symbolic locus in which nature espouses culture, the disorder of forests faces the conventional norms of a social order, the primacy of laws overflows in its own negation. "It is this paradox, this phantasmagorical project that must be elucidated if we are to understand why the sacred King is a multiplicative mechanism of productive and reproductive forces on the one hand, and a dangerous being surrounded by ritual interdictions, condemned to a premature death, on the other" (de Heusch 1985:102).

The royal actualization of incest, the legacy of Nkongolo, is the other side of the legitimization of a strict exogamy among the Luba according to Mbidi's lessons of civilization. The ambiguous body of the king encompasses these two poles. One, the negative, is linked to the memory of beginnings and incestuous unions (de Heusch 1982:26). In the royal ritual, its activity (the *bulopwe,* or sacred blood of royalty) takes place outside the inhabited space, on the margins of the society, in "the house of unhappiness": it is "a suffocating environment, without communication with the external world in the sociological sense, and without any opening in a formal sense" (1982:32). The second (the *bufumu,* or political authority) is positive and paradigmatic, while it outlines and witnesses to the conditions of social order and human survival. Kalala Ilunga, the founder of the second Luba kingdom, and all his successors inherit both the *bulopwe* and the *bufumu.*

Who is the real father of Kalala Ilunga? According to Verhulpen's version of the Luba myth, "Nkongolo who had incestuous relations with his two sisters, Bulanda and Mabela, lent these women to his guest Mbidi Kiluwe. Bulanda became pregnant and brought forth a son Ilunga, while Mabela was delivered of a boy and a girl" (de Heusch 1982:19). The story does not say more. Consequently, Ilunga can be seen as both an endogamic model (the child of an incestuous relation between a brother and a sister) and an exogamic figure (the product of a sexual encounter between a stranger and Bulanda, the child's paternal aunt). It is this exogamic model that amplifies the Luba myth. In Colle's version (de Heusch 1982:20–21), Nkongolo is the uncle of the child, and Mbidi, the father.

Clearly, the narrative conjures away something, the unspeakable unveiled in the ritual which takes place in the margins of society. At the same time, the myth obscures the forms of its own meaning. Yet a question mark is subtly preserved in the mystery of the name of Kalala's father. Hence, a founding myth and the sociopolitical institution it legitimizes amazingly confront one another. But let us be more specific. By the concept of conjuring away, I mean—be it a prereflective choice (in the Sartrean sense), an unconsciously motivated decision, or simply (why not?) a conscious desire to erase the unthinkable—whisking away (in fact, into the bush) an essential name or action and pretending to know nothing about it (see Leclaire 1971:90). As a consequence the anonymous narrator of the narrative seems really to know nothing about it, and the discourse of a collective ethnic memory can palliate an ambiguous genesis. Does not one see here in this small silence of a narrative a key to Freud's concept of original repression (*Urverdrangung*)?

Rightly, de Heusch writes that "it was necessary that Mbidi marry Nkongolo's two sisters so that the myth could oppose the only son of one to the twin offspring of the other. The true heir of Mbidi, the hyperexogamic hero, had to be an only son, devoid of a twin sibling. The incestuous relationship, which until then had harmlessly united the pairs of twins, undergoes a profound change, becoming the tragic passion of a sister who prefers her half brother, an only son, to her own twin brother. This radical alteration in kinship spells the end of endogamy, until then characteristic of human society" (de Heusch 1982:30). The price to be paid for this discontinuity articulates itself in a regicide and a possible patricide. In effect, the young Kalala enters in competition with Nkongolo, a confrontation takes place, and Kalala flees to Mbidi's country. He soon comes back leading an army against Nkongolo. According to Burton's version, his soldiers capture the king and cut off his head. In d'Orjo de Marchovelette's version, Nkongolo is beheaded and castrated. With this tragic confrontation a mythical order ends and history begins: it will develop as exogamic and patrilineal.

A careful examination of versions brings to light two startling points. First, the identification with the uncle-father is explicit: Kalala competes with the king, regularly beating him at games. The child's ambition is so obvious that the mother of the king warns Nkongolo that he might soon lose his political power. Second, in a systemic manner, the mythical narratives silence what the kingly ritual proclaims: the permanence of the *bulopwe* that Kalala incarnates and its sexual prerogatives over the mother and sisters. This deviation between myth and ritual, between the identification of the son and his fatherly figure and, on the other hand, the wish to have the mother, is highly interesting if we have in mind Freud's statement that: "His [the boy's] identification with his father takes on a hostile colouring and changes into a wish to get rid of his father in order to take his place with his mother" (Freud 19:31). Focusing on this issue and comparing *Group Psychology and the Analysis of the Ego* (Freud 18:67) with *The Ego and the Id* (Freud 19:3), René Girard notes that in his later text, "Freud discourages us from thinking that one and the same impulse — the wish to take the father's place *everywhere*—stimulates identification with the model and directs desire toward the mother" (Girard 1979:173). Yet in the Luba case, the legitimacy of the *bulopwe* is intimately thought through the *bufumu*, which seems simultaneously to oppose the very possibility of Oedipus and to proclaim it in Kalala's saga. But does this mean that Oedipus is the unthought or simply the hidden in the mysterious figure of the king? Even by supposing that the structure were more obscure, how would one account for the circumlocutions of the myths, the paradoxical conjunction of the *bulopwe* and the *bufumu*, and the highly significant confusion about the name of Kalala's father?

In order to clarify these questions, let us examine the foundation myths of the Lunda empire (de Heusch 1982:144–52). King Yala has from his first wife two sons, Chinguli and Yala, and a daughter, Lueji. The boys are asocial, lazy, and drunken. They once insult their father, beat him, and abandon him in a pool of blood. Lueji comes along, takes care of her dying father, and is finally chosen by him as successor (de Heusch 1982:147). She becomes queen and ultimately marries a Luba prince, Chibinda Ilunga, a son of Kalala Ilunga, the Luba king. In Duysters's version (de Heusch 1982:144–47), Lueji hands the power to her foreign husband and, since she is sterile, gives him a second wife, who is the mother of Naweji, the successor of Chibinda. In Van den Byvang's version (de Heusch 1981:149), Chibinda steals the power from his indisposed wife. According to de Carvalho's version (de Heusch 1982:148), "The marriage [of Chibinda and the queen] took place when Lueji was pregnant. The eldest dignitary solemnly handed the chiefly bracelet to Chibinda, enjoining him to unify and build up the country his son would rule" (de Heusch 1982:148).

In any case, despite these divergences, three things are clear. First, a patricide-regicide makes possible a matrilineality which almost immediately breaks down in a love story that explicitly brings back the Luba line of male filiation. Second, contrary to the ambiguous complexity of the Luba foundational myth, which opposes a nephew (who is perhaps a son) to an uncle (who might be the father), the Lunda foundational myth is luminously explicit: the two sons beat their father and are directly responsible for his death. Finally, the two brothers emigrate because they cannot accept the new kingly power of the foreigner who has taken over the body of their sister and her power over the land. Interestingly enough, most of the versions of the Lunda myth seem to cover the sexual dimensions of the struggle for power (de Heusch 1982:147–52). These become obvious when one opposes the Lunda myth to the Luba.

At any rate, these three facts make explicit a well-known lesson: violence is related to sexuality, and sexuality to violence (see Freud 7:125, 9:179; Girard 1979). Moreover, they maintain that blood, as a symbol or as a reality, is almost always impure (Douglas 1966), particularly when it is linked to a violent crime. "The act of regicide is the exact equivalent, vis-à-vis the polis, of the act of patricide. In both cases the criminal strikes at the most fundamental, essential, and inviolable within the group. He becomes, literally, the slayer of distinctions" (Girard 1979:74). In the Lunda myth, as we have seen, the patricide is a regicide. It brings about an overvaluation of blood relationship between the father and the daughter. This outcome, although a transformation, perfectly reproduces the Luba myth, in which the regicide coincides with a "possible" patricide.

Luc de Heusch observes this (1982:154), but unfortunately, he insists only on the asymmetrical situation of Nkongolo and Lueji: "Lueji lives with her brothers as an untamed virgin; Nkongolo lives incestuously with his sisters. An aberrant sexual relation is opposed here to an absence of sexuality, which is just as abnormal" (1982:155). I would rather emphasize another opposition. The conjunction in the Lunda myth of a father (Yala) and his daughter (Lueji), which indicates an overvaluation of blood relationships, is the other side of another opposition, a disjunction, illustrated in the tension between the sons (Chinguli and Yala) and their father (Yala). In the conjunction we have a coded incestuous relationship. It is not negated in the virginity of Lueji, and it is explicitly emphasized in a peripheral version: Lueji saw the nakedness of her drunken father, covered him, and washed him. In the disjunction, the violence and rebellion of the two brothers become significant: Chinguli and Yala oppose the power of a father over the body of his daughter, their sister, and this shows why they could only oppose the foreigner who marries her. The Lunda myth is a simple, yet radical, version of the Luba myth, in which a nephew confronts the authority of an uncle (who is perhaps his biological father) and in this gets encouragement and help from his biological father (who, in fact, could be only his social father).

Lunda Foundational Myth	
Father (Yala) + Daughter (Lueji)	Father (Yala) vs. Sons (Chinguli and Yala)
Overvaluation of blood relationships	Undervaluation of blood relationships

Luba Foundational Myth	
Uncle (Nkongolo, possible father) vs. Nephew (Kalala, possible son)	Father (Mbidi) + Son (Kalala)
Undervaluation of blood relationships	Overvaluation of blood relationships

The common point which unites the two myths in what they narrate as truth of the past outlines a meaning that states its power in a curious language: the two narratives are interdependent and echo each other. Yet the first affirms the permanence of patrilineality, and the second witnesses to a failure of matrilineality and a return to patrilineal filiation and social organization. What is the name of this game and what does it signify exactly? The centrality of Lueji may be the heart of the problem. In effect, whatever angle one takes, she is omnipresent as an essential figure in the founding of Lunda history. The master-discourse of a dying father made her queen and source of power. According to Struyf's versions (de Heusch 1982:149–50), she is an obvious symbol of an Electra whose image is transmuted into the incomprehensible knowledge of genesis. But it is in the signs of her fertility or those of her sterility that, according to all versions, she allows the now-founded matrilineal law to reformulate itself in relation to her Luba husband and the taxonomies of a patrilineal filiation.

And now, our last step, is the origin of the Bemba kingdom (de Heusch 1982:229–44). Labrecque's version reads this way: Mumbi Mukasa, the niece of God, queen mother of Lembaland, decides to marry Mukulumpe. They have four children. These young people have the foolish idea of constructing a tower which could reach heaven, the country of their mother. The tower collapses, killing some people, and Mukulumpe decides to punish his sons who are responsible for the catastrophe: Katongo, Nkole, and Chiti. They revolt. The father wants to humiliate them. They react by committing other crimes, one of which is "possibly adultery with a young wife of their father's" (de Heusch 1982:230).

The uniqueness of this fact is exemplified in the whisking away of the name of the woman. The unthought, once again, oscillates between the impossible which cannot be made explicit and the articulation of a text offering the melodrama of a polygynous structure. A possible repression in the narrative accounts for, and convincingly comments upon, desires and violence in such an extended family. Indeed, the woman cannot be the mother, can she? That is unacceptable even among Bemba. Correctly, this reading should refuse to identify the desirability of the mother in the very moment that it accepts reasons which account for the confrontation between the sons and the father. To exploit an ironic statement by Serge Leclaire which refers to something else, another thing and project, it is strange to imagine that one of the sons participating in the seduction of one of their father's women would have said: "I believe, it was a good session. . . .we shall stop here" (Leclaire 1971:122).

Ultimately, the sons leave Lembaland. Beyond the Luapula River, they build a new village. Its new prince, Chiti, regretted that his sister, Chilufya-Mulenga, had not accompanied him to assure the royal succession, in conformity with matrilineal descent (see de Heusch 1982:230). A delegation of aristocrats of royal blood is sent to bring the princess, who is a prisoner of her own father, and succeeds in its mission. Yet one night, on the way back to the new village, the prince "Kapassa lay with Chilufya-Mulenga, who was his classificatory sister. Six months later the pregnant princess confessed the name of her incestuous seducer" (de Heusch 1982:231).

This Bemba narrative constitutes the extreme reversal of the Luba founding myth and a critical rearrangement of the Lunda foundational myth. As de Heusch writes:

> Chiti's sister is jealously kept prisoner by a cruel father. . . . Chiti is obliged, to ensure matrilineal dynastic continuity, to remove Chilufya-Mulenga from their common father. Finally, we know that a second obstacle occurs to the effective realization of the matrilineal order: the excessive [incestuous] conjunction of brother and sister. . . . The prince Kapassa, who has been charged with the removal of Chilufya-Mulenga, seduces her. Chiti thereupon flies into a great rage. By banishing the guilty one from the royal clan, he clearly proclaims the fundamental law of matrilineal society which unites brother and sister in a socio-economic association devoid of erotic ambiguity. (de Heusch 1982:234)

In other words, the queen mother is, this time, an obvious institutional given; she is the niece of God. This fact is puzzling, since we know that the overconscious father, Mukulumpe, the spouse of the divine Mumbi Mukasa, was probably one of the discontented members of the Lunda aristocracy (Vansina 1966:175). On the other hand, despite the power of this divine matrilineality, the sons of Mukulumpe, in order to oppose the power of the king, commit adultery with one of his wives. She is not their mother, yet she is the wife of their father. Again, Oedipus is blurred, but can we say for sure that he is not there in that diverted sexual encounter? In any case, the proclamation of matrilineality—Chiti needs his sister in order to assure the succession—goes along with another extreme emphasis on blood relationship: to punish the guilty prince Kapassa, Chiti "gave him a degrading totem (the female genitalia). [Kapassa,] covered with shame, left the group with his close relatives" (de Heusch 1982:231).

Signs and Counterpoints

Et Nos Patimur

What should we do now with the declension of alliance and filiation in the being and life of the so-called primitive machine? Let us emphasize two problems: one, the circularity of mythical narratives as invention of history; two, the symbolism of the divine kingship as a paradoxical locus of coherence between nature and culture.

From the Luba myth to the Bemba myth the narratives recite the rhetorical unity of a tradition of alliances and its crises. At the same time, they invent and expound successive transformations in customs and rules of filiation from a strict patrilineality to matrilineality. This formulation presents also an interpretive periodization of history which expands spatially the internal diachronic contradictions of the Luba myth. For, in some versions, as exemplified in what Luc de Heusch calls a minor history of technology, the first couple is exogamic and creates architecture and pottery; then follows a series of incestuous twins who discover fishing, trapping, and hunting; finally, Mbidi Kiluwe appears in the process, bringing back exogamy and establishing a new order. The circle is closed upon itself. And then one understands the inversion in the succession of inventions: "Technical innovations follow one another in a mythical order which curiously inverts the historical progression from the paleolithic to the neolithic economy" (de Heusch 1982:28).

Indeed, one could validly argue that this inversion may signify something else. Insofar as mythical narratives do not claim to submit to the rationality of a historical genre that they do not know, the inversion could possibly be the recording of a lesson: the order of a culture can be lost, and the frightening return of a primitive space would symbolize the horror to be relived. This means that African traditional statesmen as well as the pundits of the ancient order do not necessarily expect a correct reading of their founding myths when they decide to negotiate them and offer them to the analysis of a colonial commissioner or an anthropologist. Some anthropologists have felt this and, generally, have failed to draw out the consequences of this disturbing fact. The reciting of a founding myth might be a reformulation of the origin of the state, and it almost always diachronically or cyclically opposes primitive stages to civilized ones. Let us insist that the transcription of a mythical narrative takes place on a presumption: that a radical deviation exists between two types of knowledge, the mythical and the historical. The myth becomes anthropological knowledge in the ambiguous exchange which unites the politics of an informer and those of an anthropologist. Moreover, in this dialogue, the myth, instead of being performed according to its strict social functions, is managed as an object unveiling itself to a new curiosity and imprimatur for the institution of a new knowledge. In this exchange, it is, in fact, an exegesis which is offered for consumption, and we should understand all the process as an attempt to institutionalize an interpretation for political purposes. In this exercise, it is clear that history identifies with myth and myth witnesses to an invented history on the supposition that historical narratives can duplicate (or, by the way, negate) a mythical tradition.

The second problem concerns the representations of Oedipus and Electra in our mythical narratives. It is widely accepted today that it is the adult, the father, who in his paranoia oedipalizes the son and invites him to violence (Deleuze and Guattari 1977; Girard 1979). But the father has been himself a child and, therefore, oedipalized. Where should we stop in going back? Girard insists on "the mythical aspect of Freudianism [which] is founded on the conscious knowledge of patricidal and incestuous desire; only a brief flash of consciousness to be sure, a bright wedge of light between the darkness of the first identifications and the unconscious—but consciousness all the same" (Girard 1979:177).

Specifically, our African narratives seem very clear. They address the problem at the beginning of history. It is Nkongolo, the drunken and incestuous king, who provokes his nephew/son Kalala and creates the possibility of a regicide. The mild king Yala "overflows" his daughter Lueji. In a peripheral version from the Kahemba region, we even learn interesting facts about how and why Lueji became queen: the king-father "became drunk while drinking palm wine in the company of his wife Kamonga and his children. He retired behind the hut. Chinguli found his father naked and left him in this state. His sister Lueji [Na Weji], however, covered her father with a mantle and washed him. On awakening, [the king-father] disinherited his sons in favor of his daughter" (de Heusch 1982:149). The son and his brother are drunken, and they beat and kill the king-father in the principal founding myths. Interestingly enough, in the Luba as well as in the Lunda narratives, there is an absolute silence about the desired mother who, along with the sister, are actually possessed by the *bulopwe* in the obscurity of the "house of unhappiness." Paradoxically, it is in Bemba myths celebrating matrilineality that this fact comes somehow to light. The three irresponsible sons of Mukulumpe, the consort prince, lay with one of their father's wives. And the price for maintaining matrilineality resides in the incest of Prince Kapassa and his classificatory sister.

In the Luba myth, the name of the father of Kalala is obscured, and the paternal uncle is victimized by his nephew. In the Bemba reversal of the narrative, there is no regicide, but three irresponsible brothers lie with one of their father's wives. In both cases, Oedipus is silenced. In the Luba myth there is no victimized mother. One has to forget about mythical narratives and look at the royal rite of enthronement in order to find her. In the Bemba narrative there is no regicide. Mukulumpe is only a consort prince married to God's niece. The woman possessed by the children is not their biological mother, but only one of their father's wives. The dissoci-

ation between regicide and incest cannot be more complete. The murder of
the king in the Luba myth is obvious. The incest between the sons and the
mother is remarkably covered in the Bemba myth: she is not really their
mother after all. Between these two extremes, the Lunda myth presents a
table on which "Electra" makes her own representation and clearly over-
imposes herself on the hidden Oedipus in the Luba and Bemba narratives.
On the other hand, there is an explicit overvaluation of blood relationship
in the meeting of the father and the daughter, when the daughter sees the
nakedness of the father (Struyf's version, de Heusch 1982:149–50). But
let us face the fact: the father is murdered by the sons, Chinguli and Yala
(de Carvalho's version, de Heusch 1982:147–49).

These narratives witness to a history and its beginning. Luba, Lunda,
and Bemba really constitute one ethnic community. To this day, despite the
variation of their systems of filiation, they all know that real life should, in
an absolute manner, negate the ambiguity represented by the body of the
king (in patrilineal social formations) or the consort prince and his queen
(in matrilineal ones). The origins of history signify a danger. From Mbidi's
lessons, they all think that the movement and destiny of history can be
fruitful only thanks to radical separations; the world of women should be
clearly distinguished from that of men, sons should not participate in their
mothers' activities, daughters are to be excluded from their fathers' social
and cultural milieus, and in-laws of different sex cannot be allowed to talk
to each other directly.

Let us be more synthetic. The opposition between Nkongolo and Mbidi, or
the primitive and the civilized, recites a historical succession and a major paradigm: the origin of history is linked to the foundation of the state. Both witness
to the same binary opposition that the myth emphasizes: the possibility of a
history means the invention of a refused space and its figures—those of a
primitive, which are whisked away in the name of civilization. The meaning
of this invention of a prehistory makes itself explicit in the rejection of an
original sin. In this confrontation with its own past, a civilized society establishes itself as a cultured space opposed to untamed nature and its aberrations.
There we find the power of an illusion or, more specifically, the paradox of
origins. As Paul Veyne put it, "Origins are rarely beautiful—or, rather, by
definition what we call origins is anecdotal" (1984:42).

To Deleuze and Guattari's chronologization of Oedipus and periodization of historical types (the primitive, the barbarian, and the civilized), one
could now say, after Paul Veyne:

[Can we really suppose that] primitives are too close to original authenticity
to have, in their visions of the world, the slight perspective and the touch of
bad faith that we have about our most strongly asserted theories. And then, of

Luba

1. (He) Nkongolo + (They) His two sisters
   Incest

2. *Rupture*: (He) Mbidi + (She) Nkongolo's sister
   Exogamy

3. What is the *real* name of Kalala's father?

4. (He) Nkongolo *vs.* (He) Kalala
   Regicide

5. Triumph of patrilineality and exogamy

Lunda

1. (He) Yala + (She) Nkonde
   Exogamy

2. *Rupture*: (He) Yala *vs.* (They) His sons
   Regicide
   (He) Yala + (She) His daughter
   ("Electra")
   Triumph of matrilineality

3. What is the *real* name of the game?

4. (She) Lueji + (He) Chibinda Ilunga
   Return of patrilineality

5. Permanence of exogamy and failure of matrilineality

Bemba

1. (She) Mumbi Mukasa + (He) Mukulumpe
   Exogamy

2. *Rupture*: They (Sons) *vs.* He (Father)
   They (Sons) + One of the father's wives
   Incest?

3. What is the *real* name of the woman?

4. (He) Kapasa + (She) A classificatory sister
   Incest

5. Triumph of matrilineality and exogamy

course, they are not peoples to have theories. So we pull down their cultural and philosophical productions to the level of consciousness, which finally confers on that consciousness the weight of a pebble; thus, we will have to believe that the primitive, about whom it cannot be doubted that he sees with his own eyes that one year is not like the preceding year, continues nonetheless to see everything through archetypes—and not just profess to do so. (Veyne 1984:78–79)

Claude Lévi-Strauss, at the onset of his study on American Indian myths, forcefully points out that "the initial theme of the key myth is the incest committed by the hero with the mother. Yet the idea that he is guilty seems to exist mainly in the mind of the father, who desires his son's death and schemes to bring it about" (1969:48). The nightmare is there. Mystification or truth, in the ambiguous representations expounded by narratives about Nkongolo, Yala, or Mukulumpe, directly or indirectly, the nightmare speaks out from regional histories and at the very foundation of their own dream, long before capitalism.

4
Genesis and Myth

The Luba Genesis Charter

Sometime in the late fourteenth or early fifteenth century, an immigrant, Nkongolo, organized the first Luba empire (Vansina 1965). Where did he come from? The local narratives link him to the memory of beginnings. He is the descendent of two mythical parents: Kiubaka-Ubaka (a house-building man) and Kibumba-Bumba (a pottery-making woman). Here is the charter myth as recorded by d'Orjo de Marchovelette (1950) and presented by Luc de Heusch (1982).

The Peopling of Luba Territory

In the country of the east [Buhemba], on the right bank of the Lualaba River, there once were *a man* and *a woman*. Their names [Kiubaka-Ubaka and Kibumba-Bumba] mean respectively "he who builds many houses" and "she who makes much pottery." They lived in ignorance of each other. Guided by the sound of chopping, the man discovered the woman, who was preparing firewood. They lived for a long time under the same roof, sleeping in separate beds. The copulation of a pair of jackals gave them the idea of sleeping together. They brought forth twins of opposite sex, who became inseparable companions. One day the twins found a locality which was exceptionally rich in fish. They took to spending the entire day catching fish, spending the night in the bush in each other's arms. They finally obtained permission from their parents to leave the village and devote themselves entirely to fishing. In their turn, they brought forth twins, who lived in the same incestuous manner, far from their parents. This new generation took up trapping. So pairs of twins, moving in each generation a little further westward, populated the country. (de Heusch 1982)

The Origin of Divine Kingship (*Bulopwe*)

Nkongolo, the first divine king (*mulopwe*) of the Luba, was the offspring of Kiubaka-Ubaka and Kibumba-Bumba. He brought all the lands of the west under his authority. He soon crossed the Lualaba, arriving with a large following at Lake Boya, where he built a great village, Mwibele. About the same time, a hunter called Ilunga Mbidi Kiluwe left his natal village to conquer the peoples living between the Lualaba and Lubilash rivers. On the way home he met his brother-in-law Nkongolo, who gave him a hearty welcome. In the course of the ensuing festivities, Mbidi Kiluwe was shocked to see that Nkongolo ate and drank in the company of his people. Nkongolo, on his side, was astonished to see his guest disappear behind a screen at mealtimes. He was also struck by the fact that Mbidi Kiluwe never laughed. Nkongolo mentioned this to him and Mbidi Kiluwe then burst out laughing. Nkongolo thereupon noticed that the other had his two upper incissors filed to points. He again expressed his surprise, but this time Mbidi Kiluwe flew into a rage, and retorted angrily: "You have conquered the country, but you fail to observe the elementary prohibition which obliges a king to hide himself when he eats or drinks." He thereupon took leave of Nkongolo. When Mbidi Kiluwe arrived at the Lualaba River, he told the local chief: "Nkongolo the Red has grossly insulted me and I have parted from him. I have left behind at Mwibele this man's sisters, my wives Mabela and Bulanda, who are pregnant. I have entrusted them to the care of the diviner Mijibu. I am certain that the sons they will bring into the world will rejoin me. You will recognize them by their black skins. If a red-colored man asks permission to cross the river, refuse him; but if a black man asks, agree immediately."

At the village of Nkongolo, Mabela and Bulanda each gave birth to a boy; the son of the first was called Kisula, and the second was called Kalala Ilunga. They grew up under the vigilant eye of Mijibu. As adults they continued to live with their maternal uncle. One day Nkongolo invited his nephew Kalala Ilunga to a game of *masoko*. Mijibu gave the young man an iron object skillfully fashioned to resemble the fruit employed in the game and Kalala Ilunga had no trouble beating his uncle. Wishing to save her son the disgrace of further defeats, Nkongolo's mother begged him to destroy [fill in?] the small hole into which the players threw their counters.

A short time later, Nkongolo invited his nephew to a game of *bulundu*, which is played with a rubber ball. Mijibu gave his protégé a magic ball which broke all the pots in Nkongolo's kitchen. Nkongolo's mother again asked her son not to take on Kalala Ilunga. Angered by the growing renown of his nephew, Nkongolo decided to get rid of him. He caused a pit to be dug, lined with iron spikes, and hidden under a mat. Then he invited Kalala to dance in his honor. The hero asked Mijibu for advice. Mijibu gave Kalala two spears, and told him to brandish one while using the other to test the ground during his dance. Kalala Ilunga began dancing some distance from the mat. When the drum rhythm speeded up, he leapt and hurled his spear at the mat. The weapon passed right through it, revealing the trap.

Kalala Ilunga fled, determined to join his father. Nkongolo pursued him, but the nephew had already crossed the Lualaba River when his uncle reached its bank. Faithful to Mbidi Kiluwe's orders, the local chief refused to allow the king to cross. Groups of Nkongolo's followers twice attempted to cross the river on craft they found to hand, but both groups were drowned. Nkongolo tried in vain to build a stone causeway across the river: his iron implements were useless against rock. Nkongolo then decided to lure Kalala Ilunga to his side of the river. He compelled the diviner Mijibu and a certain Mungedi to climb to the top of a great tree and call the fugitive back. One shook a rattle while the other struck a gong. Nkongolo had the ladder of vines removed which the two had used to scale the tree. There was no response from Kalala to their calls. Mijibu and Mungedi spent two days without food at the top of the tree. The diviner suggested to his companion that he jump into space with him, holding onto his [Mijibu's] belt. But Mungedi refused to take such a risk. Mijibu escaped, thanks to his magical powers. He crossed the Lualaba with a mighty leap. But poor Mungedi died of hunger.

Mijibu succeeded in joining Mbidi Kiluwe, who raised a great army and entrusted its command to his son. To defend himself, Nkongolo conceived the unlikely scheme of diverting the course of the Lomami River so as to isolate himself on an island in midstream. But his men gave up the project when they heard that Kalala Ilunga's army had seized the capital. Nkongolo then took refuge in the Lwembe gorges. A woman discovered him while he was warming himself in the sun, together with a small band of followers. When he heard of this, Kalala Ilunga reconnoitered the place by moonlight. Nkongolo's hideout was encircled. The next morning he was captured, *then* beheaded and castrated. The head and genitals of the dead king were packed into a basket (*dikumbo*), which Kalala Ilunga sent to his father. A miracle happened at the village of Lenga. When the man who was carrying the basket placed it on the ground, a termite hill formed over it with extraordinary speed, burying it under a mound of red earth. Lenga village was thereafter called Kimona.

Kalala Ilunga sent messengers to his father, seeking permission to continue his conquests. Mbidi Kiluwe gave his approval. He also reminded his son of the precise ritual observances required of divine kings. A king was obliged to take food and drink alone, and out of sight. A special hut had to be devoted to the preparation of royal meals because it was forbidden for the king to eat in a place where fire had been made. Two wives wearing special raffia dresses (*kibanga*) had to undertake the royal cuisine. The first was responsible for the cooking, the second for serving the various dishes. They had to be replaced by other women whenever indisposed. A cook was forbidden to address the king directly. Instead, she had to let him know silently and in secret when a meal was ready. Without hurrying himself, the king made his way to the dining

·room by a devious route so as not to attract attention, while the women withdrew. No one was allowed to eat the remains of a royal meal, nor to use utensils served to the king.

After securely establishing his rule over the country, Kalala Ilunga took the name of Ilunga Mwine Munza. He assumed a praise-name which said he was the son of Mbidi Kiluwe, the hunter whose bowstring broke when he was hunting at the source of the Lomami River. (de Heusch 1982)

What is the credibility of this narrative? Jan Vansina believes that it narrates a meeting between two ethnic groups (1965). Luc de Heusch agrees and notes that this particular narrative as well as other versions he used for his *Drunken King* (those of Colle, Donohugh and Berry, Verhulpen, Van der Noot, Burton, Van Malderen, Makonga, Sendwe, and Theuws) "refer to effective contact between an existing Katangan chiefdom and intruders from a more highly organized polity. After a period of marriage alliances, the newcomers inflicted a military defeat on their hosts. The new dynasty, which reigned over a great part of Katanga [Shaba] until the end of the nineteenth century, is of Hemba origin. This vague term refers to the eastern Luba, who occupy territory between the Lualaba river and Lake Tanganyika" (de Heusch 1982:9). Thomas Reefe (1981) has demonstrated the coherence of the charter by establishing a table of concordances existing between seventeen different versions of the narrative. In this one finds the essential episodes of the genesis myth: Nkongolo's physical and psychological attributes (redness and cruelty); the coming of Mbidi, the civilized prince; the pit trap; the confrontation between Kalala Ilunga and his uncle Nkongolo; and, finally, the miraculous anthill.

The narrative seems to be a memory-text in which the Luba genealogy actualizes itself as both reality and project. It used to be a social performance, and the major customs of Luba kingship claim to reenact it. Strictly speaking, it is not history. On the other hand, it cannot be reduced to a purely mythical legend. It is beyond what these two concepts imply. The charter narrative accounts for the Luba experience as a believable story about beginnings. It reflects complementary and conflicting readings of Luba history. I propose to consider this memory-text as a theoretical discourse which validates a human geography, its spatial configuration, and the competing traditions of its various inhabitants, simultaneously cementing them via this retelling of the genesis of the "nation" and its social organization. In effect, the charter does not recite exactly what happened but proposes an explanatory interpretation about how the country was occupied, a "nation" organized, and a state ensured. In sum, this memory-text presents itself as a political ratio in three operations: it duplicates a real human space amid its textuality, integrates a "nowhere" into a mythified past, and, finally, correlates actual customs, socioeconomic transformations, divine kingship, discursive practices, and displacements demanded by historical changes.

Thus, for example, proper names validate a state of social affairs and, to the extent that they are politically meaningful, propose a grid of confrontation. Most of them are symbols of something else. The East or Buhemba localizes nothing specific apart from a sense of beginning: we come from there. It is a founding vision integrated in the discourse as a major vector thanks to which the Luba can comment upon political choices and options for territorial expansions. In the same vein, the original parents can be reduced to symbols. The chart explicitly presents Kiubaka-Ubaka as *meaning* "he who builds many houses" and Kibumba-Bumba as "she who makes much pottery." This semantic classification identifies them with two techniques (architecture and pottery) which, paradoxically, as noted by de Heusch (1982:27–29), designate the last step of the historical progression from the paleolithic to the neolithic economy, the progression from hunting with bow and arrow to architecture and pottery, through first trapping and then fishing. Finally, Nkongolo and Mbidi, the central heroes, combine the illusions of a history and the political necessity of a distinction between a *mukalanga* (a self-made leader like Nkongolo) and a *mulopwe* (a king); a cruel, wicked despot and a gentle and civilized king; a social organization based on violence and an elaborate political power founded on a hereditary tradition. Nkongolo's original name is Mwamba. He is the son of Bondo wa Baleya. "There is a legend about his father being a hyena and he is consequently referred to as *Muntu utyila wadi wa malwa*, that is to say, 'A red or clear skinned man who was a monstrosity.' He was supposed to be so ugly that no one resembled him before or since. This is the reason why the hyena is now called 'the father of the chief' and why the *twite,* one of the principal counselors of the chief and one who is symbolically called 'the father of the Chief,' sits on a hyena skin when in council" (Womersley 1984:1). On the other side, his opposite, Mbidi, is known as Upemba, the man from the East, and his son, the prince Kalala Ilunga, is still known as "*Luala Misaha* or the divider of streams or nations" (Womersley 1984:9).

Clearly, proper names both colonize the past and organize the geography of current customs and traditions. They signify a dynamic political structure: the believable, the memorable, and the primitive. Referring to walking in the city, Michel de Certeau could write that "the believable, the memorable and the primitive designate what 'authorizes' (or makes possible or credible) spatial appropriations, what is repeated in them (or is recalled in them) from a silent and withdrawn memory, and what is structured in them and continues to be signed by an in-fantile (*in-fans*) origin. These three symbolic mechanisms organize the topoi of a discourse on/of the city (legend, memory, and dream) in a way that also eludes urbanistic systemacity'' (de Certeau 1984:105).

The memory-text is, as I have hypothesized, both a legend and a dream for political power. In effect, it links words and names to possessed things and spaces, designating motions of ancestors (Nkongolo, Mbidi, Ilunga) according to processes of appropriations of power and governance over new lands. It transforms foreign regions into a Luba habitability and accordingly reproduces itself in minor stories of genesis. ''Each group has its own story telling how the *bulopwe* came into the country; how they got incorporated in the Luba kingdom and became linked to the royal court. In most cases the story runs along these lines: a man came from the royal court, he settled down in this country; he governed the country, being a son of the royal court, finally he died (or was killed) and became the protecting spirit of the '*bene* so and so' '' (Theuws 1983:34).

Two literary figures operate in the charter memory, allowing its ambivalence as mythical history and historical myth: the asyndeton, or the omission of structural links; and the synecdoche, through which a more inclusive expression is substituted for a less inclusive one or vice versa. The latter maximizes the detail and in doing so reduces the complexity of the totality to a significant unity, as in the symbolism of a bed for a hotel or that of a fork crossed with a knife to symbolize a restaurant. It might also emphasize the whole and thus negate the constituting elements. Even in this process, it is a symbol which becomes a paradigm of the totality. The asyndeton omits the links between elements. It separates constitutive elements, singularizes them, and presents them as more than themselves. In the Luba memory-text, Kiubaka-Ubaka is not a man and a builder of houses, nor Kibumba-Bumba a woman and a specialist in pottery. The text has deleted the conjunctions. Kiubaka-Ubaka, it says, means ''he who builds many houses''; and Kibumba-Bumba, ''she who makes much pottery.'' They strictly represent two singularities, are separated from everything, and constitute a curious beginning, since a God-Creator is absent from this chart. They are isolated from each other and from all other human beings, if there are any. They both constitute an ellipsis. In their respective negativity vis-à-vis each other as well as vis-à-vis a before and an after, they actualize a zero point of reference. In effect, they symbolize what all origin stories have to take into account: namely, the passage or rupture from original chastity to sexual activity and matrimony, from natural isolation to social contact, from nowhere to the foundation of a history.

Nkongolo and Mbidi are, on the other hand, clear synecdoches forever linked to the history of the Luba fate. They amplify what qualifies them as individuals and appear to Luba consciousness as institutional paradigms. Their very beings as characters establish two opposed legalities or norms:

endogamy against exogamy, primitive kingship against civilized rule, violence and death against procreation and life, the *bufumu* against the *bulopwe* (see Heusch 1982:25).

It is interesting to note that Kalala Ilunga integrates the synecdoche and the asyndeton. He is a principle of contradiction, simultaneously *mfumu* and *mulopwe*. As ellipsis, he exemplifies a radical rupture with the past in his own body.

> When the boy Ilunga Luala was born he appeared still in the fetal bag and so caused great consternation. This child could be seen moving inside and so the wise man Mijibua Kalenge was consulted. He said, "Put the child on the ash heap behind his mother's hut, sprinkle chalk carefully all over it, and leave it there in the warmth of the sun. It will soon hatch out itself." The midwives obeyed most carefully and retired from the spot. Soon they heard the baby's cry and there was this wonderful baby, black like Mbidi Kiluwe. He was named Ilunga after his father together with a praise name *Luala Misaha,* that is, the divider of streams or nations. Note the parallel in the Bible record of Genesis chapter 10 verses 5, 18, and 32 — "From whom are the nations divided." (Womersley 1984:9)

As synecdoche, Kalala Ilunga identifies himself with the origin of the state. His proper name is, since his investiture on a hill (called Mwilunde wa Nkonda), Mwine Munza, or Lord of Munza. It indicates the first entry of a dynasty, and at the same time, it is a political index to a process of expansion and of naming new territories. "Ilunga Ntambo Luala Misaha Kalala Mwine Munza became the first king of a new dynasty, the first king of the Luba west of the Lualaba and, for many generations, east of the Lualaba also, as far as the Kibara mountains. Later they became known, as today, the Luba Shankadi . . . in contrast to the Luba Kasai, a section of the tribe which moved westwards beyond the Lubilash river several generations later during the reign of Ilunga Nsungu" (Womersley 1984:19).

The assortment of arguments, facts, and stories displayed by the charter myth is thus significant. It faces a memory and in this very process organizes a mythical history which at the same time witnesses to a politics of expansion. The organized memory, in effect, occupies a geographical place, which is not defined by clear boundaries. It legitimizes itself via a doubly conquered geography. The real westward movement of the Luba justifies it. On the other hand, the connection between a charter transformed into a political canon and a geography reflects itself in shifting and always adapted interpretations of the canon. Additions, variations, modifications in what I have called regional histories of genesis seem to witness to the tension between the general code (*langue*) of Luba genesis and the local dynamisms of experiences in their contingent expansion, luck, and failure accounted for by individualized recitations (*paroles*). The variations classified by Thomas Reefe (1981:32–37) in the succession or the presentation of episodes, the presence of one episode in one source and its absence in others, does not disqualify the charter as a historic monument. Yet the charter does not claim such a role and cannot. Since its invention, it only exists as a potentially conventional institution whose reality and credibility are given and emphasized in well-localized stories about the fortunes of specific Luba groups or villages. If the charter myth gets some form of concreteness, it comes from its three founding names (Nkongolo, Mbidi, Kalala) and both the semantic and political images they induce in Luba consciousness. In effect, the names of these kings triumphantly render three different things: the origin of an empire and its destiny; the geography of a political power which first captures the divine and then implements it in a divine kingship; and, finally, the unending exegesis reciting the miracle of communion between humans, a soil, and the word.

Myth, Discourse, and Cultural *A Priori*

T. Fourche and H. Morlighem, two Belgians serving the colonial administration between 1923 and 1947 circulated widely in the region of West Lomani, south of Sankuru. Their principal mission was to fight endemic diseases and by prophylactic medicine to improve the health of the inhabitants. At the end of each day they listened to the villagers, then consigned what they were taught to their journals. Year after year, they listened to their informants. They were progressively accepted as members of the Luba community, spending more time listening and taking notes than asking questions. Their knowledge of the Luba language was extraordinary. Soon they were introduced to local chapters of knowledge and were gradually given the essentials of Luba secret knowledge. This progressive knowledge of esoteric systems can be perceived in their successive publications. In 1937 the two men published in the *Bulletin of the Belgian Royal Colonial Institute* two studies on "les arbres-à-Esprits" and a descriptive analysis of the Luba dance of Tshishimbi. In the French *Journal de la Société des Africanistes*, in the same year, they gave a presentation of Luba-Kasai conceptions of the human being and the signification of death. In 1938 they presented two studies in the *Bulletin of the Belgian Royal Colonial Institute*, one on architecture and the order of the universe and the other on communications with dead people among Luba-Kasai. Ten years later, H. Morlighem signed a study on the Luba law of numbers, and in 1973 he produced *Une Bible noire* which, supposedly, offers the results of his inquiries with T. Fourche, who had passed away in Johannesburg in 1942.

In 1949 I am seven years old. My father, who works for the Union Minière du Katanga in Jadotville (Likasi), has decided to take his vacation in his village in Kasai. Our base is Lusambo, a small city, which for some time was the administrative center of the region. The Frères des Ecoles Chrétiennes have there a vocational school that my father attended. He is immensely proud of his school and of his personal achievement which allowed him to become an *ajusteur* at the Union Minière in Katanga. His dream is to turn one of his sons into a mining engineer. A river separates Lusambo from Saint Antoine, where one of my maternal uncles works as a cook for the Catholic Sisters. I regularly take a canoe to see him. The Sisters have there a school for women that my mother attended, and I am adored by one Sister Ignatius, who had known my mother as a student. She had tried hard to convince my mother to become a nun, giving up only when my mother married.

For weeks, I canoe back and forth between Saint Antoine and Lusambo. Often, in the afternoon, I have to walk with my father to the village of Bena Kankole to attend lessons. The distance seems immense. Was it really? Once there, with other boys, between the ages of five and eight, I have to listen to stories which are, to me, simply incomprehensible. They are about the universe, the human condition, life and death. These sessions sometimes last till late in the night. The following day I implore my father not to conduct me to those meetings. He smiles and says something such as: The instruction will be finished soon. If my memory is correct, however, it lasted at least two months.

In 1952 I leave my family to join a Catholic seminary in Kakanda, which, some years later, moves to Mwera, near Elisabethville (presently Lubumbashi). I am ten years old. In the seminary—which tries to be completely self-sufficient and has a minimum of contacts with the outside world—are some 120 students under the care and surveillance of ten European Benedictine Fathers. We have in common an African language, the Sanga. In effect, we live in Sangaphone area. Yet we have no contact at all with the Sanga milieu. Our real language of communication is French, and our reference mythology is Christian. No contact with the outside (no vacation, no visits from friends or parents) is allowed for at least six years. I entered the place as a child in 1952 and had my first contact with the external world in 1959. I was then almost eighteen, completely Francophonized, submitted to Greco-Roman values and Christian norms.

I thought of becoming a Benedictine monk and exiled myself to Rwanda. Fifteen years later, after several turns in my life, I was serving as the dean of the Faculty of Philosophy and Letters at the Lubumbashi

Campus of the National University of Zaire. A Dutch colleague, the late Leo Stappers, sent to me a graduate student working on the esoteric myths of the Songye tradition. The young man had just read the *Bible noire* published in 1973 by T. Fourche and H. Morlighem. It was then that I read it for the first time. Those sessions when I was a youth in Lusambo came back to mind. Yet I chose to dismiss them, and with them the book by Fourche and Morlighem. I sent the student back to Professor Stappers. After all, Stappers was more competent than I, having researched and published extensively and for many years on Songye and Luba.

The *Bible noire*—Good Lord, why is it called a bible?—is an upsetting text, not because of what it says, but for the way its content is organized. Esoteric narratives have been lumped together, arranged and translated in an ambiguous language. The authors' sources as well as the authority of their information and the level of their initiation in the Luba-Songye organizations could have been made more explicit. Nevertheless, after years of checking their interpretation, I can attest that they seem to me basically correct and fundamentally faithful to local memories, although I should also agree, and strongly, with what Jan Vansina tells me: Fourche and Morlighem's *Bible noire* is Christian-inspired. I shall come back to this point.

The voice of the tradition, according to this *Bible noire,* starts with Maweja himself, the Supreme Being. In this apparently simple foundation a law is proclaimed: from the outset any disjunction between mythical and historical spaces is made invalid. We know that this separation is, in today's scholarship, doubled by two antinomic concepts, oral and written, which in turn are usually used as criteria for distinguishing two main types of cultures. Jacques Derrida has recently noted that what is given in this opposition represents in fact an order of metaphysical opposition which itself supposes a principle of meaning anterior to the difference. Aptly, Michel de Certeau writes that "in the thought that asserts them, these antinomies postulate the principle of a unique origin (a founding archaeology) or a final reconciliation (a teleological concept), and thus a discourse that is maintained by this referential unity" (de Certeau 1984:133). Instead of questioning the immediate visibility of the tension between these binary concepts, and the silent transcendence they seem to demand, de Certeau assumes that "plurality is originary," that "difference is constitutive of its terms," and, finally, that "language must continually conceal the structuring work of division beneath a symbolic order." As a consequence, the binary oppositions such as oral versus written cannot be "raised to the status of general categories" insofar as their pertinence can be validated only from the regional historical determinations which make them possible and functional. More important, we should keep in mind that "the two terms are not equivalent or comparable, either with respect to their coherence (the definition of one presupposes that the other remains undefined) or with respect to their operativity (the one that is productive, predominant, and articulated puts the other in a position of inertia, subjection, and opaque resistance). It is thus impossible to assume that they would function in homologous ways if only the signs were reversed. They are incommensurable; the difference between them is qualitative" (de Certeau 1984:133).

This argument should be that of every credible anthropology. What it proposes is the possibility of a "new style" of analysis. Let us focus on some of its main implications and then clarify the status of a narrative such as that of the *Bible noire*. First of all, we can relativize the universal validity of the opposition between the written and the oral and reformulate carefully the paradigms about the tension between language (*langue*) and speech (*parole*). The argument, in fact, blurs the boundaries separating the scriptural economy from the oral. On the one hand, it casts a general suspicion on enterprises which in the name of the power of the written—its efficiency and its truth—reject the oral on the basis of its instability. Such projects have led to presumptuous classifications. Until recently, the method of intercultural and comparative studies consisted essentially in the manipulation of techniques (questionnaires, thematic grids, and participant observation) aimed at reproducing in a "scientific" manner what was already presupposed in the initial binary opposition, that is, in the tension between the normative and the unknown, the latter being possibly pathological. For example, many a functionalist studied African organizations, not because these were human ensembles, but, instead, because prima facie they were different from the European. In turn, the difference was at the end of a monograph accounted for by the fact that the described totality was African, primitive, or preliterate.

Within the diachronic dimension of a culture, the opposition between the written and the oral would draw strict limits by neatly separating chronologically the historical from the mythical, the latter being posited as originary and primitive. This rupture is perceived as a frontier disconnecting two different landscapes. On the one hand, there is a primitive territory in which narratives, supposedly, are in general naive, often uncritical, and at any rate can be characterized as mainly constituted by unbelievable rumors and fabulous legends. On the other hand, one finds the area and the era of the written, that is, of the perfect tool (as opposed to the imperfection of the mythical), as defined by a positive knowledge and science, insofar as this knowledge is seen as a product of the written. In its very being, the written effect makes possible an economical way of banking experiences, thus accumulating knowledge, ultimately allowing the triumph of science (see, e.g., Goody 1977). Claude Lévi-Strauss has, in *The Savage Mind* (1966), convincingly demonstrated the weaknesses and ambiguity of such a dichotomy. I do not think that I could convince those who dislike his reasons and proofs. I shall here just draw three lessons from this brief discussion.

First, the hypothesis of a linear development (from myth to history and science) negates an obvious fact: scientific discourse and practice can well coexist with myths. Claude Lévi-Strauss has aptly emphasized a powerful illustration: the most important scientific discoveries on which we are still living—the invention of agriculture, the domestication of animals, and the mastering of edible plants and their integration in human cultures—took place during periods dominated by mythical narratives and thought, long before the historical era. Another illustration is today's narrative, the novel, which superimposes itself on some mythical exigencies. In any case, since the invention of printing, the scriptural practice has taken on a mythical value in the West (see de Certeau 1984:133–39).

In contemporary Africa, one meets highly westernized and rational minds who sincerely submit to and enjoy the meaning of their mythological narratives. Each time I have used this case in public I have had to face a question from well-intentioned Westerners wondering whether those people had really assimilated the scientific habits of mind. My answer has always been the same: What is the relation between the scientific habits of mind of Christian European physicists, doctors, or university professors and their beliefs in the meaning of the Bible? In what sense could one claim that their situation is not similar to that of African scientists who relate themselves to their traditional myths? In both cases, two apparently distinct modes of thought and practice coexist: one critical, rational, aimed at mastering nature and its laws; the other, nonrational, ascientific, taking its meaning from the subjects' irrational investment in mythical propositions. As Edmund Leach put it once: "The non-rationality of myth is its very essence, for religion requires a demonstration of faith by the suspension of critical doubt" (1980b:1).

Second, the mythical as well as the historical discourses do not reenact the immediate experience of the culture they claim to unveil. In the midst of social transformations, ruptures, and developments, they arise as signs of a continuous becoming and function as "political" witnesses of a past (and its beginning) in order to mark the present. Explicitly, both the mythical and the historical present themselves as wholes, as explanatory systems. They are received by the communities which permit them as formulations of a past and as possible canons or, to use Thucydides' expression, as a *ktema es aei* (a paradigm forever) for the future. Moreover, I should insist on the fact that in the process of legitimizing what is happening in the present, they modify their ground, transform or adapt references, and constantly reinvent the very origin they account for. In fact I am here extending to the mythical what Michel Foucault calls the historical *a priori:*

> An *a priori* not of truths that might never be said, or really given to experience; but the *a priori* of a history that is given, since it is that of things actually said. . . . This *a priori* must take account of statements in their dispersion, in all the flaws opened up by their non-coherence, in their overlapping and mutual replacement, in their simultaneity, which is not unifiable, and in their succession, which is not deductible; in short, it has to take account of the fact that discourse has not only a meaning or a truth, but a history, and a specific history that does not refer it back to the laws of an alien development. (Foucault 1982:127)

In sum, I would say that in all social formations the mythical and the historical functions seem similar. They are memories whose hidden force is to refer back to what was there since the absolute beginnings and to vividly represent causalities, accidents, successes, of a culture. On the other hand, they inhabit the present as discursive practices and as such operate as political ideologies, that is, as bodies of functional ideas and truths responding to the needs of a specific community and interacting with these needs. In this dialectical process, the mythical and the historical everywhere claim to witness to a stabilizing effort.

Third, it should remain clear that the historical cannot be confused with the mythical, and I am not questioning the characteristics which differentiate them as particular and separate genres of narrative. One of the most striking is a fact: mythical narratives are not submitted to a discipline which could be compared with the demands of the *critique historique*. What I am interested in is beyond their differences. Both the mythical and the historical, despite the fact that they are submitted to a contextual authority (upon which in turn they act), establish themselves as referential monuments and as exempla. Both have practitioners, academies, and institutional rituals, because they are credible and believable.

> The credibility of a discourse is what first makes believers act in accord with it. It produces practitioners. To make people believe is to make them act. But by a curious circularity, the ability to make people act — to write and machine bodies — is what makes people believe. Because the law is already applied with and on bodies, "incarnated" in physical practices, it can accredit itself and make people believe that it speaks in the name of the "real." It makes

itself believable by saying: This text has been dictated for you by Reality itself. (de Certeau 1984:148)

Thus their irrational power: mythical and historical narratives seem always imbued with the sacred mission of carrying the nexus of cultural representation and being.

The *Bible noire* seems to be such an exemplum. It is about the derivation of Luba communities with its allegedly unbroken tradition. It is a worldview with explicit and hidden theological and historical presuppositions linking a collective consciousness and its fate to mythical roots and vice versa. Paradoxically, while defining itself as a fixed, definitive, all-embracing interpretation which proposes a high knowledge, it can also be perceived as a dynamic discourse. Beneath the surface of its propositions and their formal organization of supposedly fixed patterns, its statements, assertions, and modalities of ''consummation'' in the truth of the originary have been contextualizing the charter, thus qualifying it as a political and ideological construct. Summing up the three lessons I have just elaborated, the *Bible noire* should be seen as both an archival exemplum which is in the outside of the present and a discursive practice embodied in a presently changing culture and denoting discreet yet continuous processes of self-evaluation and adaptation. As an exemplum, it attests and represents in its own right the order of a cultural experience, its figures and their transformations through time. As a discursive practice about the originary, it is a myth, that is, ''a fragmented discourse which is articulated on the heterogeneous practices of a society and which also articulates them symbolically'' (de Certeau 1984:133–34).

But what is the authenticity of the *Bible noire?* The titles of chapters and 'sections' sound like reproductions of the Torah or of the Christian Bible: Creation of Celestial Spirits, Emanations from the Divine, Qualities of Creation, Fall of Man, Revolt of Angels, Repudiation of the Serpent, Sacrifice of the Firstborn, Institution of Sacrifices and of Communion, Resurrection of Creatures, etc. More important, the narrative revolves around some central themes—God's benevolence for his creation, man's sin, the sacrifice of God's firstborn for the redemption of humankind and his resurrection—whose meaning brings immediately to the reader's mind Christian postulations and dogmas. Here are five capsules to illustrate this statement. F.M. refers to Fourche and Morlighem, 1973, in the bibliography.

1. *God:* Maweja Nangila metamorphosed Himself firstly in three persons, thus creating two other Lord Spirits of second rank beside Him. (F.M. 12)

2. *Human Creation:* [Maweja] filled Himself up with a Breath of a potent power and exhaled it powerfully on the Earth, saying then: "Lord Man, master of all creatures, appear." Immediately, Man appeared. — After, He again filled Himself up with a great Breath, exhaled it on man and then said, "Lady Woman appear." Instantly the Woman appeared. (F.M. 40)

3. *The Sin:* Ambiguity says to Man: "Maweja Nangila created you male and female, and He did not teach you how to make love and procreate." Man answered: "Show me." Ambiguity committed this crime. In front of the man, he coupled himself with the Woman; after, he helped them to copulate. And Ambiguity told the Man: "you see that Maweja Nangila did not create you in His own image: He did not give you all His powers." (F.M. 112)

4. *Redemption:* Initiated people still call him [the Firstborn Son of Maweja] the "Great Flesh." In effect, Maweja Nangila, before sacrificing Him for all his creatures, metamorphosed Him into [human] flesh. He died and resurrected, resurrecting at the same time with all creatures. (F.M. 224)

5. *Communion:* In sacrificing his Firstborn to creatures, in giving them to share and eat the Flesh from his Forehead, Maweja Nangila instituted ceremonies of Sacrifice and Communion in species. He demonstrated its virtues and powers. (F.M. 139)

Finally, I should insist on another fact: the rigorous completeness of the narrative and its intellectual systematicity arouse suspicion. An incidental reference (F.M. 224) to Europeans (who, according to the narrative, witness to the grandeur of Maweja, our God, because without knowing him, through their Lord Jesus, they speak in fact about him) may, at best, logically lead one to wonder about the age of the narrative and question its authenticity. At worst, one may think of rejecting simply the whole thing as a mystifying fabrication and indict Fourche and Morlighem for having concocted it. Does not the narrative in its governing formulations and symbolism presume the Christian Bible, and does not it, at least once and explicitly, make reference to a thorough confrontation with Christianity?

I personally see no reason for suspecting the good faith of Fourche and Morlighem. Indeed one regrets that they do not include in their book a detailed account of their "fieldwork," which would have reported on their informants, the circumstances in which they began collecting the *Bible noire,* and the techniques used for recording it and fixing it in written form. Yet we should keep in mind that when Fourche and Morlighem began their research in the 1920s, it was not customary to introduce ethnographical studies by the

exposition of one's personal experience and subjective feelings. Even a preliminary discussion of techniques did not often seem necessary. The works of
Frobenius, for example, and the collection of *mémoires* of the Académie Royale
des Sciences Coloniales are concrete illustrations. In the late 1940s a respected
French scholar, Marcel Griaule, still used this approach, as exemplified by his
Dieu d'eau (1948). In itself, the method is neither good nor bad, but usual in
the anthropological practice. Predicated on the "scientific rationality" of the
nineteenth and early twentieth centuries, it pretends to balance a reasoning
about and a description of human cultures between universal norms and contingent experiences. In this perspective, ethnography is a matter of cognitive
classification and its possible political exploitation. From this framework, the
Bible noire is, after the imaginative *La Philosophie bantoue* (1945) of Placide
Tempels and *Dieu d'eau* (1948) of Marcel Griaule, remarkable, since it presents itself as the articulation and translation of what is out there in a contingent experience with a significance that can face universal paradigms. Yes, the
book was published in 1973. By then ethnography and anthropological methods had profoundly reelaborated their methods and rules. I think it is uncalled
for to reproach an old man for remaining faithful to the methods and techniques of his time.

One might add: How do we know that the *Bible noire* is genuinely the
exposition of what is out there as a secret knowledge in the Luba tradition?
Such an interrogation could bluntly become: Is not this so-called translation an arrangement or simply a lie? We know how for years a similar
suspicion was manipulated against Marcel Griaule's work, unfortunately often
in a dishonest manner. The most recent example of Griaule-bashing is in the
August 1988 issue of *African Arts,* a special number on Dogon art edited by
Kate Ezra. In any case, I believe suspicions like this to be fruitful if properly
used, and they should be applied to all anthropological descriptions. Specifically, one should question the credibility of any anthropological "reason" and
"imagination" and also the validity of any anthropologist's constructions. Particularly problematic is the conceptual bridging, or the translation, of a given
"place," or experience, and its own rationality with the "space" of scientific
discourse. Even present-day reflexive anthropology, so concerned with the
anthropologist's *états d'âmes,* is questionable if it cannot prove that it does a
better job in bridging conceptually two languages (*langues*) or two speeches
(*paroles*). The test of validity of an anthropological construction has little to do
with complacent self-analyses and certainly less with fashionable psychological exhibitionisms about fieldwork, intersubjectivity, or other spurious concepts. The credibility of today's anthropological concepts (beyond all the
modes and openings that they suggest in metaphors, litotes, or hyperboles)

cannot but unveil itself in a validity-test: a dialogical confrontation between the native original place that the concepts exceed and, on the other hand, the scientific space in which they valorize themselves.

Two criteria contribute to the validity-test of an ethnographic study: first, confirmation of results by subsequent explorations on the same topic or on closely related themes; second, conformity with the conclusions of indigenous people, specifically the local intelligentsia which is critical of both local opinions and anthropological reason. Griaule, for instance, made such an achievement. Dogons today recite his saga. And subsequent researchers—Dieterlen, de Heusch, Cissé, and others—have evaluated Griaule's translation of Dogon cosmology and furthered his hypotheses.

The *Bible noire* presents a similar, although more discrete, outcome. Its overall effect in the field of anthropology seems to have been one of shock and disbelief. This may account for the silence which surrounds the book: even learned professionals remain cautious about its content. On the other hand, the Luba and Songye popular reception has been overwhelming. They have recognized their traditional discursive practice and its cultural *a priori* well mirrored in the translation. Respected local scholars and students of the Luba past have guaranteed the relative credibility of the narrative. In the aftermath of the publication of the *Bible noire,* Mabika Kalanda, a specialist of Luba history and culture and one of the foremost influential thinkers in Central Africa, transformed himself into a publicity agent of the book, urging his fellow intellectuals to read carefully the *Bible noire*. By then, the Reverend Marcel Tshiamalenga, a doctor of theology from Louvain University, Belgium, and a doctor of philosophy from the University of Frankfurt, Germany, a long-standing professor at the Faculté de Théologie Catholique in Kinshasa, had, in an unprecedented move for a Catholic priest teaching at an ecclesiastical institution, integrated the *Bible noire* into the corpus of serviceable means for the reconstruction of latent and unconscious Central African systems of thought. His essays on linguistic and anthropological philosophy (1973) and on the philosophy of sin in the Luba tradition (1974) are supported by explicit references to the *Bible noire*. To my knowledge, Henri Maurier, a professor at the Institut Catholique de Paris, was the first non-African to trust the *Bible noire*. In the first edition of his *Philosophie de l'Afrique noire* (1975), he refers to it apropos of classificatory imagination and its relation to African symbolism (Maurier 1985:208).

The credibility of the *Bible noire* imposes itself as a fascinating question. Yet can we really say that it also founds the authenticity of the narrative? Referring to my own exceptionally early "initiation," I have noted the *basic* consistency and general correctness of the narrative. I have said nothing about its authenticity as discourse in the Luba-Songye continuum. To do so at this stage of analysis would demonstrate nothing. Anyway, my own experience is not, and cannot in itself be, proof of authenticity for a mythical narrative spelling out its linkages with primordial beginnings. I have already mentioned my scepticism about the unusual completeness of the narrative. Let me specify now the issues regarding authenticity. Three questions will suffice: Did the narrative edited in French spring from Luba imagination as it is offered? Who is really speaking about, signifying, and metaphorizing Luba origins in the written document articulated by the language and voices of translators? Could we pinpoint what exactly the translation from Tshiluba to French has extinguished, ruined, reorganized, embellished, or explicated?

Unassumingly, Fourche and Morlighem offer us keys for this critique. Introducing their work, they write: "All these documents of observation and orality have been collected through conversations [*à bâtons rompus*] during our mission of prophylactic medicine" (F.M. 7). "We used to write down on the fact, or immediately after, in the *very local language* what we heard. When we had indigenous peoples accompanying us, we used to ask them to repeat the conversations so we would not miss points" (my emphasis, F.M. 7–8). So far, so good. The gaze and the ear of the observers have no mediation. They are really parts of a dialogical exchange, and the verbal communication takes place in Tshiluba (or in a proximate dialect) and is afterward transcribed in the same local idiom. And a control version by linguistically more competent partners (or observers) then takes place (but how often?) to guarantee the exactness of the received message. After the establishment of a provisional draft, each author separately made a second control, first focusing on confused or litigious renderings (*expressions troubles et litigieuses*), then making new inquiries until he could be certain that he had absolutely understood and tightened up the meaning and intention (*compris et serré le sens et l'intention au plus près*) of controverted concepts and sequences. The information was then card-indexed. Finally came the moment of writing the book. We can follow the authors' process and comment upon the three main stages they invoke: the exploitation of their bank of information, the translation, and the organization of the narrative in French. First, the exploitation: "*We have therefore reexamined our notes,* confronting and cross-checking them. We have sorted out the most solidly confirmed and explicit. *We have then reclassified them, dividing* their parts when they dealt with various topics, and we *completed* them by each other when a connection imposed itself as natural" (my emphasis, F.M. 8).

The endeavor proposed here is not a simple reproduction or reflection of what was given in dialogues, but rather a different level of exchange. I think that I am right in my supposition that the critical analysis which here reexamines and reclassifies notes uses concepts and grids coming from outside the local language and place. Something amazing is happening here. A reading seems to need its own reformulation about what it has understood through subsequent dialogues and examinations. It imposes its own reconversion by reviewing its own first construction (in an African language), and then by jumping to theoretical exigencies for reordering (to reclassify, divide, complete) the lines of real dialogues and what knowledge they have brought about. Nowhere in this process does it reflect on its own movements and its consequences. In effect, a rupture is being created between a first narrative (which has already been mutilated through card-indexing) and a second text undertaken as an analytical reading. This leads to the second point: the translation. I hope it is by now clear that this operation takes place after an elaborate work of intellectual rearrangement (classification, divisions, and completions) of the primordial discourse. Strictly, what is being translated is not the ordinary material which came out of hesitant conversations, but a second-level discourse submitted to both a control, verifying its faithfulness to the origin, and an evaluation of its rationality vis-à-vis a silent grid. A translation takes place.

> *We have reconstructed* the [traditional] texture [of the narrative] worn out in certain places, and by lack of information *we have patched it up* in other places with indications from "profane" sources, but by strictly using indigenous glosses, without modifying a phrase or a word. We have avoided the easy picturesqueness of exotic terms and translated everything we could possibly, commenting upon rendered terms, using approximate words or other expressions. In brief, *we have tried to be in conformity* with the blacks' thought [*la pensée noire*]. (my emphasis, F.M. 8)

The *Bible noire* seems thus a kind of violence on another discourse. It is a reconstruction, a *patched* narrative which sincerely *tries to be in conformity* with the story that allows it. Yet it has conceptually freed itself from it. Metaphorically, one could say that it is a new space. In fact, it defines a transformation of the privileges of a dialogue which, by the way, was based on commentaries in Tshiluba about other discourses which themselves referred to others and so on. Where could one find the real initial source or center? Fourche and Morlighem, putting aside exoticism, believed that they could localize in their dialogues with Luba persons schemata that, methodically analyzed and carefully used, would permit a critical translation that could render in French the essentials of Luba knowledge. The published text obeys the authors' authority. "The organization [of the *Bible noire*] in chapters, their titles and disposition are our responsibility. That was the price to be paid for clarity, and we think that such a division alters nothing, since it faithfully espouses the logical sequence of blacks' conceptions. Yet this division does not suggest that natives make classifications or distinctions which are foreign to their spirit, as happens when worldviews are classified as dynamism, animism, etc." (F.M. 9).

The deviation is now perfect and given in good faith. The sovereignty of an analytic reason justifies its power in establishing a text submitted to the order of an organizing clarity. This, believe the authors, is completely extraneous to the first-level discourse they had from Africans. Does this translation suppose the classical theme of the colonial library: Where does the light come from? Let us just remark that the authors repeat and insist on their fidelity to local conceptions and their admiration for this oeuvre. "The *Bible noire* is really an indigenous work. The book is not more marked with shortcomings than many other sacred books which express multiple and successive voices whose different tones accord to each other in a more or less harmonious way. The *Bible noire* has on them a neat superiority: it is exempt from foreign interpolation" (F.M. 9–10). One could easily agree about the originality of the *Bible noire*. The real problems are the significance and authenticity of the translation. Analogically, this might be the place and moment to refer to a magnificent passage of Jacques Derrida apropos of "Edmond Jabès and the Question of the Book": "The necessity of commentary, like poetic necessity, is the very form of exiled speech. In the beginning is hermeneutics. But the *shared* necessity of exegesis, the interpretive imperative, is interpreted differently by the rabbi and the poet. The difference between the horizon of the original text and the exegetic writing makes the difference between the rabbi and the poet irreducible. Forever unable to reunite with each other, yet so close to each other, how could they ever regain the *realm*" (Derrida 1978:67).

Fourche and Morlighem say they translate an indigenous experience. Yet as they recognize it, they also comment on difficult issues, explore and interpret meanings. Who is the "rabbi" and who is the "poet" between the informant who unveils an esoteric knowledge and the commentator? What should we do with the tension between the two possibly opposing texts? Fourche and Morlighem have a potent explanation: there is not a complete originary text, but only fragments. They write: "This work is not really balanced. We have been forced about certain secondary topics to make developments which might seem disproportionate because they give rise to interesting cross-checkings. The work has the length of a narrative that one individual could not have composed. There is probably no native who possesses this knowledge in its entirety. On the other hand, the recollection and patience of the rare men of memory have their limits" (F.M. 9). Things become clearer. The highly positive reception of the *Bible noire* by Central African intellectuals (particularly Luba), simply means that the authors succeeded in arranging pertinently the themes of their constructed narrative by aptly exploiting more authentic fragmentary narratives.

The achievement is remarkable. The other writings which in Central Africa had a similar impact, and with which Fourche and Morlighem's success can be compared, are works by Van Wing on Lower Zaire's Bakongo, Colle in the east, and Tempels in the southeast. How to account for the fact that all these authors are, as were Fourche and Morlighem, "amateur" anthropologists or ethnographers? They seem to succeed where professionals fail. They render an African configuration to the point of speaking almost perfectly the language of an unrecorded history and its fantasies. They do it in such a way that indigenous intelligences, even the most demanding and intolerant, agree about the general correctness of their constructs. The fact raises serious questions apropos of the practice of African scholastic anthropology.

Though Fourche and Morlighem's translation may not be authentic in the strict sense of the word, it nevertheless integrates harmoniously the themes, effects, and spirit of local fragments and their indigenous rhythm. This is the ultimate test of its credibility. I shall evaluate it systematically in the following section by comparing and checking the content of the *Bible noire* with exoteric texts. Regarding the significance of the surprising five capsules presented earlier, the coming pages should demonstrate that very probably they are, to use Lévi-Strauss' language, only mythemes, that is, universal motifs occurring in mythical narratives throughout the world in varying cultures and traditions.

Creation, History, and the Sex of Beings

> In the beginning of all Things, the Eldest Spirit Maweja Nangila, the First, the Eldest and the Great Lord of all the Spirits who appeared afterward, manifested Himself, alone, and by His own power. Then He created the Spirits. He created them not in the way He created other things but through a metamorphosis of His own being, dividing it magically and without losing anything. That is why the Spirits participate in Maweja Nangila's divine nature.
>
> F.M. 11

Maweja is the proper name of the Supreme Being. Nangila comes etymologically from the root word *nanga,* which means "to love." Other divine names include Mulopo, also used as adjective in expressions such as Mulopo Maweja, "Lord God," and Mulopo Maweja Nangila; Mvidie, Mvidi, or Vidye, names that designate God but also any immaterial spirit; Mukulu, a concept that includes the meanings of primordial, the first, fertilizing power, etc., which often appears in conjunction with Mvidie, as in Mvidie Mukulu; and Nzambi, or God (see, e.g., Van Caeneghem 1956:10–24).

At the origin of everything, there is thus Maweja, alone, a self-created being who at one moment transforms himself and begins consciously a complex creative process. A close reading of the narrative shows that he creates successively two major orders, that of heaven first, and then that of the earth. Let us synthesize the whole story. From himself alone, Maweja, whose complete name is Mvidie Mukulu Maweja Nangila, engenders two Lord Spirits: Mvidie Mukulu wa Tshame and Tshame wa Mvidie Mukulu. The former, known as the Elder Spirit of Tshame, is commonly qualified as the Firstborn and the Flesh of Maweja's Forehead. Tshame wa Mvidie Mukulu is known as Tshame the Lord Spirit, born from the Elder Spirit. "Maweja Nangila therefore created . . . first of all three Elder Spirits having the rank of Lords and they are: Himself, Maweja Nangila, the first and the greatest among them, the Lord of all Spirits and All Things. The Elder Spirit . . . , second Spirit in lordship . . ., and Tshame Elder Spirit or Tshame born from an Elder Spirit who is the third Spirit in lordship" (F.M. 13). The narrative metaphorizes the paradoxical unity of this divine grouping. Maweja could be considered as "a male Lord in a [human] family." The second spirit who sits to his right, his firstborn, is like "his first son born from the first wife." The third spirit sitting on his left would resemble a wife. In effect, says the text: "The firstborn sits to the right of the father, the first wife to the left of her spouse; thus one is on the male side and the other on the female" (F.M. 12).

The metamorphosis of Maweja into three is followed by another, producing a fourth spirit, Mulopo Maweja, commonly called Maweja's emissary. Afterward Maweja creates two sets of four other main spirits. Then they are twelve. The text insists on the symbolic meaning of this number: "[Maweja] created twelve remarkably perfect spirits in three by four, for Maweja since the beginning has created by using numbers three and four" (F.M. 14). Next, gigantic winged and intelligent animals emanate from the Creator. These celestial beings are analogous to the terrestrial lion, man, eagle, leopard, buffalo-antelope, etc., and have an exceptionally great vital force. They can be seen as symbolic representations of the great spirits: the heavenly lion would reflect Maweja; the man, the firstborn; and the eagle, the third spirit. Finally, Maweja also generates basic celestial elements in pairs, such as energy and breath, water and fire, high heaven and earth, light and darkness, the two major luminaries (the sun and the moon), and the stars.

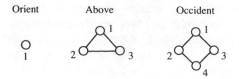

Figure 3. The classification of Lord Spirits. After
T. Fourche and H. Morlighem, *Une Bible noire,*
(1973, Brussels: Max Arnold).

A second creation takes place immediately after the organization of the celestial space, this time on the earth. Twice in five stages, during two different seasons, Maweja brings life on the earth, doubling the magnificent things already existing in the high heaven. In this creative process, two features are new. First, Maweja operates with the assistance of the two Lord Spirits he brought into existence; second, he no longer creates by emanation, but by convocation: he calls or breathes in order to bring beings and things into existence.

> [Maweja] was creating; the First Spirit of Tshame was ordering created things, as a firstborn would organize the goods of his father; and Tshame the Spirit was making them grow, as a first wife would care for her husband's goods. . . .
> In reality, when Maweja Nangila brought the creatures to existence, he did not create all of them by convocating them in the same manner. According to their nature, he created them by using one or the other of the following three great secret knowledges: speech [*parole* as *kuela diyi,* that is strictly: summoning verbally], call by gesture which realizes acts it imitates, and finally breathing which is divine in its nature. (F.M. 33–34, 39)

Mvidie Mukulu Maweja Nangila divides himself then through metamorphosis in three, then in four, Elder Lord Spirits.

The fall of the fourth spirit brings the number back to three. Mvidie Mukulu Maweja Nangila created two Elder Lord Spirits in order to be assisted by four, as in the house of a polygynous man living among his four wives.

1. Mvidie Mukulu Maweja Nangila
2. Mvidie Mukulu wa Tshame
3. Tshame wa Mvidie Mukulu
4. Mulopo Maweja
5. Mvidie Nkimba
6. Mule Mwedi
7. Tshiushikulu
8. Muntu Lufu
9. Tshiukula
10. Tshela Mpungi

11. Mwadia Mvita
12. Kadia Bilu

In exoteric versions and syntheses (see Van Caeneghem 1956:38–43), three man spirits come after the Supreme Being, Mvidie Mukulu Maweja Nangila, described metaphorically as simultaneously his equals and his sons. They are Kabale, Mikombo wa Kalewo, and Bende. Kabale is celebrated as "God, Kabale, God's Son, God of Tshilele." Tshilele is a highly persecuted woman who survived all the miseries of a challenging life, avoiding all the traps thanks to a special divine protection; she is known as the mother of a Kashidi. Mikombo wa Kalewo, the equal of God, begot himself and lived among humans who harrassed him. Tired by the naughtiness of humankind, he went back with his followers to his father for advice on how to save humans despite themselves. Of Bende it is said, "Bende is God, God is Bende." He is the spirit, the voice, and the counsel of Maweja. Let us note that in a controversial concordist move, Van Caeneghem writes: "A number of Black Christians say: Mikombo was our Jesus-Christ. . . . a number of Black Christians say that Bende is the Holy Spirit" (Van Caeneghem 1956:41–42).

During the first season, a dry one, Maweja creates the fundamental terrestrial order with its basic pairs of elements:"Naming possesses . . . the power of metamorphosing [the named]. In effect, in giving names to things when he was creating them, Maweja Nangila conferred upon them their form, or character, virtues, and particular modes of behavior" (F.M. 42). The first creation reproduces heaven's geography: energy and wind, water and fire, sky and earth, light and darkness, the luminaries (sun, moon, stars). During the next season, a rainy one, Maweja successively brings to existence paired things. They are qualified as elder and principal creatures. The norm of this cycle is symbolized in a human name, Nkongolo Kamukanda, and the rain. We should note the link between this name, which means reddish and is also associated with the rainbow, and with rains. It is in effect the metaphoric brother and the negation of the rain. Other creations include vegetables and savanna trees, stones and forest essences, birds and aquatic animals, terrestrial animals and human beings. The creative process did not stop here. It's still going on today, according to the narrative. "Afterward [Maweja] subdivided principal species in a continuing successive process, sorting out two by two, in twin pairs, particularized species; then subdividing these, and in the same manner from principal things producing more particular entities until he created the multitude of all the smallest creatures" (F.M. 60). In brief, in the last phase of his creation, Maweja operates imaginatively by virtue of a life principle, the power of schizogenesis impressed on certain creatures.

The creation in its order as well as in its meaning remains perfect until the moment humans rebel against their Creator. The heavenly and the terrestrial espouse each other so intimately that they reflect in each other the complementary purity and immortality of a peaceful and virtuous universe. But human disobedience opens the era of corruption. In anger, Maweja destroys his creatures. Yet in an afterthought of compassion and love, he decides to bring them back to life and sacrifices the life of his Firstborn as the price for redeeming the corrupted world.

The first creation takes place through divine emanations. The second creation follows afterward by convocation in the vocative. The divinity brings to life *ex nihilo* terrestrial creatures. The principal or elder beings come into existence during a first dry season, and during the second rainy season, the junior or earthly creatures are engendered. To complete his oeuvre, Maweja brings to light new and well-particularized entities by dividing up previously created species. The first creation by emanation concerns spirits (primordial spirits, celestial animals and beings) and heavenly things (such as energy, breath, water, fire, the high heaven, earth, light, darkness, great luminaries, stars). The second creation is structurally opposed to the first. It gives life to terrestrial creatures through Maweja's summons (naming, calling, breathing). During the dry season principal and elder terrestrial creatures appear; during the rainy season, junior beings and things. This creation itself is completed on earth when Maweja brings to existence new entities through schizogenesis, thanks to already created species. Broadly, this is the general order:

First Creation	Second Creation
Emanation	Convocation
High Heaven	Earth
Emanated Spirits	Created Beings
Primordial Things	Junior Things

The code of the second creation produces a balance between its order and that of the first creation. It brings about primordial binary oppositions: dry season versus rainy season, terrestrial elder things versus terrestrial junior things, or earth's creatures. We have now, on the one hand, earthly energy, wind, water, fire, sky, world, light, night, luminaries; and, on the other hand, junior creatures created later, during the rainy season: Nkongolo Kamukanda (the norm of the law), rain, stones, vegetables, savanna and forest trees, aquatic and terrestrial animals, human beings.

Dry Season	Rainy Season
Terrestrial Elder Things	Terrestrial Junior Things

Let us pause one moment and briefly look in another direction, by going back to the very beginning, to Maweja himself. I have been using so far masculine qualifiers apropos of Maweja. They are debatable, since Maweja is, according to the narrative, both male and female. Maweja is simultaneously father and mother. All the creatures Maweja brought into existence in the first originary universe (before human rebellion) were hermaphrodites. The primacy of the elder always transcends the tension between masculinity and femininity: "Each of all created things was made hermaphrodite as in the case of elder things, or simultaneously male and female as in the case of animals and humans. In specific couples, the male generally [but not always] appeared first and thus is the elder of the female who comes afterward" (F.M. 43).

During the second creation, in the dry season Maweja creates two twin pairs in five stages. They are: energy (male and elder) and wind (female and junior); water (female and elder) and fire (male and junior); the sky (male and elder) and the earth (female and junior); light (female and elder) and darkness (male and junior); the major luminaries (the sun and the moon, which are male and elder) and the stars (female and junior). During the rainy season, creations appear also in five stages: Nkongolo Kamukanda (male and elder) and the rain (female and junior); vegetables (female and elder) and savanna trees (male and junior); stones (male and elder) and forest trees (female and junior); birds (female and elder) and aquatic animals (male and junior); terrestrial animals (male and elder) and humans (female and junior). The following table synthesizes the second creation. M means male, F is for female, and u symbolizes union.

Second Creation

	Dry Season		Rainy Season	
Stages	Elder	Junior	Elder	Junior
1	Energy (M)	u Wind (F)	Nkongolo Kamukanda (M)	u Rain (F)
2	Water (F)	u Fire (M)	Vegetables (F)	u Savanna Trees (M)
3	Sky (M)	u Earth (F)	Stones (M)	u Forest trees (F)
4	Light (F)	u Darkness (M)	Birds (F)	u Aquatic Animals (M)
5	Luminaries (M)	u Stars (F)	Terrestrial Animals (M)	u Humans (F)

Careful readers might observe that my interpretation and this synthetic table give to birds a female and elder status and to aquatic beings a male and junior status, whereas Fourche and Morlighem do exactly the contrary. I believe my interpretation to be the correct one. The rainy season's creation transforms the dry season's creation. Both constitute an order reflecting the primordial creation which took place in the high heaven and whose organization became a paradigm in Maweja's creative process. Here is the code of celestial things' creation:

Energy (M)	u	Breath (F)
Water (F)	u	Fire (M)
High Heaven (M)	u	Earth (F)
Light (F)	u	Darkness (M)
Luminaries (M)	u	Stars (F)

The second creation reactualizes structurally the first. Twice, in five phases, it reproduces the model of the first creation according to a very simple formula: the union of a male and a female is followed by a reversal, a union of a female and a male.

Thus, male and female, Maweja created all beings and things. The narrative adds a major point: "It is because Maweja excellently made the creatures creating them in twin pairs as brother and sister, or as husband and wife, that ancient lords used to marry their own sisters" (F.M. 45). This explanation refers to a problem we analyzed earlier and which concerns the incestuous pattern of the first parents up to Nkongolo's time (see de Heusch 1982). The general code supporting both the Luba founding charter and the esoteric tradition on beginnings follows:

Male	u	Female
Brother	u	Sister
Husband	u	Wife
Elder	u	Junior

We should note here that gender qualification does not signify an absolute sexual determination. Instead, it only marks the primacy of one gender over the other. A female always includes a junior male side, and a male possesses in itself a discreeter female aspect. In sum, the body of Maweja's creatures is always hermaphroditic, or simultaneously male and female. Yet the male always has precedence over the female by virtue of its intrinsic qualities. These are, in the tradition, rendered in three categories: aggressiveness and imperiousness; fullness, toughness, and sharpness; violence and strength. The tradition opposes them to the order of the female's qualities: passivity and fecundity; roundness, hollowness, and welcoming; and mildness and beneficence.

Interestingly, the gender opposition which is given as natural operates also, since the first moment of creation, at a symbolic level. It thus accounts for the transformation of gender status and qualities. Two examples will illustrate this. The paired luminaries and stars created during the dry season include in themselves a number of logical transformations. In a first operation the masculine qualities of the conjunction of sun and moon are posited vis-à-vis the feminine intrinsic qualities of all stars. In this relation, the moon is male. A second operation, that is, the confrontation of the sun and the moon, makes the former a symbolic brother or husband of the latter, who, being a sister and wife, is therefore female. The same type of symbolic gender transformation takes place in the ensemble of stars. The second illustration is a quotation from the *Bible noire:* "When a human couple has twins, very often one of the children is male and the other female; if the two of them belong to the same sex, usually the elder is given his real sex and the junior the [symbolic] quality of the opposed sex" (F.M. 22).

To use Foucault's commentary on this type of knowledge linking semiology and hermeneutics, the interpretation of the natural and the symbolic makes a distinction "between observation and relation almost impossible. This results in the constitution of a single, unbroken surface in which observation and language intersect to infinity. And the second, the inverse of the first, is an immediate dissociation of all language, duplicated without any assignable term, by the constant reiteration of the commentary" (Foucault 1973:39). Foucault links the fact of these two forms to the primacy of the written. We have just seen how well they are actualized in an oral tradition.

The symbolic duplication of resemblances and transference of qualities through sexualization of features communicate. The human body as commented upon by the tradition qualifies and distributes them well. Three main types of discrimination intervene. Transcending the natural, they all formally oppose the "right" side, male and elder, to the "left" side, female and junior. The first type establishes a spatial distribution by qualifying the gender of elements on the basis of allegedly empirical observations. The following deductions offer an example:

Entities	Male/Elder/Right	Female/Junior/ Left
Eye	Strong Vision	Weaker Perception
Ear	Sharp Hearing	Poor Hearing
Nostril	Excellent Flair	Confusing Flair

A second discrimination seems more functional. It opposes entities by virtue of their functions and ways of operating.

Male/Elder	Female/Junior
Mouth has the creative power of speech, articulation, and absorption.	Anus has the negative power of eliminating impurities.
Epigastrium possesses the power of the verb and that of intuition about invisible things.	Penis and vagina have the power of reproducing human flesh and life.
Front of the head (*lubombo*) has the analytical capacity of discernment about future events.	Occiput (*kabakentshi*) has the capacity of discernment about events.

The third and last genre of discrimination is excessively metaphoric. It opposes human organs on the basis of symbolic classification using a basic oppositional formula: male versus female, brother versus sister, husband versus wife.

Male/Elder	Female/Junior
Brain: conceiving and reflective gift	Women's ovaries and men's testicles: power of physical reproduction
Heart: the father of life and vitality	Lungs: wifelike organs that "cook" heart's meals

The three types of discrimination in this presentation of human organs obey a very simple structure. Observed natural phenomena such as the opposition of sexes are transformed into symbolic signs of a second order. A positioning symbolism imposes itself (see Maurier 1985:187–211) by reuniting entities in the dynamism of a theoretical circularity through the mediation of gender qualification. The process seems to transcend (or to negate) the distinction we can make between semiological and hermeneutical approaches. By *semiology* I mean the knowledge and methods which allow one to observe, describe, and relate social and cultural signs in a given culture. By *hermeneutics,* I mean the knowledge and technical norms which permit one to read, relate, and interpret relations and meanings in a given culture (see Foucault 1973). The three types of discrimination are organized according to the same pattern: two different elements or entities are joined on the basis of their opposed natural functional or metaphoric qualities. The gender qualification operates as a paradigmatic mediation in the linking and separating process of the virtues of beings and things.

The symbolic classification of colors may help us to further our analysis. The *Bible noire* contrasts two fundamental pairs of colors: the white and the red (F.M. 88). Let us note that Luba traditionally reserve the white color for God's celebrations, and the red or a mixture of red and white are generally used for the cult of *bakishi*, "spirits" (Van Caeneghem 1956:22). On the one hand, the white symbolizes strong life and the red signifies a strong death; on the other, the black symbolizes a weaker life and the imprecise color signifies a weaker death. The first couple is male and elder; the second, female and junior. The *Bible noire* gives concrete examples of white "waters," such as brain fluid, semen, and breast milk. Examples of red fluids are blood, menses, bile. Black fluids include secretions from the prostate and Bartholin's gland; the uncolored "waters" include tears, urine, and saliva.

Male/Elder	Female/Junior
White (Strong life)	Black (Weak death)
Red (Strong death)	Imprecise (Weak life)

A second level of distinction opposes two new couplets: an imprecise white (or whitish) and an imprecise red (or reddish). The first is characterized by a weak life, the second by a weak death. Opposed to them are the vague black (or blackish) with its weaker death and the absolute imprecise color which is of a weaker life.

Male/Elder	Female/Junior
Whitish (Weak life)	Blackish (Weaker death)
Reddish (Weak death)	Absolute Imprecise (Weaker life)

When we compare the second level of oppositions to the first, we learn a number of things. Most obviously, although the second level reproduces the first, the new variations of colors all have weaker values in the tension between life and death, male and female. The second thing in effect consists in the structural transformation represented by the second level. A vertical relation of opposition exists on the first level between the white and red, black and imprecise. It symbolically opposes a strong life to a strong death and also a weak death to a weak life. In fact, the message can be read as follows: the white is to the red as a strong life is to a strong death; in the same way, the black is to the imprecise as a weak death is to a weak life. The second level transforms the message into a new economy: the whitish is to the reddish as a weak life is to a weak death. Likewise, the blackish is to the absolute imprecise as a weaker death is to a weaker life. The message seems repetitive. Horizontally, the message reads: the white (strong life) is to the black (weak death) as the red (strong death) is to the imprecise (weak life); and the whitish (weak life) is to the blackish (weaker death) as the reddish (weak death) is to the absolute imprecise (weaker life).

Vertical Articulation		
1st Level of Classification	White (Strong life) vs. Red (Strong death)	Black (Weak death) vs. Imprecise (Weak life)
2d Level of Classification	Whitish (Weak life) vs. Reddish (Weak death)	Blackish (Weaker death) vs. Absolute Imprecise (Weaker life)

Horizontal Articulation		
1st Level of Classification	White (Strong life) Red (Strong death)	vs. Black (Weak death) vs. Imprecise (Weak life)
2d Level of Classification	Whitish (Weak life) Reddish (Weak death)	vs. Blackish (Weaker death) vs. Absolute Imprecise (Weaker life)

When we compare the vertical arrangement with the horizontal by paying strict attention to the second-level disposition of values, the message becomes tautological. Vertically it reads as follows: the whitish is to the reddish as a weak life is to a weak death; the blackish is to the absolute imprecise as a weaker death is to a weaker life. Horizontally, exactly the same statement comes out of the oppositions. The redundancy is striking.

It is possible to consider the two levels as two tables classifying both colors and symbolic values. Using the semantic tension between life (universally positive) and death (universally negative) which distributes colors in value categories, let us construct a kind of symbolic square for a logic game that could permit other hypotheses about the relationships existing between colors. The white would have in the model a universal affirmative value of life (strong life) opposed, in a relation of contrariety, to the universal negative value of red (strong death). A relation of subcontrariety could reactualize this tension by opposing the partial positive value of the imprecise (weak life) to the partial negative value of the black (weak death). To continue this analogical interpretation, a relation of subalternity would exist between the white (strong life) and the imprecise (weak life) and also between the red (strong death) and the black (weak death). Finally the symbolic square posits the white and the black, the red and the imprecise, as contradictory.

White	Red
Universal Positive	Universal Negative
Strong Life	Strong Death

Imprecise	Black
Partially Positive	Partially Negative
Weak Life	Weak Death

By introducing the gender and seniority qualifications of colors, the symbolic code could witness to the following (purely analogical and not at all logical) relations: a relation of contrariety between the male elder white and the male elder red; a relation of subcontrariety between the female junior imprecise and the female junior black; two relations of subalternity, between the male elder white and the female junior imprecise and between the male elder red and the female junior black; and two relations of contradiction, between the male elder white and the female junior black and between the male elder red and the female junior imprecise. Schematically, we can represent them in this manner:

White	Red
Male	Male
Elder	Elder

Imprecise	Black
Female	Female
Junior	Junior

It is interesting to observe that the second-level table does not reproduce the basic organization of the first. It cannot be put into the model without producing nonsensical statements about the tension existing between colors and their symbolic values of life and death. Duplicating the first-level organization on the basis of semantic correspondences existing between terms (white-whitish, red-reddish, black-blackish, imprecise–absolute imprecise), because of the type of symbolic qualifications of the virtues of the vague and intermediary colors (whitish, reddish, blackish, absolute imprecise), the table would produce bizarre propositions such as a weak life (whitish) is in a relation of contradiction with a weaker death (blackish); or a weaker life (absolute imprecise) is in a relation of contradiction with a weaker death (reddish). In any case, even apropos of a symbolic table, it would not make sense at all to consider a weak life (whitish) as a universal affirmative symbol and a weak death (reddish) as a universal negative symbol.

Whitish	vs.	Reddish
Male		Male
Elder		Elder
(Weak life)		(Weak death)
vs.		vs.
Absolute Imprecise	vs.	Blackish
Female		Female
Junior		Junior
(Weaker life)		(Weaker death)

This second table is strictly a commentary on the basic model. It indicates that all intermediary colors are symbolically weaker than their basic equivalents. We can consequently put aside this general statement and focus on other qualifications, those of gender and seniority. Redundant and strong messages come from both horizontal and vertical tensions. Horizontally, the tension between the whitish and the reddish is one of complementarity: one is a weak positive in life, the other a weak negative in death; yet they are both male and elder. In the same way, the absolute imprecise and the blackish oppose and complement each other: they are both female and junior; yet one symbolizes a weaker life and the other a weaker death. Vertically, the table posits clearly the superiority of the whitish and reddish, both male and elder, over their reciprocal subalterns, the absolute imprecise and the blackish, both female and junior.

This analysis of a Luba-Kasai esoteric symbolism sheds interesting light on the Luba historical charter as presented by exoteric Luba-Shaba narratives (e.g., de Heusch 1982; Reefe 1981; Womersley 1984). The charter, already analyzed, begins the history of the Luba by opposing two individuals, Nkongolo and Mbidi Kiluwe, who symbolize in the Luba collective representation two opposed types of leaderships which took place successively in the beginnings of Luba history. Nkongolo is a *mukalanga* (self-made man), violent and incestuous. His praise name is Kongolo Mwamba mujya na nkololo, that is, "Nkongolo who dances with a scimitar." "The implication of this, the people say, is that he delighted in chopping off the ears, noses, and even heads of those who ventured too near him. He also had knives, for it is said that when he sat in state he always had two kneeling female slaves, one at each side of him, into whose necks he plunged his knives to raise himself up when rising from his throne'' (Womersley 1984:5). His ambition and power sprang from a natural model: ''It is said of this Nkongolo that when a boy at his home near the present Lukungu, east of Kamina and near the sources of the Lumami and Lubilash rivers, he watched the *black* driver ants fight and devour the termites, or *white* ants, and thus was fired with an ambition to be a great leader of men and a conqueror of others'' (my emphasis, Womersley 1984:1). Traditional narratives give his familial background. His father was a hyena, universally known as Muntu utyila wadi wa malwa, that is, ''a *red* or clear skinned man who was a *monstrosity*'' (my emphasis, Womersley 1984:1). Nkongolo, the reddish son of his father and a *mukalanga,* succeeded in becoming a great leader by realizing his will to power in a manner imitating the primitive violence of the black driver ants he studied.

The other character, Mbidi Kiluwe, is pictured by the charter as a refined man (the son of a hereditary king) who is highly civilized. As de Heusch rightly observed (1982:23), Mbidi makes a discreet use of his mouth and has highly sophisticated habits of drinking and eating. Womersley's text specifies well Mbidi's appearance. The two sisters of Nkongolo, Mabela and Bulanda, are just back from the river where they have met Mbidi. '' 'What was he like did you say?' asked [Nkongolo] the King. 'Wonderful,' breathed Bulanda, 'tall, lithe, handsome — *shiningly black* like the great buffalo of the forest' '' (my emphasis, Womersley 1984:7). The qualification of color is repeated in the version at least twice. It is first mentioned when Mbidi, having decided to leave Nkongolo's kingdom, meets the official ferryman on the Lualaba River, who turns out to be a longtime friend. He confides in the ferryman a major responsibility: ''One of these days a young man will flee from Nkongolo, for Nkongolo will be jealous of him. If he is a *brown or reddish man, light colored,* do not ferry him over, but if he is *black,* tall, and strong like me, ferry him over with all speed that he might reach me at the capital, and whatever you do, do not ferry over Nkongolo the Tyrant, who is sure to be not far behind'' (my emphasis, Womersley 1984:8–9). The second time the qualification of color appears, it is when the charter describes the birth of the son of Bulanda and Mbidi: ''This wonderful baby, *black like Mbidi Kiluwe.* He was named Ilunga after his father together with a praise name *Luala Misaha,* that is, the divider of streams or nations'' (first emphasis mine, Womersley 1984:9). Womersley adds immediately: ''Note the parallel in the Bible record of Genesis chapter 10 verses 5, 18, and 32 — 'From whom are the nations divided' '' (1984:9). The remark is interesting, but not pertinent in this chapter, which is concerned with the symbolic opposition of Nkongolo and Mbidi.

The following two tables will illustrate these oppositions. The first I discussed in my last chapter, which exploited heavily de Heusch's study (1982).

Nkongolo	Mbidi Kiluwe
Primitive Royalty	Refined Royalty
Incest	Hyperexogamy
Sterility, Death	Procreation

The second transforms this set of oppositions into a new table by integrating the tension of colors we have just observed in the Womersley version of the same charter.

Nkongolo	Mbidi Kiluwe
Mukalanga	*Nfumu*
Primitive Royalty	Refined Royalty
Primitive Violence	Civilized
Red	Black

The last table confirms the symbolic tensions that we found in analyzing the colors in Fourche and Morlighem's esoteric narrative. Nkongolo is red and as such symbolizes a strong death and represents a negative paradigm. Incestuous, wicked, and violent, he incarnates all the universal negative virtues of a male. He is not in a relation of contradiction with Mbidi. Mythologically and historically, he is the elder. Mbidi comes after him, an antithetical paradigm in a position of subalternity: he is black, junior, and symbolically female. It is not an accident that two women, Mabela and Bulanda, meet him and subsequently bring him to existence in Nkongolo's world, and thus positively actualize the tension as subalternity. The women's action ultimately makes possible an evolution from the primitive violence of Nkongolo to the civilization brought about by Mbidi.

The sign (if we need one) is given in the charter. A woman (symbolically, a weak death or a weak life) makes the historical rupture possible. Kalala Ilunga, the son of Mbidi, because of his intelligence, brilliance, and success, becomes a living challenge to the authority of King Nkongolo, who decides to get rid of the young man. Kalala is smart. Moreover, he has the support of his father's faithful friend, who happens also to be King Nkongolo's close adviser. When Kalala's life is in danger, he flees in time. Nkongolo goes after him. Soon, the situation is reversed. Kalala has indeed successfully reached his father's kingdom, and he returns with an army to fight Nkongolo. The latter understands rapidly that he is finished and hides in a cave with his two wives.

One day one of the two wives spied movements in the bush along the plain from this hill. Hoping this might be the vanguard of Kalala Ilunga's army, and being tired of the lonely life in the cave, she went out, ostensibly to collect more firewood but actually to see if she could make contact with any of Kalala's warriors.

As the sound of her ax rang out, chopping away at firewood, the first of this war party, actually a young relative of Kalala himself, crept cautiously up to surprise the woman, hoping to obtain some news of the whereabouts of Kongolo's hiding place. To his amazement the woman was just as glad to see him as he was to see her, and in answer to her questions she said that she was none other than one of Kongolo's wives and that she was tired of living in a cave and longed for the busy life of the capital. Moreover, she promised to reveal the hiding place if the young warrior would promise that her life and that of the other wife would be spared. Kongolo was old and had had his day, they would be only too glad to welcome back the conquering Kalala Ilunga.

The young warrior promised this and so the woman advised him to hide until the next day at dawn, then wait with a large party near the cave, which she pointed out on the distant hill. "When the trees begin to show red in the early dawn," she said, "Kongolo will come out to warm himself. The other wife and I have been collecting firewood for a long time ready for such a time as this. It is all stacked up by the mouth of the cave. As soon as we see Kongolo emerge from the cave and make his way up to the steep path to the top as his custom is, we will quickly jam all this wood in the mouth of the cave so that he cannot quickly get back in again. The whole hill is honey-combed with caves and if he got back you would have difficulty in finding him. So, as soon as you see us run the wood into the cave's mouth, seize him, for Kongolo is yours!" (Womersley 1984:16)

Kalala's people catch Nkongolo, and they sever his head and place it in a *dikumbo dia kipao,* " that is, a round basket with a lid, both beautifully woven, and a large bunch of *white* cocktail feathers fastened to the top" (my emphasis, Womersley 1984:17). Kalala Ilunga becomes the new king. With this a primitive era ends, a history begins.

The Luba Kasai, and indeed other Kasai tribes, usually refer to Kalala Ilunga by the name of *Kongolo Mwana* or *The Young Kongolo* because he followed Kongolo and was in fact his nephew. Because he was related to both groups— the incoming Luba and the Kalanga or old inhabitants of the land—through his mother, and because he did not slaughter the old in favor of the new, he was able to integrate the two peoples although the new, powerful, and more numerous became completely predominant. The *old strain of lighter-colored* people can often be seen here and there, and mothers watch anxiously for their pinky-brown newborn babies to turn the lovely shiny black they so much admire, which they usually do after a few days. A child who grows up to retain the lighter brown color is often called Mutoka, the white or light one. Wherever a subchief of the original pre-Luba people was loyal and efficient, he was allowed to retain his position, such as chief Bunda and chief Kilumba of the Mwanza District, and Madia near Kabongo. All intermarried and all were completely integrated. Odd families who came over on their own, either pioneers who came before the great migration or others who followed after, are still known locally as Hemba or Bemba, while a large section of the Luba nation who left the shores of Lake Tanganyika and crossed the intervening mountains in a more northerly direction, but who did not cross the Lualaba, is known as the Hemba. (latter emphasis mine, Womersley 1984:19)

By this name of Kongolo Mwana, the new king interiorizes the very ambiguity of his birth. In effect, Kongolo Mwana can be translated as "Young Kongolo," as Womersley does, or as "Son of Kongolo." The polysemy conveys clearly, as we observed in chapter 3, the unbearable junction of the *bufumu* and the *bulopwe* in the king's body. In any case, with this polysemic sign, a new community is born. It integrates harmoniously two traditions: that of Nkongolo's light-skinned Kalanga, the first inhabitants of the region, and that of the black-skinned Luba invaders. The new king, Kalala Ilunga, appears then as the sacred paradigm which transcends opposed terms. Son of Mbidi and nephew of Nkongolo, he belongs by his blood to both ascendencies.

Nkongolo	Mbidi
Kalanga	Luba
Light-skinned (or reddish) people	Black-skinned people
Short	Tall

An eccentric version of the chart, that of Van Malderen, analyzed by Luc de Heusch, reproduces the opposition between less- and more-advanced cultures. On his way back to his country Mbidi meets with the Tumandwa twa Maseba, who are red and very short and inhabit termite caves. "They appear to have been driven onto the high plateau by a slightly taller, less hairy, darker people, the Twa, under the rule of Nkongolo. Mbidi Kiluwe, a tall black man, is said to have taught the Tumandwa twa Maseba how to cook food, use the bow and arrow, and build huts" (de Heusch 1982:26).

Tumandwa	Nkongolo's People (Kalanga)
Red	Reddish/blackish
Very short	Short
Very hairy	Less hairy

The line of evolution from nature to culture (represented by Mbidi) is thus given in two main formulas: from red to black through a reddish or blackish intermediary; from Tumandwa's culture to Mbidi's through Nkongolo's. It is, says the charter, Mbidi, a tall black man, who sets in motion the process which technologically and politically transforms the Tumandwa and Kalanga societies. By marrying in both societies (first the sister of Nkongolo, then the daughter of the Tumandwa chief), he confuses their physiological distinctivenesses through his children, who are tall and black. Ultimately his descendants take political power and forge the whole of the Luba empire.

The charter opposes two antithetical models. Nkongolo's is closer to nature, and his power metaphorically reproduces natural violence. You will recall that Nkongolo's ambition is founded on a natural lesson: he studied how black driver ants fight and eat white ants. The second model represents a cultural horizon: exogamy and a new art of ruling. In transcending the two models, Kalala Ilunga, along with his successors, affirms himself as Nkongolo Kamukanda, as the tension between nature and culture. I used this expression in the description of that part of the second creation taking place during the rainy season. The concept, according to the *Bible noire*, refers to the elder and male being of the first pair of twins created by Maweja during the rainy season. The junior and female equivalent entity is the rain. Provisionally let us accept Fourche and Morlighem's comment: "In some western regions, the word still designates the *rainbow*, but rainbow is probably not an exact translation. Nkongolo designates in reality 'something which is reddish'; Mukanda includes a double meaning: that of imperative 'law' and that of 'stoppage' with the value of opposing a movement. Etymologies of Nkongolo can, on the whole, include the following renderings: 'Master of the Law' or 'Cycle of the Law.' We have chosen the first, which agrees with the primordial character of ambiguous and primordial being" (F.M. 43).

5

The Practice of an Ordinary Life

In the preceding pages I have invoked cultural frontiers without explicitly discussing them. What does it mean to focus on the coherence of the Luba experience? Despite its specific geography and past, the domain is vast. My project however, has nothing to do with scholastic anthropology. In effect, I have chosen to take seriously some texts published by a few specialists whose approaches I consider correct and whose interpretations seem dependable.

One may ask: Whence comes this authority? And what does it mean to use it apropos of Luba or Songye peoples and tradition? My answer will be simple. It is true that I am not an anthropologist and do not claim to be one. I spent at least ten years of my life studying ancient Greek and Latin for an average of twelve hours each week, with more than that amount of time devoted to French and European cultures, before being eligible for a doctorate in comparative philology (Greek, Latin, and French) at Louvain University. I do not know many anthropologists who could publicly demonstrate a similar experience about their specialty in order to found their authority in African studies. This is indeed, despite its emotional efficiency, the worst argument I could have invoked. I had to go through these years of education as did my European codisciples who chose to specialize in philology and philosophy. The real problem is one of power between cultures that I shall address in the last chapter of this book apropos of the exemplary case of Peter Rigby's study of Maasai: in effect, its objectives, methods, and operations directly witness to this fact, and it simultaneously, in its enunciations, defines the authority of its practitioners. Should I add, in perfectly bad faith, that I know some anthropologists such as Mary Douglas or Edmund Leach whose opinions are respectfully considered even when they make pronouncements lying outside their fields of formal competence? My experience would define itself somewhere between the practice of philosophy with its possible intercultural applications and the

124

sociocultural and intersubjective space which made me possible: my Luba-Lulua mother, my Songye father, the Swahili cultural context of my primary education in Katanga (Shaba), the Sanga milieu of my secondary education from 1952 to 1959 in Kakanda, near Jadotville (Likasi), and, later on, at the Catholic seminary of Mwera, near what was then Elisabethville, and my brief sojourn in a Benedictine monastery in Rwanda.

I have been using texts of a few specialists of Luba culture in order to meditate on functions of cultural interpretations and the ways in which these constantly renew and oppose one to the other. I have checked the texts used and would like to guarantee here their soundness. From them, I developed my own commentaries on the general practice of the Luba culture. So far, I have restricted my attention to structurally organized narratives. They signify a starting point, and simultaneously these archival narratives cadence both rhythmic literary keys and ancient memories. Indeed, the poet or specialist of memory who recites the past adds, transforms, and adapts. Yet the fundamental message (a mythic one) and the stylistic frame of the recitation (a codified one) obey basic traditional formulas. In this chapter, I focus on the practice of an ordinary life and examine popular statements which unify events and discursive enunciations. In the description there is no chronologically linear line.

In a Regional Voice: Anastasis

The essential message of the curiously named *Bible noire* (Why is this text called a bible?) edited by T. Fourche and H. Morlighem could be perceived in its coincidences and contrasts with Christian beliefs. When initiated Luba, at the end of the last century, heard European missionaries expounding the Bible, they had every reason to rejoice. They thought: Maweja Nangila, God, is omnipotent. Even these foreigners know of his deeds and witness to his marvels. They submitted to the order of Christianity, the colonial rule, and decided to collaborate with the new power. Yet they kept secret the fundamentals of their knowledge and restricted its transmission. It is a mystery how T. Fourche and H. Morlighem would have had even partial access to it. On the whole, the initiated Luba-Songye believed that in the long run Maweja Nangila's power would triumph openly. They were probably right, considering, as we have seen in chapters 1 and 2, the present politics of mainstream churches and the basic teachings of independent churches.

The central message in this regional knowledge is Maweja's love for humankind and its sign: the death and resurrection of his Son. Here is the traditional text:

Maweja Nangila created everything in good faith and with good intentions. He also created animals and humans with the same disposition, that is, with good intentions. As in the case of a magnificently fragile and beautiful cloth having a delicate texture, He has forgotten that in creating life, He also created death and has left it among His creatures. That is why up to this day when we compare something perfect to something else, an imperfect one, we say: "*Maweja Nangila* created one thing in good state and forgot about the other."

Thus, Maweja brought from death for a reunion all His creatures. They were all silent, but He could read their thoughts. . . . After a long meditation He spoke to them and said the following: I am establishing a pact between you and Me. In order to fulfill my Lordship, and in order to perfect my creation and erase the flaw of death existing in what I have brought to life, I am sacrificing My own Son, the Flesh of my Forehead, my Firstborn Spirit. So, this is the pact, and you will respect it by behaving and acting according to your obligations and I shall keep my promise and follow my own obligations. If you do not, after your terrestrial death, you will be damned and go into the depths of the Earth and you will remain there forever experiencing a second death and incapable of incarnating in another life. . . .

Maweja designated his Firstborn Spirit who was in the assembly, that is the Second Spirit in Lordship because He was the First of all Spirits after Maweja himself. . . . He said to Him: become a human being. Instantly, the Firstborn became Flesh, while conserving his own appearance. And Maweja Nangila gave an order to present Spirits: sacrifice Him so that everyone can share his Flesh. He was sacrificed. He died because Maweja, God the Omnipotent, had ordered it. All the present Spirits participated in the sharing of God's Son's flesh. Then Maweja said to the assembled Spirits: with this sacrifice of an Eternal Flesh, the Flesh of my own Spirit, the Flesh of my Firstborn Son, I have suppressed the flaw which was still there in my creation and fulfilled my great Lordship.

In effect, our ancestors' tradition teaches that through, and by, this very sacrifice of His own beloved Son Maweja sanctioned His pact with the Spirits and the Human race, and erased the flaw that he put in his creation by allowing death to exist. The sacrifice sanctioned Maweja's covenant with His creatures. . . . We also do know that after participating in the sacred meal, all the spirits went into Death's sleep. But the following morning at daybreak, the Firstborn Son came back to life. He resurrected and appeared not as Flesh but under his form as heavenly Spirit and in his appearance as the Elder Spirit of God, the Son of Tshame as He has been since all beginnings.

This myth presents itself as a totality. It is almost a rigid canon (in the way a written text would impose itself upon a reader). It is a polynomia, insofar as it pluralizes meanings through different and complementary orders, and a naming code which enunciates the absolute beginnings of the human experience and accounts for the tension between life and death, by offering the central sign of human redemption: the bloody sacrifice of God's Son and his coming back to life.

The concept of intertextuality may help to specify the signification of this "epicized myth" which is simultaneously a nexus between and a fusion of the sacred and the profane. Let us compare the esoteric version of Fourche and Morlighem with exoteric narratives from the Luba area. Intertextuality designates the transposition of one system of signs, symbols, and meanings into another. The movement can be analyzed from the viewpoint of the original system as well as from that of the new system which reactualizes and adapts the first code. In this reading, we should not postulate a relation of dependence, or even suggest that exoteric versions are somehow translations of the esoteric canon. I would tend to think that in the Luba-Songye tradition they have been interacting upon each other to the point that the question of knowing what is the original is not really pertinent, insofar as basic structures are concerned. They are, simply said, transformations of each other. They all bring to light the same type of oppositions and distinguish categories of beings, facts, and things according to the same fundamental rule: A is what not-A or B is not.

Here is a synoptic schema of the six narratives I would like to comment upon, focusing on three themes: God's creation of humankind, original sin, and punishment. The narratives come from the following sources: N_1, Fourche and Morlighem's *Bible noire* (pp. 112–29); N_2, "The Story of the Lord Father Creator" (Theuws 1983:141); N_3, "The Story of the Lord" (Theuws 1983:142); N_4, "Story of Kaleba, Father Creator" (Theuws 1983:143); N_5, "Story of the Lord and the Three Men" (Theuws 1983:144); and N_6, "Story of the Spirit Who Gives Life" (Theuws 1954:59–62).

N_1	N_2
1.1 It is said "Maweja Nangila created man" or that He created men. This means that Maweja created the first or the ancestor of all humans and he created him twinly, that is male or female, a couple known as Bende.	2.1 The Lord first started cultivating trees and herbs. He also left two people, a man and a woman.
1.2 Maweja left the man and the woman in an area dominated by a *dibondo* [a raphia palm tree] or, according to other versions, under a *Dibwe*, an Elais palm tree. The Lord told them: Stay here, this is the space of your Lordship. And this is my order: Never bless my palm tree, never slash it in order to drink its wine. If you do, you will die.	2.2 He said to them: Eat of all the food that is here. When you hear the rain coming, that is water I give you to drink and to wash with. Early next morning the rain blackened overhead. . . . The morning rose and another day. They found the lake and beds where the water flowed.

1.3 Ambiguity, that is the Serpent named Nyoka, told the man and the woman: Maweja created you male and female but did not teach you how to copulate in order to reproduce yourselves. And man said: teach us. And Ambiguity the Serpent copulated with the woman and afterward invited the man to do the same.

1.4 Maweja sent the Spirits, the sun, the moon and the man to look for and bring him a jar of palm wine. They went. The sun came back first, the following day. Then, the moon, after three days. Man was the last to come back after five days. And the Lord confronted him: why have you drunk my wine?

1.5 Maweja Nangila thought that his creatures had become bad, although by his creation he wanted them to be good. In great anger, he decided to destroy them all. In truth, he did and they all died. It is in memory of this that all creatures became mortal and that today we have proverb stating: Maweja Nangila created everything good but the Bad Spirit Kavidividie falsified his plans.

N_3	N_4

3.1 The Lord came with his people . . . from the East.

3.2 He left them in the countries. . . . He gave them fire and split many rivers . . . and told them: Now eat all the things I left you. Do not eat, however, the fruit of the red trees. If you do, you will die.

4.2 The Lord built a fence through the middle of the bush. The whole country was thus cut in two. Game was caught in it.

One morning . . . men found a white animal caught in a pit. They carried it and brought it to the Lord. The Lord said to them. . . : Its name is Good Luck.

3.4 When the Lord returned, he found these peoples eating the red fruits which he had said to be taboo. The Lord said: Stay here, wait sixty days and then follow me. I will show you how to free yourself from the taboo.

The men went again to the fence. They found a black animal caught in a pit. . . . The Lord questioned them: Do you know this animal? And they said: We do not know it. And the Lord said: This is . . . Bad Luck.

3.5 The people refused to follow. And so they remained with the everlasting misfortune.

4.5 First good luck and then bad luck.

N₅

5.1 Long ago the Lord created three peoples: the sun, the moon, and the man.

5.2 One day he brewed beer and poured it into a jar. He told them. . . : Nobody will drink that beer without dying.

5.3 They did not listen to his advice. They stayed, took the beer, and drank it with their children and wives.

5.4 The Lord came back and found them mourning. He questioned them: Why are you mourning? The man said: We mourn for nothing. But the sun and the moon said: We mourn for our children who died. The Lord said to them: What did they die of? Perhaps you drank the beer? But the man said: No, they just died. The moon and the sun said: indeed, we did drink it.

5.5 Thereupon the Lord told the sun and the moon: Your children did not die, they are sleeping. . . . We men died and will die altogether, because the first man told a lie to the Lord.

N₆

6.0 The Spirit [Vidye] created a man. He gave him an arrow and told him: this will help you to feed yourself. You will get fair game.

After four days, the man decided to hunt in the bush. At a river he met a woman. She was living alone. He asked her: Who are you? She said: I am Pamba. And he said: Where do you come from? Pamba answered *Vidye* sent me and told me: Go and give birth. Pamba asked the man: who are you?

The man said: My name is Ngoi. She asked: "Where do you come from?" His answer was: *Vidye* sent me to live here.

Then Pamba asked: What do you eat? Ngoi's answer was: I eat meat. *Vidye* gave me fire and moreover an arrow telling me that I could kill animals. And Pamba added: To me, He gave fire but also *lulindu* [flour], *nyumu* [peanuts], *maraba*, [maize] and *nkunde* [beans]. . . . They lived together for one month. Pamba gave birth to two children, a boy and a girl. One month later, she again gave birth to two children, a boy and a girl. They sent their children to other rivers where they inhabited and had their own children after being married among themselves.

The structural organization of the esoteric version (N₁) is similar to that of the alternate exoteric transformations (N₂–N₆). There are three remarkable features in the narratives. First, God is described as a benevolent Creator whose epiphany is not dazzling. The impression given is that he dwells among the creatures he brought to life. He cultivates trees and herbs (N₂), gives fire and water to his people (N₃), constructs a fence so that they can catch game (N₄), and teaches them how to nourish themselves (N₆). God is acknowledged as the Creator and the Lord, yet the image in the narratives is that of a Father. This strikes the imagination when one knows that the benevolent, just, paternal figure of God is the very opposite of that of Luba kings and chiefs, most of whom are known for their authoritarianism, cruelty, and wickedness. Commenting upon Luba-Kasai fables and legends concerning God, Van Caeneghem wrote: "In all these stories, Luba attribute to God the same quality before anything else, namely His goodness toward humans and his paternal sentiment. Although they consider Him as the Omnipotent Lord and the Great One who is above everybody, they think of Him and go to Him with confidence and without fear" (Van Caeneghem 1956:120).

The second feature concerns God's lordship. It distinguishes him from other creatures and posits him as an absolute master of taboos. You cannot bless my palm tree, nor drink its wine, he says in the esoteric version. In N_3, the order is of the same nature: Do not eat the fruits of the red trees. Finally, in N_5, the Lord's prohibition textually almost reproduces that of N_1: nobody will drink my beer without dying. The third feature which unites the narratives is man's disobedience. Because he has not respected God's order, he is punished, and his descendants become mortal, in N_1, N_3, and N_5. In a variation presented by Van Caeneghem (1956:186–87), death seems more directly linked to both human disobedience and choice. God wants to know who drank his beer. The sun, the moon, and the human all claim not to have touched it. God lets them go and orders them to appear before him. The following day the sun came first in the morning; the moon came the third day. The human, feeling guilty, never did.

Textual divergences should also be noted. N_2 and N_6 chronicle only the goodness of the Lord toward his people. God domesticates the new world by cultivating it, growing grass, and bringing water to the first humans. In N_6, he puts the first man in a situation of nomadism and gives him an arrow. The woman is created as a food producer, thus an agriculturalist. On the whole, the image of the Creator is that of Father and Lord. He offers everything: the happiness of a beginning in which there is no prejudgment that could lead to major accident. N_2 and N_6 witness to this. In N_2, the gift of life and existence is given simultaneously to the female and the male. At the same time, nature is offered as a dominion to the first parents. Similarly, in N_6, the man and the woman are masters over the surrounding nature. But contrary to N_2, the narrative in N_6 presents the woman as culturally more advanced than the man: she is already a sedentary agriculturalist, whereas the man is a nomadic hunter. Here is Theuws's version:

Ngoi [the man] said to Pamba [the woman] is your [vegetarian] food tasty? Pamba answered: "it is good, and I am satisfied with it." Then Ngoi said: "meat is good." And Pamba asked: "could you bring me some meat so I can try it?" Ngoi went to hunt, killed a eland. Pamba cooked it, ate it and said "it

is good.'' Then, she prepared *nsima* [flour] with vegetables and offered it to
Ngoi: eat, she said. He did. Then he said: ''it is not good at all; it is not tasty.''
He tried the peanuts, and liked them. Thus, he ate only the peanuts. Pamba,
then, said to Ngoi: ''I am going to cook the meat.'' ''We might die'' was Ngoi's
reaction. Pamba tasted. And Ngoi added: ''let us try it with your *nsima*.''
Pamba cooked a *nsima* and they ate it with the meat. Both thought: ''It is
wonderful, both the *nsima* and the meat fill one up.'' (Theuws 1954:60–61)

The encounter takes place at the river where the woman obviously lives.
We have already seen that the descendants of the first couple spread all over
the country, establishing their settlements around sources of water, rivers
and lakes. N_2 explicitly describes the gift of water as a major event. Another
important fact actualized by the dialogue between the man and woman in
N_6 is their contrasting complementarity. The arrogance of Ngoi (''Your food
is not good at all'') opposes Pamba's will to cooperate and identify with the
man: she wants to taste his food; she cooks for him despite Ngoi's fears
(''We might die'') and invents the combination of *nsima* and meat in order
to please him. In brief, the woman completely submits to the man. Everything happens as though the narrative should synthesize a patrilineal
ideology. Man needs the woman in order to evolve from primitiveness to
an agriculturalist culture. The woman, on the other hand, is from the outset
depicted as dependent on the man, who appears as the master of a history
in the making (see Mwamba 1972). She says to the man: Vidye sent me and
told me, ''Go and give birth,'' summing up an essential vocation which is
the very condition of human survival.

Now what is said about the woman both as a culturally more advanced
being compared with man and as the condition of human life itself becomes
more complex when one considers the exoteric cycle of stories about
Mikombo wa Kalewo, ''Mikombo, son of woman named Kalewo.'' The
fellow is also known as Mwana wa Maweja (God's Son) and Mwana wa
Mulopwe (Lord's Son).

It is said of Mikombo that he begot himself in the womb of the woman
Kalewo, because in his time male humans did not exist yet. We should note
that blacks do not represent God as the physical father of Mikombo; the
anthropomorphic representation of God has not been elaborated to such a
point, but they acknowledge that it is through the woman's body that one
comes physically to life. That is why Mikombo gave a body to himself in the
womb of his mother. From the viewpoint of their ontology that conceives
Beings as Forces (each being is in itself an immaterial force existing with or
without its visible envelope) to give a body to oneself signifies nothing impossible; although extraordinary, the fact coincides with their metaphysical

universe. In any case, God is not considered to be the physical father of the firstborn Mikombo, yet the latter is called his child because the vital force of Mikombo and that of his mother Kalewo proceed from God. It is God who created and fertilizes their life forces so that they can achieve their complete integrity and fulfillment in the visible world. (Van Caeneghem 1956:39–40; see 120–28)

In sum, the primordial mother, to use Jung's expression (1980:183), is present at the genesis of both life and history. Her body marks the division of the earthly life from the divine and its capacity for giving birth, a differential character vis-à-vis man.

This absolute beginning is framed in a mythical space in which the Creator interacts directly with his creatures. He speaks to them, they answer back. He teaches them and organizes their cultural economy: you can do this and not that, you may do this and you should absolutely not do that. In N_3 and N_5, the confrontation between the Lord and his creatures is violent. Humans refuse to follow the Lord and by this very fact remain in their deadly misfortune (N_3); since then humans are mortal (N_5). Let us note that N_1 dramatizes the event: "Never bless my palm tree, never slash it. . . . If you do, you will die," says the Lord. The order is duplicated in N_3: humans cannot eat fruits from red trees. On the other hand, the order redundantly repeats itself in N_1 and N_5 as a prohibition to drink the Lord's wine or beer. The ensuing punishment for the human race is death.

One should also note a notable divergence. In N_1, death (*lufu*) is a flaw which from the very beginning parallels life. In N_3 and N_5, it becomes the direct consequence of human disobedience. A careful analysis of the original versions indicates that *lufu* cannot be reduced to the strict meaning of death. *Lufu* includes death, and at the same time, it signifies everything unpleasant in the human condition. As Theuws notes, "The unhappiness expressed by [these texts] is indeed death. But the term *lufu* has a much wider signification. Every impoverishment of life force is already *lufu*. A difficult work: *i lufu*; a meal without fish or meat: *i lufu*; a disease: *i lufu*; anger: *ileta lufu*, it brings death" (Theuws 1954:63).

Finally, it is noteworthy that the esoteric N_1 clearly links the freedom of humans to sexuality and the bliss of existence. The theme is, interestingly enough, reverberated in verses of N_1 and N_2 in which one finds a Lord enjoying brewing and, we can guess, drinking beer. It should also be noted that the same Supreme Lord gently (and forgivingly) in N_1 and N_5, as well as in Van Caeneghem's version (1956:186), gives immortality to the sun and the moon and punishes the liar, our ancestor.

The motif of redemption transcends all these mythical stories, but N_1 is the only narrative which accounts for the sacrifice of the Lord's Son.

Maweja decides to erase the flaw of unhappiness that is linked in a relation of necessity to the gift of life. His Son is put to death and then comes back from the realm of the dead. In the meantime, the sharing among spirits of his body has revived a hope: eternal life has become again possible. A new era opens up, and Maweja imposes upon his people a new set of laws:

> You shall not kill nor hurt your fellow humans
> You shall never take someone else's goods or wife
> You shall never ruin the life of another human being
> The woman should never commit adultery.
> (F.M. 137–38)

In man's rebellion and its consequences, there is something mysterious: he has learned sexuality from Nyoka, the serpent (N_1), enjoyed the tabooed wine of beer (N_1 and N_5), and eaten the defended red fruits (N_3). The confrontation with Maweja is dramatic. Man dares to say to the Lord: "You have not created us in your image" (F.M. 118). The rebellion provokes a disaster in heaven. An army of spirits led by Maweja's envoy to the earth mutinies against Maweja. They are, indeed, crushed by faithful spirits and damned for eternity under the earth. To his former envoy, Maweja says: "All the powers I gave you in the past and that you have personally transformed into negative powers, you can now exercise them only on the wrong side of everything" (F.M.).

The narratives analyzed clearly agree on the three points we have chosen to focus on: the creation, humans' disobedience, and the punishment. The universe is created by a benevolent Vidye. He establishes a natural and a cultural order and proposes to humans ways of integrating themselves into these orders. They do not obey, and by their acts they bring about death and disorder. This basic message stems from a simple pattern: an initial collaboration between the Spirit and his creatures is followed by an antagonism only transcended in N_1 and in the cycle of Mikombo wa Kalewo, thereby exhibiting the heavy price of reconciliation between divinity and the human race.

"The Lord came with his people. . . . He came from the East" states N_3. Theuws notes that "one thinks about the hunter chief, Mbidi Kiluwe, who came with his people from the East and journeyed through Lubaland. He left some of his people in several areas. He founded the royal dynasty of the Baluba" (Theuws 1983:142). The narrative would thus structure two orders of meaning: the Spirit's saga and a postcreation enterprise by Mbidi Kiluwe, the founding father of Luba history. They seem to reflect upon each other, universalizing the narration through the Lord's acts, prohibitions, curses. On the other hand, the same narrative individualizes itself as a metaphoric recitation of memory. In effect, the Luba claim that Mbidi came from the East, traveling throughout the region between the Lubilash and the Lualaba rivers. The esoteric version of Fourche and Morlighem's also confuses the mythical dimension with the historical. The Lord's story about creation is repeated in its entirety as a mythical and historical event. This absolute discourse becomes apparent in the memory of original beginnings. Its project is the expression and illustration of a theological order. God, indeed, subjects himself in the form of the second Spirit to the human condition. Can the human, from this sacrifice, deploy a history?

In fact, there is desire for it, but as yet no alternative, since history does not exist, save in God's speech and system. It is, to use Kristeva's language, a monologism in which the subject who speaks is the same as the one who enunciates the story, in which the locutor coincides with the enunciator and is, simultaneously, the addressee (Kristeva 1980:87). Nothing can be subversive in such a discourse. The subject might be anonymous, yet it "assumes and submits to the rule of [God]. The dialogue inherent in all discourses is smothered by a *prohibition*, a censorship, such as that this discourse refuses to turn back upon itself, to enter into dialogue with itself" (Kristeva 1980:77).

Monologic texts as mythical narratives have a similar and universal system of meaning: they tautologize between tradition and oblivion and in so doing induce principles of exclusion and integration in a narrative formation. The practice of tautologization is one of reproducing the grammar of a basic memory and manipulating it as source and object of interpretation. As narrative, our corpus indicates in its very being its own politics. It defines its own constellation of meaning, constitutes itself as the other side of discursive practice, and by its own value makes problematic all correlational logics, dialogisms, or even phrases that might challenge it. The political demand is here the other side of a theological systematization.

These monologic versions constitute an *a priori* and function as both archive (thanks to rhythmic formulas which structure them) and living memory. Théodore Theuws writes that "stories about the first human beings, about procreation or about the domestication of animals are in a different style" (1983:52). But which style? Then, he adds, "Everywhere people take it for granted that they are just stories" (1983:52). By this statement, Theuws distances himself from Luc de Heusch, who "treats the traditions on the origins of kingdom as myths" (Theuws 1983:52n1). Yet about these traditions, Theuws remarks: "The first ancestors, who brought all kinds of seeds, fire, arts and crafts, and death into the world, were sent by God to start things and establish the kingdom. So Luba society, once again, was legitimized by its supernatural origin" (1983:53).

Those stories are narratives that maintain control over the past and the future. They are used, invoked, exploited in order to protect an ethnic identity. Throughout the history of the Luba empire, claims Thomas Reefe, the Bambudye society had as its mission to keep and proclaim the body of the tradition (Reefe 1981:13–14). This statement might be too strong insofar as this tradition has been a permanent object of political negotiations. Strictly speaking, adapting Foucault, I would say that these "stories" about beginnings, traditions and archives as well as their analysis, "involve a privileged region: at once close to us, and different from our present existence, it is the border of time that surrounds our presence, which overhangs it, and indicates it in its otherness; it is that which, outside ourselves, delimits us" (Foucault 1982:130).

The question of time is here immediate. It colonizes cultural settings and even claims to decipher a geography: "The Lord came from the East." On the other hand, a series of signs, mainly in N_1, clearly appear to negate both the authority and the credibility of the charter. At any rate, by their presence they question its antiquity and authenticity. In effect, some of the themes seem to presuppose the Bible and the missionary's gospel. Other versions, such as N_5 and N_6, refer to beer and *nsima*, a porridge of cassava, millet, or banana flour. We can, using "state of the art" techniques in the field, propose very general historical timeframes for the appearance of these products and thus localize them in historical contexts. One might begin, historically, by noting that according to some specialists "typological studies indicate a close relationship between the Western Desert Terminal Paleolithic groups and the Arkinian and the Upper Capsian in the Maghreb, implying a broad zone of very general cultural similarity across the semiarid Nolocene Sahara." More precisely:

The first known settlement with pottery, which is firmly dated within one standard deviation of 8100 B.P., consisted of two long rows of saucer-shaped house floors each with one or more adjacent bell-shaped storage pits. . . . Nearby was a deep walk-in well. Clearly, a complex and highly structured society is represented, and one which was strikingly different from that of the immediately preceding Terminal Paleolithic. Rare bones of cattle, morphologically within the size-range of domestic forms, indicate a herding economy, although apparently they were kept not for meat but for blood and milk, a widespread feature among modern African cattle-herders. Instead, gazelle and hare, to judge from the frequency of their bones in the refuse, were the main sources of meat. Associated floral remains include domestic six-row barley and weeds usually associated with cultivation, as well as several trees and bushes, including acacia and both dom palm and date palm. (Wendorf and Schild 1984:95)

To go farther southward in an area close to that of our myths, D. W. Phillipson hypothesizes that "the only part of the Bantu-speaking territory where there is any convincing evidence, either archeological or linguistic, for the possible practice of food production prior to the advent of the Iron Age is lower Zaire. Here . . . the so-called 'Leopoldian Neolithic' industry dates from the last few centuries B.C. and may (although it must be emphasized that the evidence for this remains entirely circumstantial) have been based upon some form of food production" (1984:277).

Regarding the origin and spread of crops, two conflicting hypotheses oppose each other. The first, more traditional, links the Central African expansion of agriculture to the migration of Bantu-speaking people. Between 3000 and 5000 B.C., these groups would have moved from the northwestern region around the Cameroon-Nigerian area toward the south, and by the first millennium A.D. they would have reached the eastern coasts and the Transvaal. Their language included words for goat, gourd, yam, pulse (see Meeussen 1956), and they used cotton, millet, sorghum, and sesame. Murdock deduced his thesis from a comparative analysis of nine western Bantu lexical lists: "Bananas, taro and yams appear in every one of the nine, and in nearly every instance as staples, whereas no crop of the Sudanic complex except the oil palm occurs in more than one list. One can scarcely conceive of stronger proof that the Northwestern Bantu could not have entered their present habitat until they received [these] Malaysian food plants" (quoted in Stahl 1984:17). These would have been introduced some time during the last two centuries B.C., replacing almost completely more traditional foods (e.g., *Dioscorea rotundate, D. cayenensis*), much as, some centuries later, colonial contacts led to the adoption of cassava and maize (see Stahl 1984).

Other researchers have hypothesized an African domestication of some crops, such as West African rice and Ethiopian teff. An African scientist, Lwanga-Lunyiigo, has even advanced the possibility "for an independent origin of agriculture in the interlacustrine area of East Africa." Others, more numerous, "have allowed that African populations may have been 'pre-adapted' to seed-cultural systems of agriculture (i.e., they were intensive grain collectors)" (Stahl 1984:11–12). In any case, A. B. Stahl aptly notes the weaknesses of both the diffusionist and independent invention hypotheses.

The evidence in support of . . . diffusionistic hypotheses is scanty. Evidence pointing to independent invention is equally scanty, if not nonexistent, but it can no longer be assumed that diffusion is more likely than independent invention. Among those who favor the invention mode, there is a lingering tendency to identify the development of crop complexes in the African subcontinent with specific linguistic or "racial" groups. The problems of identifying "racial" type from skeletal material is manifold; indeed, the concept of "race" is a questionable one. Hypotheses regarding the racial affiliation of archaeological populations remain untestable, for it is difficult, if not impossible, to determine the genetic affiliation of skeletal remains precisely enough to identify "race."

Too often, archaeologists have attempted to use their data to test hypotheses generated by linguists. An example is the attempt to correlate the spread of iron-working, of agriculture, and of Bantu-speaking peoples. The association of these three factors has met with overwhelming and uncritical acceptance by archaeologists, an association which, so far as language is concerned, the archaeologist can never demonstrate satisfactorily. In the author's opinion, the attempt to attribute cultural remains to a particular linguistic group represents an archaeological cul-de-sac.

Available evidence bearing on the origin of African agriculture is meager. Hypotheses have most often been formulated on the basis of plant geography and on linguistic and ethnographic evidence. A striking characteristic of most of the published studies is their lack of supporting archaeological evidence; that which has been put forth is usually of an indirect nature (e.g., the presence of ceramics or of tools assumed to have been used for cultivation). Most of the direct evidence (e.g., carbonized seeds, seed impressions) has been recovered as a by-product of investigations focusing on other issues, since few research projects in Africa have been devoted specifically to the elucidation of agricultural origins. (Stahl 1984:20)

Most of the hypotheses mentioned by Stahl are simply surprising. They witness more to racial tensions existing in the field than to scientific demands. D. W. Phillipson in his synthesis of African Archaeology (1985) offers a sensical and prudent deduction from meager archaeological data. His position includes two observations:

Food-producing communities making pottery and ground stone artifacts are known to have been living in the Sahara for at least two thousand years before any of these traits is attested to in West Africa. Their apparent southward dispersal into West Africa seems to have occurred at about the time of the major period of Saharan dessication, when climatic and vegetational zones would have shifted to the South. . . . [But] there is as yet no evidence to suggest that all food-production in West Africa began as a direct result of contact with more northerly areas. It appears certain, however, that domestic animals were so derived, and probably cereal agriculture also. Yam cultivation, however, although nowhere conclusively attested to in the archaeological record, may well have been an indigenous development and perhaps one which pre-dated any other form of food production in this region. (Phillipson 1985:139)

In fact, there is no convincing reason for supposing *a priori* that most crops cultivated in Africa (several types of yams, and cereals such as sorghum, bulrush millet, teff, finger millet, African rice) are not indigenous, since they "are derived from plants which grow wild in the sub-Saharan latitudes" (Phillipson 1985:114).

In any case, less controversial is the fact that the Chipumbaze complex, or Early Iron Age, in East Africa comprised stable Bantu-speaking communities, organized in villages, producing food, manufacturing pottery, and using iron in the region of Lake Victoria during the last centuries before the Christian era (Phillipson 1985:171). They progressively expanded throughout Central and Southern Africa. Their original homeland has been located in the region between eastern Nigeria and Cameroon.

> The consensus of linguistic opinion suggests that the dispersal of the Bantu languages from their north-western homeland took roughly the following course. From the Cameroon area expansion initially took place either through or along the fringes of the equatorial forest, eventually leading both to the interlacustrine region and to the country around the mouth of the Congo River. In this area a second dispersal took place that gave rise to the Western Highland languages. Subsequently the Eastern Highland languages were dispersed, most probably from somewhere in the vicinity of the Zambia/Shaba Copperbelt. (Phillipson 1985:179; see Senghor 1988:29–73)

When Nkongolo receives the visit of Mbidi, the man from the East, Nkongolo's community has been agricultural for centuries and knows how to work iron. The meeting itself is probably a mythical story and reproduces other narratives about the foundation of various communities that are, according to lexicostatistical analysis, much older. According to Thomas Reefe, the percentages of lexical correlations between Luba and Bemba "suggest that the parent languages of the Luba of Shaba and the Bemba diverged some 2,000 years ago. The language of the Luba-Kasai diverged from that of the Luba of Shaba some 1,200 years ago, while Hemba separated as recently as 500 years ago" (Reefe 1981:74).

Living; or, The Body of the Woman

Marcel Détienne and Jean-Pierre Vernant's *Les Ruses de l'intelligence* (1974) has demonstrated an intelligence "immersed in practice." About this practice, Michel de Certeau wrote that it is marked by a combination of "sagacity, foresight, intellectual flexibility, deception, resourcefulness, vigilant watchfulness, a sense for opportunities, diverse sorts of cleverness, and a great deal of acquired experiences" (de Certeau 1984:81). Let us follow the Luba practices about living and dying by focusing on marriage, birth, and death.

A man and a woman decide to marry. In fact, their families have betrothed them to each other or at least arranged the happening. The families have actualized the interplay of their complementary interests. The advising of the bride by the mother or, more generally, by an older maternal aunt, divorces the bride from her original family. Her husband will be her king and master (*mfumu*), and his family must be pleased and conquered. Such is the price she must pay to a social order she could one day symbolize. By so integrating herself, she is not only the wife of her husband but primarily the mother of his children. The mother or the maternal aunt of the bride tells her that she is now an adult (*muntu mukùlumpè*) since she is marrying. She might be fourteen or fifteen years old, but with the consent of the two families, she will become automatically an adult and fully responsible for a husband, his home, his tradition, and, the families hope, his children. Nobody invites her to become a subject of a possible history in the making. On the contrary, she has to promote the respectability of her original family by practicing an ordinary life which fits into a discourse of obedience. A master charter is given to her as bride; it specifies and individualizes her major duties toward her spouse and his family and in so doing maintains the configuration of a patrilineal tradition.

Today is your last day in your father's home, henceforth you will stay in your own.

Now you are an adult, you will have a home of your own; you will meet with all kinds of people.

You will make us known as respectable people to your husband and his people, if you follow the advice we give today.

But you will also cause us to be insulted by your husband and his people if you don't pay heed to what we tell you.

What are we going to tell you? It is this.

There is the work for your husband; there is the work for his brothers; there is the work for your parents-in-law; there is the work for your husband's friends.

And in connection with the work for all these people, some will come together with your husband and some will not.

The fact that your husband came to fetch you means that he left his mother's house, having his own from now on.

In this house he has a right to give what orders he likes; he tells you all he wants, and that is exactly what you must do.

It is becoming for you to serve his brothers in the same way as you serve himself, and to serve his friends as well, whether he is at home or not.

But all this must be done according to his wishes, as he says: that is the way I want it. All these things will show, if you do them properly, that this girl of ours received sound advice from her parents.

Thus, even if your husband treats you badly and you go on doing what he wants you to do, the people of the village will speak for you.

Your husband is like your child. It does not befit you to roast a piece of cassava and eat it all by yourself while your husband looks on.

Whatever you eat you have to share with him; it is not becoming to eat alone by yourself.

It is your duty to know the proper time to prepare his meals.

If there are visitors your husband ought not to have to remind you saying: these visitors, are they going to eat something?

To serve your husband does not mean just to feed him.

In the past, your fathers dressed in animal skins. Nowadays your husbands follow European ways and dress in clothes.

A man likes to dress neatly so he may show himself among his fellow men.

He wants the house where he receives his friends properly swept, and the bed where he sleeps well shaken and made.

When your husband says to you: how is it that this thing is in such a state, it is improper for you to answer: haven't you got hands yourself to fix it?

You will run the risk of causing your parents to be reviled, because some husbands are correct; some others, however, are not.

And at the end you will come and tell us: that husband of mine called you names.

But you ought to know that your husband does not start calling us names without reason, and if you do your work properly he will not. If your husband calls us names it is you who made him do so, because you don't work as he wants you to.

It is not befitting for you to come and tell us the disputes you have with your husband.

Now that you are married don't tell your husband: tomorrow your father will come to return the bridewealth. You get married to stay with your husband.

If God grants you his blessing you will bear children and you will raise them as we raised you.

Obedience to your husband is peace and joy in married life; to satisfy his wishes, to do the work your husband wants to be done and to do what he tells you to do is the way to bring joy in your home.

It is not befitting you as a woman belonging to other people, to return every word your husband speaks or to raise your voice continuously against your husband's as if you were a man yourself.

It befits you, woman, when talking to your husband, to speak in a restrained voice. Never say anything which could put him to shame in public.

If you have a word with your husband, even if he puts you in the wrong in public, it becomes you to restrain your tongue from speaking your mind. Back home, between yourselves, you may ask him questions.

If you have words with your husband it becomes you to talk to his grandparents. If he has none, speak to one of his other relatives.

It is wrong to tell other people the words you have had with your husband, because this is to slander him. Don't you dare!

Your first duties are towards your father-in-law.

After staying in your own place, your own home, for a few days, you will prepare an early meal for your father-in-law.

But this first cassava-porridge you will prepare for your father-in-law, shall not be prepared with greens; this porridge must always be prepared with meat or fish.

While cooking this food for your father-in-law, you must know about his ways: whether he takes his meals in his own fenced-off kitchen or eats in some other place.

If he eats in his own kitchen, you will have to do exactly as your mother-in-law does when she cooks there.

Be it a particular way of dressing during that work, or a special way of calling him when the meat is ready.

When you bring the food, it is proper also to bring some drinking-water and a bit of salt, so that he may add some if the food is not to his liking.

When calling your father-in-law, always approach him from the right, kneel down saying: father, I call you. Keep on your knees until he looks at you and says: yes, my child, thank you, or: yes, I am coming.

Then go ahead to the kitchen to wait for him until you see him arriving, then leave.

Don't go too far, by no means. Remain near enough to see him retire.

When he leaves the kitchen, return there to clear away the pots.

Then, after a few days, cook another meal for him exactly as you did the first time.

Thus, if one day your mother-in-law is away, you will be able to cook for your father-in-law, because you will have done it before.

These are your duties towards your mother-in-law.

You daughter of man, it is not befitting for you to sit down with outstretched legs while your mother-in-law tires herself pounding flour.

You daughter, as long as you stay in the house of your mother-in-law, do things in such a way that she always finds the house swept, the jar full of water, the meat cut, and the water for the porridge boiling on the fire, so you can prepare a meal for her as soon as she comes home.

These are your duties towards your husband's other relatives.

A good wife does not wait when her husband's brothers are hungry saying: I will cook food for them only when my husband is here.

Except when your husband himself told you so saying: I don't want my brothers or cousins coming near the house when I am not here.

When strangers call at your house, it is not right for you to wait until your husband reminds you, saying: did I see you preparing food for these people?

You ought to know that, even if they have already eaten before leaving, the food they took was not yours; and you must cook your own food for them so that they may eat it. (Theuws 1983:127–31)

Marriage realizes an order of representations. The ritual has been subjected to well-delineated obligations. The bride is to integrate herself in the interests of a patrilineal lineage. The long text quoted as illustration is ancient in its regrouping of a patrilinealist ideology and its motifs. It is also modern, and directly relates to a new truth. "In the past, your fathers dressed in animal skins [*bisèla*]. Nowadays your husbands follow European ways and dress in clothes'': ''bèènu banùme ké bà kizungu, kèbavwàlà bisandi.'' The new type of cloth does not change the tradition, since the husband incarnates this very tradition and through the children reproduces both its power of the past and its permanence. In any case, this text makes transparent the grammar of an ideological system: the husband is a king, and children bring with them the continuity of the future (Theuws 1983:177).

Childless women often kill themselves when they discover with age that their chance of becoming mothers is over. The song of a ''childless mother'' is an excellent paradigm. She lives in a village of childless women. Theuws notes that ''moulding pots and jars is women's work. Not every woman, however, is trained in the potter's art'' (1983:179). This particular village formulates thus a special place and a discreet discourse, something like the domestication of the abnormal. These childless women confine themselves in the perpetual emergence of both utensils and art. At the same time, their confined accommodation suggests a strange order: their physical infertility links itself to an aesthetic creativity. The surface of their activity and life is a pure negation of the usual and normal village. Yet their ordinary rule seems strange: ''They cook pots and jars.'' From the practice and on it emerge a question and a mystery. There is, indeed, in the village a superartist.

> One day she made a fine jar. She put it in the corner of the house.
>   While the jar stood drying she said continuously: Yo! Yo! I poor wretch! I know modelling all right, but I have no child; what shall I do? All the time she complained like that. (Theuws 1983:177)

She goes out to attend to another business, then comes back to find that her beautiful jar has metamorphosed into a girl. The new mother is happy and accepts the child's taboo. ''It is my taboo, says the child, not to wash with water or to get wet. That is my interdiction because I am the unfired jar'' (Theuws 1983:177). In fact, the message is transparent. The child is raw, because she has not been cooked as all children are. An obvious correlative of this is the textual abnormality offered: this is happening in a space where cooking jars and pots is the norm. Such a miracle cannot but be unthinkable. The song establishes thus a logical conclusion: the child has gone to dig mice in the field with other children. The rain surprises them, and she melts and returns to her original condition. The mother ''found only the head nearly melted. She grasped it and at that moment it broke up entirely. All that remained was mud. The mother hanged herself, and so both of them died'' (Theuws 1983:178).

The structure of the song presents the fundamental arrangement I have been discussing. It opposes the raw and the cooked, nature and culture. The miraculous girl, although a magnificent product of knowledge and art, has remained a natural phenomenon. The mother, an artist in cooking jars, knew that her daughter was inevitably in danger. The abnormality of the living space of the childless woman witnesses to what is missing: male adults whose presence could establish a new tabulation between the raw and the cooked, nature and culture, the continuity between the past and the future.

A stereotyped prayer of a sterile woman illustrates this. Life and its permanence through successive generations is seen as God's endeavor. She confronts him. The recitation follows an interesting schema opposing the supplicant to God, a finite being to an Eternal Spirit, and more directly a submissive creature who has obeyed divine rules to the one who imposed them.

> Oh, my Lord Kaleba, Father-Creator! who created me with my hands
> and feet.
> All my friends have their [reminder] to leave on earth.
> What have I done? I never steal, I rob nobody.
> Now I am in trouble, what is the reason I see misfortune?
> If I am to die, kill me, you Father-Creator.
> It is you who placed me here on earth,
> how could I resist you anyway?
> (Theuws 1983:82)

Another prayer from a childless woman illustrates how a child signifies in a Luba woman's life. The prayer specifies what she has tried. There is, in the supplication, which is also a confession, a gradual tension about the efficiency of human means versus the divine, and their respective virtues in the woman's despair translate implicitly a major sign: fecundity as a paradigm.

> You, my God,
> I have invoked my Spirits, in vain
> I have made charms, in vain
> My God, Lord of humans,
> All that I am abandoning it;
> Now, I count only on You,
> Give me also a child
> that I can live with it
> In my home, at my place.
> (Van Caeneghem 1956:99)

Here is the husband's prayer:

> Lord God,
> The bride price I paid for my wife,

I got it normally thanks to my work.
But you, heavenly God,
How come that I cannot beget a child?
I have done everything that was to be done, in vain;
And now, I am submitting to You my distress,
You, the Master of everything,
Help me in my marriage
So I can have a child who is mine.
(Van Caeneghem 1956:99–100)

Around the child, a rhetorical transaction normally takes place. Songs and prayers make public statements. They might seem improvised, yet structurally they are closed texts, expressions of a collective and traditional effort. In fact, with each happy pregnancy, they repeat the expectations of an old memory, reciting both the biological fate of the species and the symbolic laws of a tradition. The poet, or more specifically the supplicant, is everybody, every adult, who happens to be at the center of this major event. The woman condenses in her pregnancy the productive quality of the future and the articulation of the past. The temporal dimension, as event and symbol, visualizes itself as spatial pertinence: her *lubanza*, that is, both the real space around her house and the family, stand now publicly as a communal representation. The woman sings:

You who followed me, father, mother, or brother,
I do not know
I know only the blessing they follow me with,
and that is enough
He says: let me warm myself at a fire
on earth
so I may appear a second time
among the people
. . . .
So I know that you followed me to end my disgrace among the people
Let it be as you intended it to be
Now as I conceived you
may I go with strength
until I give birth to you.
(Theuws 1983:83–84)

The dialogue brings face to face the pregnant woman and a deceased member of the family. Has the deceased person revealed himself or herself to the pregnant woman? This blessing brings back to life the vital force of an older generation. The child will be given the name of a member of the family to mark the continuity of life. The new existence relieves from the mother the disgrace of infertility. The woman's womb as a fecund body valorizes the confrontation of life and death, nature and culture, and this specific fact reenacts the foundation of her own being: she is the mother of the tradition her fecundity witnesses to. Her blessing rules another major sign: an ancestor can symbolically leave the cold kingdom of the deceased and settle again in a maternal womb that ultimately will liberate the warmth of life.

Does the song shape also a belief in reincarnation? Does it simply reformulate the stability and mysteriousness of the gift of life? (See Stefaniszyn 1954.) In any case, it grounds an absolute beginning, jams a memory, unites antagonistic forces. One then understands why the supplicant should be terrified by what she both represents and symbolizes. She insists in her prayer: in order to become pregnant, she did not use divination practices, she did invoke the dead, the child she bears came naturally. And in this benediction it is the will to live of a tradition that she names.

> I did not become pregnant because I wanted to give birth to you,
> it is you who followed me of your own accord while you wanted to warm
> yourself at a fire on earth. (Theuws 1983:84)

The husband joins his spouse in supplication, identifies with her and prays:

> You who followed, be you my father or my mother,
> did you not say:
> I will follow those I left on earth so that I may warm myself at a fire?
> Now, we don't like to be followed with trouble.
> Be good and protect this freeborn woman,
> that she may walk with strength,
>
> as she was before.
> We will submit to all the taboos you want
> either that of the fire or that of vegetables or that of meat.
> We already knew, you wanted to come to warm yourself here on the earth.
> Well, come straight on then, without twisting. (Theuws 1983:84)

About the surprising expression—this freeborn woman—used to designate the pregnant wife, Theuws notes that the "wife is a daughter of free people, she comes from another lineage. [The husband] is responsible for her life and her health. If she dies in childbirth, he will have to pay the heavy death fine for her" (1983:85). The interpretation is correct. The original says:

> Wikalè biyampè, ne ùno muntu wa bênè,
> nândi ùmulamè ênkâ biyampe
> wiendela ênkâ nè bukomo

This textually should be rendered as: "Protect well this *muntu* who belongs to someone else and keep her well, perfectly well that she may walk with strength."

Indeed, she belongs to a different lineage, and she has always been a free person. The text, in fact, says much more. First, one notes that the song uses *muntu* instead of *mukazi* (woman), instituting the pregnant wife as a given and present being who here and now transcends the concepts of man and woman. I have already noted in a preceding chapter that *muntu* provides the most basic and all-encompassing concept of a being of intelligence. Even God is often called upon as a *muntu*. Second, the woman is qualified as *muntu wa bênè*, the equivalent of the Luba-Kasai expression *muntu wabende* that we found in the analysis of the creation. In effect, Maweja (God) created the first ancestors of all humans and created them as twins, a male and a female, a couple known as *Bende*. In the quotation, the best rendering of *muntu wa bênè* would thus be *His*. In the expression, *muntu wa bênè/bende*, the meaning conveyed marks a distinction: the husband, in using it, relates the woman to an order of both lineage and freedom that institutionally escapes him.

But there is more: *bende* is a felicitously equivocal word. It can, as pointedly demonstrated by Van Caeneghem, refer to one of the Elder Spirits, and as such it is a proper noun. It can also, as I have been trying to show, designate someone who belongs to someone else or to a different lineage. Van Caeneghem notes:

> The word *Bende* is first used as personal pronoun, then as a qualifier adjective which signifies: who belongs to someone else. *Bende* [one of the Elder Spirits] proposed once to God [Maweja] to question human beings about what they think is their origin. Thus God asked them: from whom do you come? They answered: *tudi ba bende*, we belong to someone else, that is to say our origin is not in ourselves, but in someone else, which means God. In the response, the word *bende* [*babende*] is used as a qualitative pronoun. But *Bende* [one of the Elder Spirits] explains the response differently and interprets the word *bende* as a substantive, that is to say a personal name, his own: we come from *Bende*, we belong to *Bende*. Thus *Bende* affirms that his authority is the only one recognized by human beings. (Van Caeneghem 1956:42)

Thus, a linguistic polysemy participates as a work of meaning in the articulation of a pregnancy, transforming it into a semantic performance. And this process in what it connects and unveils refers back and explicitly to the very foundation of creation at the level of a manipulation of signifieds as well as that of signifiers.

Finally, there is a strange symbol in the prayer: the woman and her husband make a striking statement. In positing a possible ancestor as the possible child, they actualize a paradoxical memory: the pregnant woman appears to be simultaneously the daughter-child of an ancestor (in the past) and the mother of the very tradition which reactualizes itself with her child. What such an ambivalent connection formulates as a motif of a tradition brings to mind Dante's formulation about the Virgin Mary: "Virgin and mother, daughter of your own son, humble and grand, and more so than any other creature."

Linked together, the three points I have just made might designate a silent, ancient, and extremely strong rule. A work of meanings coincides with the ambivalence of a woman's body. A metonym explodes: what is referred to in songs and poetry proclaiming both the genesis of life and its future promises blurs. A specific sex, the female, offers itself as womb. It seems a locus in which the contradictory tensions of a cultural identity and its configuration unveil themselves as projects performing God's will and words. In *Desire in Language* (1980), Julia Kristeva, referring to Ferenczi, Freud, and Marie Bonaparte, has a proposition which fits my intuition. She writes:

> From the point of view of social coherence, which is where legislators, grammarians, and even psychoanalysts have their seat; which is where *every body is made homologous to a male speaking body,* motherhood would be nothing more than a phallic attempt to reach *the mother who is presumed to exist at the very place where* [social and biological] *identity recedes.* If it is true that *idealist ideologies develop along these lines urging women to satisfy this presumed demand and to maintain the ensuing order,* then, on the other hand, any negation of this utilitarian, social, and symbolic aspect of motherhood plunges into regression—but a particular regression whose currently recognized manifestations lead to the hypostasis of blind substance, to the negation of symbolic position, and to a justification of this regression under the aegis of the same Phallic Mother-screen. (my emphasis, 1980:242)

Let us pause one moment and relate these statements to our analytic interpretation of Luba relations to motherhood. First of all, Kristeva accounts for an ideological social coherence which supposes, at least theoretically, a distinction between the subject of consciousness and the object of a social manipulation within a social formation. The plane of her discourse witnesses to this particular separation. On the other side, how could we say that Kristeva's positions could illuminate the grouping of Luba propositions? In effect, these seem to belong to and speak about a patrilineal and paternal authority. An unlimited memory which includes Maweja (Syakapanga) defines itself as patrilineal and paternal. Second, about "the mother who is presumed to exist at the very place where identity recedes," I would say that in texts I have been exploring she seems to be the very focus where identity finishes or begins. The force of mythic narratives and stereotyped prayers adhere well to this locus about which Kristeva found a magnificent metaphor: "An excursion to the limits of primal regression can be phantasmatically experienced as the reunion of a woman-mother with the body of *her* mother. The body of her mother is always the same Master-Mother of instinctual drive, a ruler of psychosis, a subject of biology, but also, one toward which women aspire all the more passionately simply because it lacks a penis" (Kristeva 1980:239). Again one could refer to the fact that in our song-poem, the woman emerges as the one who transcends the polarities of gender and is constituted explicitly as *muntu*, whereas her supplicating husband is given as *munume* (Tshiluba: *mulume*), as a male. She is a cultural construct from the outset compared with the naturalness of her husband's masculinity. There is here a syntagma which sums up a tradition: God gives life, the phallus actualizes it, and the woman witnesses to it.

The last point in the quotation ("idealist ideologies develop . . . urging women to satisfy [a] presumed demand and to maintain the ensuing order") recomposes important interferences. Instead of facing them here, I would like to correlate some of them with an examination of two types of traditional reactions: first, when the child who is now a young adolescent has to leave the village in order to strengthen his life elsewhere before the maturity rituals; second, when there is a death in the family.

Before that, let me quote Jung, who first generalized the question from the context of his European psychological practice:

As we know, there is no human experience, nor would experience be possible at all, without the intervention of a subjective aptitude. What is this subjective aptitude? Ultimately it consists in an innate psychic structure which allows man to have experiences of this kind. Thus the whole nature of man presupposes woman, both physically and spiritually. His system is tuned in to woman from the start, just as it is prepared for a quite definite world where there is water, light, air, salt, carbohydrates, etc. The form of the world into which he is born is already inborn in him as a virtual image. Likewise parents, wife, children, birth, and death are inborn in him as virtual images, as psychic aptitudes. These *a priori* categories have by nature a collective character; they are images of parents, wife and children in general, and are not individual predestinations. We must therefore think of these images as lacking in solid content, hence as unconscious. They only acquire solidity, influence, and eventual consciousness in the encounter with empirical facts, which touch the unconscious aptitude and quicken it to life. They are in a sense the deposit of all our ancestral experiences, but they are not the experiences themselves. So at least it seems to us, in the present limited state of our knowledge. (I must confess that I never yet found infallible evidence for the inheritance of memory images, but I do not regard it as positively precluded that in addition to these collective deposits which contain nothing specifically individual, there may also be inherited memories that are individually determined.) (Jung 1972:190)

I am concentrating on situations of crises in which a Luba woman would face the representation of her tradition to the point of physical exhaustion. This choice implies nothing more than an intellectual demand. In effect, the ambiguity of the woman is there at the outset of all the stories: genitrix, yet eternally second; threshold of culture, yet reduced to the works of nature. This system claims to formulate itself since the foundation of myths. Should not I know that a textual interpretation can operate either as retranscription of meanings from their genesis to their blossoming or as qualification of texts from the viewpoint of the truth of their context? I would like to insist on the fact that what I am facing and reading in the Luba *context* is not a *library* of texts thanks to which one could describe, for example, a history of mentalities. I am using circumstantial documents, "archival discourses" built up as practical knowledge, whose controversial authority comes from their supposed age and their rigid structures. These archives and the discursive practices which actualize them witness to a political discipline. Generally, anthropologists have tended to comment only on the interplay flowing from the most visible relationships and conjunctions between Luba sociohistorical organizations and their corresponding interpretative discourses. I thought it might also be useful to look at what a patrilineal discipline silences in the representation of its own solidity.

As we have seen, the socially and culturally distinguished woman is defined as the mother of her children and the daughter of her own children. Fertility outlines a being, and motherhood diffuses it as a common location in the tradition. Yet here she is, a real human being with feelings and fears. How do the "archives" reveal her when her children are taken away in accordance with the tradition she founds? Here are two exemplary ruptures: the *Kulaya mwâna* ritual and the blessing of children by a dying father.

Customarily, a young adolescent before his initiation has to leave his father's village for his mother's "nation," that is, her original place. Theuws notes that "people are jealous of a man who has children, and jealousy is the source of witchcraft" (1983:98n3). The custom declares what seems in the culture to be an obvious fact: fecundity and life are such wonderful things that their emergence suscitates joyous bewilderment (from those who illustrate them) and negative desire (from those who cannot). This is why, for a fertile woman, the succession of days reflects itself in a permanent confrontation with the divine in order to safeguard her home and her children. Each of her mornings begins with a stereotyped rite and invocation to Maweja. In front of her house, at dawn, she is the first outside. She has her child in her arms, orients it successively to the East and then to the West, reciting the following formula:

> God, Supreme Being
> Give us health for our bodies
> That my children may be happy.
> It is You who gives
> To each what is his or hers.
> (Van Caeneghem 1956:91)

At night after dinner, while the family is enjoying the end of the day around the fire, the mother often leaves first and retires into the house. There, she blesses the child and says:

> Lord God,
> Please give us a peaceful sleep
> Till the moment when
> You shall awake us in peace.
> (Van Caeneghem 1956:92)

Thus, fertility calls in its own order its possible negation: infertility. Its presence backs a tradition. The impotent and the infertile might confront the totality of the tradition by questioning their exclusion from the positive network and, possibly, challenge the very deviation by harming what represents most clearly their apparent failure: the children of a fertile couple.

A young adolescent is to be sent away. The ritual consists of an official blessing by the father. The mother stands in a corner, probably crying. An invitation determines itself as wish, desire, and pact. The father has a hand on the front of the child when he says:

> All the misfortunes, all the hatred they have
> for me, your father,
> is just because of fecundity
> with which I begot you.
> Well, go and leave for a while,
>
> that you may leave all this behind.
> Go that you may be happy

And the Lord [Vidye] lays his hands on you
. . . .
I or your mother, after a while, will come
to see you

Do not think you left your mother,
Your mother will also come to see you
We want you to be strong.
(Theuws 1983:98)

The father accumulates Vidye's prerogatives. The fecundity of the woman becomes a sign of his power, and its fruit (the child) should leave for the exteriority of his power in order to maintain strength, grow in vitality, and mature. The Lord, recites the father, lays his hands on you. One might also observe that in the same recitation, another note arises. The father states a usual course of things: "I or your mother will come to see you." Almost immediately, he neatly dissociates the centrality of the landscape in which the blessing is taking place from the country the child will be soon discovering: "Do not think you left your mother." Which mother is really referred to? I shall come back to this issue. In any case, the formula of the blessing maps parables through three major elements: a patrilineal territory, a woman's fertility (the child represents in its being a statement), and finally the social function signified by the father and the mother in their community.

The protective locus where the child is being sent is the mother's ethnic territory which offers itself as a new but symbolic womb. It will protect the child. At any rate, a duplication of the natural mother exists there: she might be a sister or a cousin, and she is usually already present during the *Kulaya mwâna* ritual. She is the one who will act out the impossible: going beyond the geographical and spiritual boundaries of two traditions that in the long run should ensure the linearity of this same tradition. In another blessing formula, the father might say, addressing this female parent of his wife:

Look, you sister, go well with the child. There is nothing to worry about.
This child is yours, born to you, your own blood.
Now then, child, go with your mother,
go in the health that you enjoyed here.
Do not be sad.
You are going with your mother.
She is no stranger.
(Theuws 1983:99)

The field articulated here is a symbolic one. It unifies what should be divided, lineages whose individuality accounts for the move of the child.

What is stated supposes the interethnic collaboration which made possible the marriage of the blessing father and the mother of the leaving child. The female parent of the latter, whoever she is, is called sister by the father, who immediately imposes her on the child as mother: "You are going with your mother. She is no stranger."

The collaborative structure between different ethnic groups seems reversible. Yet the ethnic identity of the child will remain always within his father's affirmation and its past. The ritual is thus only a prerequisite condition to preparing the initiation operations. The child will come back, supposedly stronger, from the mother's culture and will enter ritually and actually into the horizon of his patrilineal tradition. The mother, her family, and her culture have submitted to the symbolic politics of these exigencies which guarantee the ideological equilibrium of the father's culture.

Here is another illustration. A dying man restates the "law" of his system in the strongest imaginable terms. Saying farewell, he recites an unchanging lesson that has been repeated for generations:

Stay well, don't be arrogant, don't make the living curse me.

Now I leave you. My brother whom you know will be your father.

I don't leave you any palaver. I did not insult anybody.

Take care of your sister's business, because women have no sense.

Don't follow their advice. All my possessions go to your father. The wives go to your father.

With regard to goods, only your father will hand them out with his own hands. You will respect him for my sake, you will tell him your worries. . . .

You, brother, stay well with the children I leave to you.

The man who has children is always envied by the others.

Don't listen to all kinds of talk, don't nurse any bad feelings.

If my wife refuses you, lead her home, they will give you what is yours.

Later on when you will leave, will I receive the inheritance?

I shall have already decayed where the termites are.

So I leave you all the things as did my father when you were still a child.

Did I insult you? I raised you properly. You stay here and also raise children properly.

When I shall be dead, shall I come back? This path is not trodden by people coming back.
(Theuws, 1983:105–6)

This last blessing of a father formulates three main demands. The subject of the tradition is a male one, and the father's brother will enunciate his rights now that the end imposes itself. Indeed, to the brother go all the goods and wives. Do not trust women, says the dying father to his son, and, more specifically, help your own sisters: they are women, and "women have no sense." Yet we need women, and "the man who has children is always envied by the others." In order to specify the particularity of this case, I would say—and I am playing on one of Foucault's phrases (1982:95)—the subject of the lesson, that is, the dying father, should be considered as identical with the author of the formulation. But who is really the author of the formulation if not the very tradition of the dying subject giving a last lesson for the continuity of the order?

Similarly, the lamentations of the husband for his dead wife could be regarded as expounding a rupture and its possible impact on the order of customs and the ordinary course of things. Rhythmic sentences balance the woman's virtues, duties, and signification with social pacts, summarizing the logic of a relationship and its emotional economy. The woman's dead body marks here the end of interacting codes between nature and culture, and within the latter generates possible hallucinatory violences.

Funeral Song for a Wife

This freeborn woman, o father, this freeborn woman!
Alas, where am I going to bring her, this beloved wife of mine?
Where shall I discuss this issue so they may agree with me, your poor friend?
They have already worried about you, first wife of mine.

You who now lie down at full length, o wife, brave with the pestle.

They took hold of me. The yard became too wide. Who is left to give me a bit of cassava?

Mother of lions, mother of giants.
Beloved, bewitched for your beauty,
who was told: she will bear children, she will be famous.

She will be like the others, famous
daughters of mother Kalamba,
brave with the pestle, if they fight with
the bow they fail.

Beloved wife, now that you rejected me altogether,
where shall I place the children?

Alone on the road, sad at home, lonely I will lie down on the bed.

Beloved wife of mine, where did you rest your head?

I might put mine beside yours, so that we may unite our dreams and upon awaking say: o dear! o beloved!

Beloved wife of mine, you who came to put an end to the sorrow in our house.

I wail like the cicada who digs a hole and goes inside, but I go on and am laughed at.

O woman, deferring to me, beloved wife of mine!

You who can't be planted in a gardenbed,
else I would plant you beside the road so I could look at you!

My friends with their families like forests, o strong woman;
mine is already thinned out.

They lie down with their families. I just look
at the sky, but it is locked, and on earth
there is mumbling for fear.

I see somebody passing by with his wife,
but my heart doesn't want to call her.
I die lonely as a dog; even a dog's smell is recognized by people.

I am thinking about the places where we sat down, o wife,
where the prints of our bodies remained,
and the grass was left crushed.

I see those who sleep with their wives.
My heart is burnt out inside me.

Alas, where shall I see you, beloved wife of mine?

I am consumed by fire.
You beloved, who was never lost in a
crowd, even if all were standing up.

Light-skinned as the white eagle so that even the white cowrie seemed dark!
(Fair! Fair! She didn't use up the water even if she washed in a mug!) (or:
Black like the *munywa*-bird, white her teeth like the raffia.) Parting for ever!
I call and call!

I am tired, o dear, how did you treat me today? My beloved, though outside
you were unassuming, inside the house you were full of play and laughter.

You were of a natural beauty! The artificial beauty resembles the sweet
potato, full of shoots.

They hate me, all of them. I stole nothing of other people.

My little spatula, you raised children;
hardly have they grown up and you are blamed!

This is my own funeral song! I, your friend, am the small *kitengu*-bird killed
out of wickedness,

it did not pick the rice, it did not eat the millet.

I wish I had preceded you! You would have followed in my steps.

Mother, who never went far away,
mother, even when you lay down, the
children wanted to be nursed.

Mother who never says anything against her child, even the retarded is his
mother's child.
You leave me with them, what shall I do?

The woman who does not give birth to a child is sterile, but the children of
other women call her.

I wail like the cricket; the cricket cries and goes inside, but I stay at the
entrance without seeing it.

O Lord, to whom one does not complain of his sorrow, look, he would give
you still more of it.

Now, sorrow at home and sorrow from afar have fallen on me!

I rack my brains thinking about my joy that died.

Where did those misfortunes come from?
Those who have seen you, will mourn over you. I poor wretch!

Those who never met you only laugh at you,
thinking no more of you than of a dog.
Begged food cannot satisfy a hungry person,

what appeases one's hunger is only what he cultivates himself.

So whose death was this in reality?
Death has overtaken me, miserable, dragging my life out on earth.

The world underneath refuses the thin, even if only the bones are left.

Handsome with your graceful gestures, o mother, dancing with a fan;

the heavy-bodied dance with a rattle.
This is my own funeral song, o wife!

Go ahead! I follow you, even before the moon hides in the woods; this is also
my death!

The tears of misery don't stop flowing,
I groan and they just drip on.

I died myself, beloved wife of mine, lady who is not praised when she is
sleeping.

Rouse her so you may see for yourselves.
(Theuws 1983:111–15)

This is a magnificent love text by its formal and semantic organizations if one remembers that it is always acted out as a declamation in which voice, gesture, and formulas interact. Formally, it is a more or less fixed farewell piece submitted to a relatively strict pattern of parallelism, temporal contrasts, and such binary oppositions as inside versus outside, male versus female, husband versus wife, fertile versus infertile, yesterday versus today and tomorrow, etc. The husband cannot radically modify the constructional schema during the performance, particularly the order of repetitive themes and their amplifying effects. Doing so might then weaken the efficiency of his words and the pertinence of the ritual. The pedagogical dimension of the song operates on the whole exercise: the song, in effect, has to be a sound language of a tradition. Even what could seem to be highly personalized references to a loving relationship enunciates in reality already given paradigms. The husband has only to choose the correct formulas that should apply to his wife, as apropos of his wife's pigmentation: "Light-skinned as the white eagle" or "Black like the *munywa*-bird." Yet let us insist, after Theuws, that "here again, some particular situation may need a few words spoken in a less formal way, but still, much in all these more or less institutionalized forms of speech is traditional, well-balanced and rhythmical. If somebody coins a good phrase, it may quickly become common knowledge, and the original speaker is soon as nameless as the old, long forgotten people, who began things and spoke the first incantations" (Theuws 1983:49).

The semantic level parallels the formal arrangement of words, paragraphs, and fluctuations in the intonation and accents of the speech. It exposes itself as an organic and complementary voice of the formal structuration only if it can subject itself to that first order and operate in accordance with its forms. As in the case of many West African cultures (see, e.g., Maurier 1985:155–60), what one finds here is a representation of the efficient speech which links itself to the constancy and the hidden veins of a past. It imposes itself as a pronouncement invested by a traditional vitality which, recapitulating the past, is also future-oriented and has the power of reaching and confronting beings in their essences.

Confronting the Body of the Earth

A division of labor based on gender seems universal in traditional societies. In Lubaland, agriculture is a feminine activity, whereas hunting and smelting are masculine. This is interesting to stress by reintroducing the curious reversal of the history of technology already discussed (see de Heusch 1982:26–29). The first parents—Kiubaka-Ubaka, the man, and Kibumba-Bumba, the woman—are professionally specialized. He is a builder of houses, she is knowledgeable in pottery. They meet accidentally and live together chastely until the day they observe two animals making love. They do the same, and give birth to several generations of incestuous twins. One of the founding fathers of Luba history, Nkongolo, is still caught in this incestuous spiral. It is Mbidi Kiluwe, the hunter, who closes the cycle by following the law of exogamy and ultimately organizes the Luba empire. Luc de Heusch writes:

> Mbidi's very name [Kiluwe] shows him to be a skillful hunter. He distinguishes himself by a new way of hunting, evidently more effective: he uses a bow and arrow. Technical innovations follow one another in a mythical order which curiously inverts the historical progression from the paleolithic to the neolithic economy: architecture and pottery, fishing, trapping, hunting with bow and arrow. Bringer of food and bearer of a refined culture, Mbidi Kiluwe crowns the series of technological achievements evoked in the prologue to the myth. His sudden, enigmatic appearance puts an end to a history which has been going round in circles. Given over completely to labor and reproduction, men were denied the wider horizon of exogamy, just as they were ignorant of the customs of divine kingship. The dreary repetition of incestuous pairing up to the time of Nkongolo has no other function than to highlight this abrupt change in mood. A recital devoid of dramatic tension and literary interest gives way to a helter-skelter succession of complex events leading to the necessary victory of the central personage, now elevated to heroic status. The scene overflows with violent and passionate action, extremes of love and hate. The heroic tale of Kalala Ilunga marks the beginning of true history, which emerges from the ancient mold of mythical thought in the shape of a national *epic*. In it, we see above the clash of arms a people politically united and in full possession of the necessary technology. (Heusch 1982:28–29)

De Heusch's interpretation is excellent and accurate (see also Roberts MS1). In what it clarifies, other possibilities of interpretation come to light. Nkongolo the incestuous and the cruel comes from a well-established family. His father, Bondo, according to the tradition, was known as the Muntu utyila wadi wa malwa, or the clear-skinned dangerous one. The name of his mother was Nseya, and his own name was Mwamba Nseya. The stories of his beginning and life situate him in a relatively sedentary, agricultural context. As one example, when his two children die by his fault—he has submitted them to a poison proof—he is then living in his capital city between Kalumbu and Kimona, which is not very far from Kabongo. The children are buried, and we are told that "groves were planted around the grave and in each a *mpafu* or wild olive tree" (Womersley 1984:2). The man and his culture have, by then, gone beyond nomadism. The narratives present Nkongolo as a highly mobile general. He conquered, ravaged, and plundered from permanent bases. One of his three centers was located between Kampemba and Kipukwe. In order to protect it, he planted a ring of trees all around it. Nkongolo Island was his second and northernmost residence. Finally, Katonkele on the Lomami River was his third base, where a ring of trees is still visible; according to the local tradition, the ring is the remnant of a fence built by Nkongolo. These factual references indicate that Nkongolo's culture was far beyond an original primitive organization. The domestication of plants had already been introduced. Moreover, Nkongolo's people are relatively stable and build houses. When Nkongolo receives Mbidi, the foreign prince, immediately after noting the distinction of the visitor who declines to eat and drink in public, he consults his oracle, whose response clearly indicates that Nkongolo's culture has already reached the age of architecture: "This is no ordinary visitor but a great prince, the eldest son of a king. Such a man can never eat before others. You must build him a hut at once—a special hut. . . . Nkongolo ordered his men to hurry without delay to the nearest woods for sticks and poles, and to the plain for thatch grass. Quickly a temporary eating hut was constructed for his exalted guest" (Womersley 1984:7).

Yet this highly civilized prince is portrayed as a hunter and thus paradoxically incarnates a less-advanced civilization. He is tall and remarkably black, and for years he has been traveling westward from Niembwa Nkunda in the southern region of Lake Tanganyika. Mbidi is looking for his sister's dog. "His sister Mwanana's famous hound, so big that she had named him Ntambo or lion, had disappeared. She had blamed him so he had set off with his own two hunting dogs . . . and a party of retainers to look for it. At the same time, he was anxious to explore as much of the country as possible before the death of his aged father" (Womersley 1984:7). Indeed, he found the dog, sent it back, and, enjoying his exploring, continued his travel. Womersley writes:

An official history of the Lunda compiled by District Commissioner Van den Byvang at Sandoa 4 September 1926 declares that the Muluba Ilunga Mbidi Kiluwe, or Muluba Tshibinda Illunga (*tshibinda* in the Lunda language is the equivalent of *kiluwe* in Kiluba, i.e., hunter) was regent for his young son

Mwata Yamvo for twenty-five years before leaving the area. The Luba historians give no exact number of years but give the impression that it was a short period of just a few years. However, all agree that, after some time, Mbidi Kiluwe and his party of followers returned eastwards, crossing the Lubilash, picked up the Lumani and following it downstream, hunting as he went and enquiring for Kongolo's capital until he came abreast of Lake Boya and struck east to this famous little lake where, as we have recounted, he met Kongolo's sisters, Mabela and Bulanda.

Now when Kongolo had learned all that he wanted to know about the ways and behavior of a royal chief, his interest in Mbidi Kiluwe waned and he began to seek some means of getting rid of this stranger. So he began to be casual towards him, finally becoming insulting, remarking openly, "How can I put up all this time with a man whose teeth are filed to points?" Mbidi Kiluwe thought: "This is too much. . . . I have taught him all the customs a royal chief should follow—now who has sharpened his teeth but I? It is time I took my departure." So the royal stranger packed up his few remaining possessions, called his *mwadi mishi* and prepared to depart, deciding that he had overstayed his welcome. (1984:8)

Let us face the paradox. Mbidi is systematically presented as hunter, while Nkongolo, the cruel one, is an agriculturalist. More than that, he has already mastered the art of smelting iron. His own name witnesses to that: "In fact, one of his praise names was *Kongolo Mwamba mujya na nkololo. Nkololo* is the name of a curved, knife-like instrument which is used for scraping out the insides of founding mortars. . . . Iron-working was a rare profession in those days, and an iron-worker was considered to be a very important man. The progenitor of the royal Luba line was called . . . Sendwe Mwalaba, which means Mwalaba the Iron-worker" (Womersley 1984:5).

The opposition between Nkongolo and Mbidi manifests both the odd reversed history of technology and the creation charter of the first human beings and their culture. The civilizer Mbidi seems to come from a primitive stage, and he is glorified as a magnificent hunter. He succeeds in transforming, for the better, a culture which has mastered agriculture, architecture, and smelting technologies. On the other hand, this reversed canon reflects another model, the primordial genesis, that of the first couple which appears in an already specialized division of labor: Kiubaka-Ubaka, who builds houses, and Kibumba-Bumba, who makes pottery. We already know that in the "Story of the Spirit Who Gives Life" (N$_6$), the man is a hunter, and the woman, an agriculturalist. Synthetically, focusing on paradigmatic subjects, we can construct the following table:

Genesis	
Male (Kiubaka-Ubaka) Architecture	Female (Kibumba-Bumba) Pottery

N_6	
Male Hunter	Female Agriculturalist

History	
Male (Nkongolo) Agriculture, architecture, iron-making	Male (Mbidi) Hunter

The ordering in successive lines of Genesis, N_6, and History has no particular meaning. It is just a summarizing device. N_6 could have been considered first, since it is about the world's creation. Yet History, in which Mbidi is opposed to Nkongolo, comes chronologically after the first two whatever they might be. Two remarkable conclusions can be drawn from this table. First, the relationship between gender and labor: women are linked to agriculture and to pottery. Second, men are indistinctly associated with all the known phases of technology. In sum, one could now hypothesize that the surprising reversal of technology analyzed by Luc de Heusch (1982:27) should be interpreted from the background of this division of labor and its social implications.

Let us briefly concentrate on a number of prayers used until recently, which are related to specific technological practices: hunting (masculine), agriculture (feminine), smelting (masculine). My understanding is that they constitute an ideological constellation which recites the authority of a tradition and the grammar of its gender division in the mastering of the body of the earth.

Hunting is a liturgy (see Bouillon 1954). A female Spirit, Mwadi wa Nfwana, presides over its procedures. The professional hunter belongs to a closed association and has undergone a special initiation. Often, his wife has participated in it, and since then, she is known as Inamakola (or Inazinga, if she is not the hunter's first wife). A series of taboos link the hunter and his wife and objectively constitute a statement through which a cultural system claims to dominate natural signs. They include absolute faithfulness, purity of the heart, regular periods of celibacy, and submission to the female Spirit. An unfortunate hunter might pray:

I wronged you [Mwadi wa Nfwana]
when I omitted "to count you your days."

You destroyed my virility.
Now that I have appeased you,
give me back my strength,
that I may sleep well with my wives.
I want you to unlock my rifle.
(Theuws 1983:64)

The ritual specifies clearly that, before hunting, the man spends three or four nights with each one of his wives, and then he dedicates a specified number of nights to the Spirit, generally three or four. Behind his own house, a small hut is built. Depending on the area, above or along the hut a simple altar of branches displays the Spirit's symbols. The hunter has to spend the required number of nights alone in this retreat and count well that the Spirit has her due. Indeed, according to belief, if he does not respect the rules, his rifle will be locked and his hunting will end as a failure. Metaphorically, "if he does not take care and forgets to 'count the nights' of the spirit, he will be 'killed' in his genitals" (Theuws 1983:64n3). In any case, let us note provisionally the following fact: Hunting begins and ends as a ritual. This stipulates also a guideline for the hunter's active and passive sexuality. The latter, which corresponds to a period of chastity, reveals itself as a symbolic sign of a sexual union between the male hunter and the female Spirit.

After an unsuccessful hunting preceded by a carefully coherent ritual, the following prayer would be addressed directly to God and ancestors:

Oh, you Father-Creator, wherever I go in the
bush, I find nothing. . . .
I am not a stranger in this country.
It is the land my father and forefathers left
me, how could I be a stranger?
I do not rely upon the charm,
I call upon the spirit of the land.
I call upon my tutelary spirit,
both of them go together.
You, father, forefathers, brothers who died
help me that I may find a little game
that I may eat and feed the children.
(Theuws 1983:65)

The invocation here operates in a more visible and simpler apprehension of both the space and the tradition. The hunter traces his male genealogy, thus reciting his rights to the sovereignty over the land. The two movements transform his unsuccessful hunting into a natural contradiction, for which he demands an explanation from God himself. In the same vein, after a good hunt, the hunter will thank God publicly and occasionally include his fathers and forefathers in the ritual invocations. Here is another example in which God and ancestors are called upon after an unsuccessful hunting:

> God
> You who give game to men
> You who give goods to humans
> Why do I experience only misfortunes?
> The high herbs bother me.
> You, God, are not you there?
> And you, my father, my grandfather
> Are not you there?
> (Van Caeneghem 1956:98)

Cultivating, an eminently feminine activity among the Luba, is another dynamic in which a socioreligious liturgy duplicates and interlaces with a simple process of production. There is a multitude of rituals concerning the preparation of the field, the fixing of the limits of the field, the sowing, and the harvesting. One of the most elaborate is that of the celebration of first fruits. When the harvesting period arrives, the king's first wife, or the wife of a minor chief in smaller villages, visits the fields around the village. She is solemnly and ritually dressed, rubbed with earth that is white, the color of innocence and of the universe of the departed. She longingly fills a basket with the ripest and the most beautiful ears of millet and maize. Back home, she brews beer and offers it to the king. The latter has invited his advisers and his important officers for the rite. He ceremoniously dedicates the first cup to the spirits and then pours its contents on the ground, claiming his past and celebrating his ancestors. Later on, the cup will be placed at the limits of the city and the fields, thus uniting in a reciprocal interaction the inhabited space and the endless natural territory open to an agricultural economy. Before drinking his first cup of beer, the king solemnly invokes the Lord. The assembly listens silently:

> Well, gentlemen,
> truly for many years already
> I have cultivated the land
> without getting much of a crop.
> Now this year the Lord did me also a favour.
> Kaleba [the Lord] does not give to one alone,
> He gives to the elder.
> He gives to the younger.

I thank him for the food He gave me.
Let us drink this beer, let us rejoice.
Nkungwa Banze [our Lord], made me a present.
(Theuws 1983:74)

If the crops are poor, the king will use another formula which may begin as follows:

Alas, oh Forger of the mountains,
all this misfortune I am meeting year after year!

What shall I do?
The house is full of children.
How shall I feed them?
Should I go and steal for them?
Or should I send them to my relatives to be looked after?

The soil I am tilling,
is it not the same soil, all my friends are tilling?
Who directed his malice toward me,
spoiling my crops?
Who is he in the village?
(Theuws 1983:75)

These formulas are remarkable. They powerfully bring under the responsibility of the man the work of women. The man directly faces the Lord. He acts as one who tills the soil, produces and grows the fruits of the earth. He is also the one who immediately after the offering to the spirits and ancestors drinks the first beer, reiterating in this rite the past, its representation, and hope for the future. The fecundity of the earth as well as its occasional unfruitfulness seem to confront in his body God's motives and the language of nature. The female voice, even apropos of an essentially feminine activity, has been since the founding myths pushed into the margins of the society.

The ritual prayer before smelting ore (an exclusively masculine work) actualizes this cohesion. Piece by piece, each sentence points to the sacredness and the importance of the activity. Its space identifies with a logical sequence in the creative process: God gave the fire to man and accordingly a power and a duty.

Oh Lord . . . who gave me my little fire
You are the reason why I rub with earth
on my face
Help me, please,

so that the ore may come out nicely smelted
That I may get food and wealth.
(Theuws 1983:89)

This last prayer, as well as the preceding ones quoted, are sequences of a representation. They are, first, accessible only to men. Second, they witness to a common place, a mythical beginning, in which the transparency of a Creator's gifts unifies in the primacy of the masculine all modes of existing on earth. Finally, their message deploys itself as an obvious fact: living and mastering the body of the earth do not seem to require anything other than a permanent refoundation of God's law. The most ordinary tasks for survival, such as hunting, cultivating, smelting, are formalized in rituals in accordance with formulas which interpret them mythically, and at the same elicit a whole space of cultural and political orthodoxy.

The necessity of mastering the body of the earth in order to perpetuate the human race provides a reason and an explanation for the absolute power of a collective consciousness. The grid of order, despite the political manipulations which through time have modified it and adapted its statements, claims to refer to the beginnings. Human bodies, remarkably female bodies, are *intextuated* in an original law. Michel de Certeau found a magnificent expression: "Give me your body and I will give you meaning, I will make you a name and a word in my discourse." In our context, it is an imperative diktat: You should submit your body in order to get a meaning, have a name and a function in the discourse. De Certeau put it well in noting: "These two problematics maintain each other, and perhaps the law would have no power if it were not able to support itself on the obscure desire to exchange one's flesh for a glorious body, to be written, even if it means dying, and to be transformed into a recognized word. Here again, the only force opposing this passion to be a sign is the cry, a deviation or an ecstasy, a revolt or flight of that which, within the body, escapes the law of the named" (1984:149).

In Luba stories which comment upon the "glorious body" of the tradition and thus double mythical and political knowledge, women indeed frequently cry, often go mad, and, in general, tend to withdraw in ecstasy and other witchcrafts. The missionary interpretation of the Luba stories and their implications has mainly looked for stepping-stones of something else. Let us thus look at a Marxist proposition which claims to be both better and more efficient.

6

Anthropology and Marxist Discourse

Peter Rigby's *Persistent Pastoralists: Nomadic Societies in Transition* (1985), which focuses on Ilparakuyo Maasai of West Bagamoyo District in Tanzania, is an extremely well-executed research project and a remarkable piece of thinking on Marxism and the practice of African anthropology. It qualitatively advances our understanding of the dynamics of nomadic societies and challenges the canon according to which pastoralism is necessarily a historical step toward an agricultural social formation. The project unfolds from an observation that becomes a thesis: "The historical uniqueness of the East African pastoral formations is radically affected in a most fundamental sense by any trend towards any form of cultivation, although this does not represent a transformation of the mode of production" (Rigby 1985:173). Hence there follows, according to Rigby, a "reluctance of these pastoral social formations to adopt cultivation, despite the mounting pressures at all levels for them to do so, and their consequent search for other methods of 'dealing with' the encroachment of commoditization and the penetration of peripheral capitalism" (1985:174). This is often suggested (but not really demonstrated in detail) in a highly competent chapter on pastoral production and socialist transformation (Rigby 1985:123–67). The conclusion summarizes Rigby's interpretation. Pastoralists "have long been faced with a diminishing resource base of suitable grazing and water facilities. As a result, herd size has decreased, and there is a consequent increase in dependence upon agricultural products. This has been accelerated in recent years by such government policies as villagization" (Rigby 1985:174). Thus, a technical and highly convincing argument becomes a crucial element in a set of proposals on how to handle the already existing interdependence between pastoralists and their agriculturalist neighbors and, in more general terms, how to evaluate government policies of economic integration.

166

It is not my objective to "review" Rigby's book, but instead to assess three central points that contribute to its coherence and strength: his critique of fieldwork; his reflection on history and time; and his Marxist method and its implications for both anthropology and the social formation concerned. Although these themes constitute the essence of Rigby's chapters 2, 4, and 6, I shall also consider elements from other chapters. Let me be clear here. Such an analytic and systematic reading is a sign of respect for an excellent, thought-provoking, and imaginative book. In fact, *Persistent Pastoralists* is one of the few books in African anthropology I have read during the last ten years that has not obligated me to face at least one of the following nightmares: doubts about the author's sincerity, knowledge of the field, or psychological balance; or, more important, the authenticity of the data interpreted.

Critical Participation; or, A Question of Place

The title of Rigby's second chapter is "Critical Participation, Mere Observation or Alienation." It is a reflection on the ambiguities of fieldwork. The concept of a critical participation might not seem surprising at a superficial level. But it appears provocative, even scandalous, given the opening paragraph written in July 1976: "I have been doing what is conventionally known as 'fieldwork' among Ilparakuyo of West Bagamoyo District for just over one year; the number of days I have actually spent 'in the field,' however, add up to just over two months. Owing to the exigencies of my other duties, the longest single period I spent in the area in which Ilparakuyo live was two weeks, this being almost immediately followed by a further week. All the rest of the trips I managed to make to the area have averaged two or three days each" (Rigby 1985:25). How can one dare to write even a paper on the basis of such a limited experience? Indeed, those who know Rigby's background have smiled, thinking or stating: This is sheer showmanship. And so it may be. But those who do not know him continue reading, perhaps hoping to learn tricks from an avowed scoundrel. They are immediately taken aback by Rigby's "indigenous roots," which directly challenge their competence about their own fieldwork and the credibility of their *parole* as Africanists.

Perhaps the most important is that I am, and have been for some time, a relatively full (if largely absentee) son and member of an Ilparakuyo homestead (*enkang'*). Furthermore, my younger Olparakuoni brother (*olalahe lai*) is a full (and more frequently present) member of my homestead in Dar es Salaam, which is also the periodic venue for gatherings of Ilparakuyo *ilmurran* (young men) and junior elders (*ilpayiani*) who may happen to be visiting Dar es Salaam for a day or two from the home area. This fortunate eventuality lessens the participatory gap caused by my work-enforced exile from my Ilparakuyo environment. My descent and affinal status in this particular *enkang'* has its roots in much earlier circumstances, in the days when I was of the *ilmurran* age-grade, and which need not detain us here. But it could be said with some accuracy that I am among those researchers who chose their specific area of research upon the grounds of an adoptive affinity and kinship rather than for strictly "scientific" reasons; for personal interest rather than exclusively in the pursuit of knowledge. (Rigby 1985:25–26)

This confession could account for the confusion between scientific observation and policy proposals suggested above, and to which I shall return. Rigby's self-described personality raises the issue of "authority." He contends that he speaks from an African insider's experience; scientific reason would be, in his case, submitted to this decisive fact. Here are some statements illustrating Rigby's vision of fieldwork. Some readers will find them romantic; others might take them seriously and follow me in my interrogation of his project.

I have walked through the bush in the middle of the night with a group of *ilmurran* . . . listening to songs that could never be sung in or near any Ilparakuyo homestead. (1985:26)

I have sat for many hours with elders (*ilpayiani*) drinking gallons (literally) of beer, listening to them discuss almost everything: sex, morality, politics, religion, the weather, the qualities and quantities of beer, marriage, death, birth, and each other's initiation, usually joking. (1985:26)

My brother and I have walked 16 miles or so in blazing sun in search of our father's homestead, which had been abruptly and forcibly shifted several miles from its original site while we were away in Dar es Salaam. (1985:27)

I have also seen the joy of an old man with his sons and discovered, without any probing questions, how many others had died and who now would perhaps have been older than his eldest. (1985:27)

If Rigby is lying in these statements, then we are missing a potentially magnificent novelist. The problem is precisely that the description of his experience is very probably correct. Its goal is to unfold progressively what Rigby calls a "pastoral praxis" or "a *dialectical relation* between various ideological elements and the constantly changing imperatives of the material base of pastoral existence'' (Rigby 1985:4). It disorients the functionalist practice of describing the native in the accusative, in which the native cannot be but a grammatical direct object. What it brings to light most visibly is a subversive question directly related to the initial provocation: how many anthropologists could speak through Rigby's voice about their own fieldwork? The ''mystique'' of field presence invented by Malinowski—who was obliged to actualize it by the force of circumstances—is a difficult ideal for many researchers. Most of them, for quite respectable reasons, spent less time ''in the field'' than they claim to have. In any case, a small number of them have the philosophical tools that can enable them to confront from their own contextual grid of existence what it means to speak in the accusative (in a descriptive manner about an object) or in the vocative (in a dialogue with someone) about a cultural body which is not theirs, or is theirs only accidentally. Exceptions exist, though (e.g., Beidelman 1986; Riesman 1977), in which one can observe how a remarkable mastery of a cultural place is transformed into a discursive invented space (see Wagner 1981).

I am distinguishing here *place* from *space*. The first, as already indicated in this book, can be understood as a locus, specifically as a plane which is ''the order [of whatever kind] in accord with which elements are distributed in relationship of coexistence'' (de Certeau 1984:117). On the other hand, space is rather a geography constituted by dynamic elements which meet, intersect, unite, cross each other, or diverge. As Michel de Certeau put it, ''Space occurs as the effect produced by the operations that orient it, situate it, temporalize it, and make it function in a polyvalent unity of conflictual programs or contractual proximities'' (1984:117). To expand de Certeau's illustrations, I would say: As a street is a place that a walker transforms into an active space, or as a text is a locus of organized signs obeying the logic of a proper place that every reader can change into an intellectual or aesthetic space of learning and enjoyment, so the ''object'' of an anthropological curiosity (a culture, its institutions, rituals, or mythical narratives) constitutes a place with its proper rules that the anthropologist's activity and interpretation transform into a new space. This new product is a ''practiced place,'' something which is different and, in any case, could hardly claim to compare its dynamics with what de Certeau called ''the law of the 'proper' which rules in the place'' (1984:117).

It should be clear by now that it is more than a question of the duration of fieldwork that Rigby is challenging in exploiting so dramatically his existential authority. The problem resides in the participant observation which in itself (as activity and as project) as well as in discourses it allows (doctorates, books, lectures, etc.) obliterates major issues. Let me be more specific. One of the issues is given in the very concept of *native*. It is circumscribed as both a substantive and an adjective. What it designs and qualifies at the beginning of fieldwork is the anonymity of something like "beings in themselves" that, at the end of the fieldwork through the magic of the anthropologist's words, are spatialized in a proper noun and a supposedly cultural body. But what is the significance of this metamorphosis?

> Any theory constructed from them must of necessity be flawed in some way, or still retain implicitly the false dualism between theory and practice which Marxism sets out explicitly to demolish. Such a theory would, therefore, remain "alienated" from the social reality it purports to explain, and practice based upon it would be false. I am not saying here that statistical data collected in this fashion are irrelevant to sociological analysis and explanation. On the contrary, I am attempting to clarify the uses to which they may be put by exposing the epistemological and ontological assumptions that underlie their collection. . . .
>
> The very term "participant observation" implies the false ontological objectivity, derived from the natural sciences, which I have been trying so strenuously to dismantle. In the sociological context, it allows the logical possibility of being an "observer" without being a "participant" or a "participant" while not being an "observer"; both postulates are patently absurd. All participants [actors] must be observers in their own right, interpreting and analyzing the situation, or else they would be unable to act or "participate"; similarly, all observers [social scientists?] must, if only by their very presence, participate [act?]. Unfortunately, some social scientists have either ignored or deliberately denied these fundamental elements in any data collection process. . . .
>
> My unequivocal stance upon the matter of the methodology of data collection and interpretation is that, as far as his limits take him, the social scientist's full participation both intellectually and emotionally in the day-to-day activities of any community, within the context of its language and culture, is indispensable to any *critical* understanding of the structures and processes he is trying to elucidate, and *ipso facto* the foundation any practice which may derive from such knowledge. (Rigby 1985:31, 35–36)

All this is fine and perfectly relevant insofar as Rigby intends to bind the intersubjective context of data to discursive practices interpreting them. Rigby is correct when he insists on the fact that all problems arising in the intersubjective context (his examples: we don't have enough cattle to feed ourselves; our children don't obey us any longer; our wives are going astray) concern the social scientist and cannot be reasonably divorced from the anthropologist's interpretative discourse. And he adds: "*But* this *trans-*

lation must be meaningful to all parties concerned, not only to some esoteric coterie of inspired individuals" (Rigby 1985:43).

Some implications of this well-intentioned position are arguable. What the last sentence proposes is, at best, confusing. I am not convinced at all that Rigby's book is *meaningful* to his Ilparakuyo friends and parents in the manner it might be to his American and English Marxist colleagues. The Belgian Marxist Benoît Verhaegen faced the same predicament and elaborated a method he called *histoire immédiate* (1974). My scepticism has nothing to do with the fact that Rigby's African friends may not speak English or might be incapable of making sense of Rigby's technical jargon. I contend that Rigby's text unveils a conceptual space which does not have the stability of the original locus. This does not imply a doubt about the correctness of the translation. On the contrary, I am impressed by the careful way in which his interpretation tests itself against the original locus (e.g., the discussion of the economy of "sharing," particularly pp. 79–86; and the history of alienation of Maasai land, pp. 92–122). My concern has nothing to do with that, but with what Rigby seems to resist: the best translation is always a reflection, or, more specifically, a metaphoric construct. It can identify with what is prior only figuratively and, in any case, witnesses to a dubious power. Let me specify what I mean. The everyday experience of Ilparakuyo (or Ndebele, Luba, Mande, or whatever) locus articulates itself as being, as text (in the full sense of the word). What a competent translation such as Rigby's does is not to apprehend the being-there, not even to unveil it, but to organize a reflection and specify a commentary, a new order of meaning. I do not question the pertinence of specification. The point is to recognize the fact of a jump and, thus, understand the power of Rigby, that is, the power of the anthropologist. In reality, his interpretive practice witnesses to a metapower: a capacity of transforming a place into a conceptual space and of moving from this space to the original place. In this context, to state that "the translation must be meaningful to all parties concerned" does not seem to make much sense. In effect, Rigby the anthropologist began by terrorizing everybody with his authority: he is the only perfect bilingual among his fellow anthropologists and his Ilparakuyo elders, *ilmurran,* and family. And this suggests another dimension of his authority: he is, when he is critical, the only real master of symbolic and conceptual linkages existing between the "laws of the place" and all interpretive operations that can spatialize the being and the body of the Ilparakuyo place.

This issue of the meaningfulness of the translation is probably more complex. I suspect Rigby of using the adjective *meaningful* in a highly specialized sense, if I take into account the relative importance of some of

Jürgen Habermas' theses in his reasoning and, specifically, the discreet presence of the concept of ideal communicative action. Let me quote Habermas: "The virtual totality [knowledge] that is sundered by splitting-off is represented by the model of pure communicative action. According to this model, all habitual interactions and all interpretations relevant to life conduct are accessible at all times. This is possible on the basis of internalizing the apparatus of unrestricted ordinary language of uncompelled and public communication so that the transparency of recollected life is preserved" (Habermas 1971:232). This virtual totality speaks from a place. Indeed, it is not an African one, and there is nothing wrong with that. It expresses itself in the diachronic dynamism of spatializing the original locus, a beginning and its history. Its present fulfills a past and its future; this future, to use Jean-Paul Sartre's expression, is "the continual possibilization of possibles" (1956:186). The collective meaning—if it exists—operates within a regional tradition through signs of the virtual totality. Synchronically, the virtual totality would actualize itself in the efforts of active subjects, who seek to transcend the tension between their "inside" and the "outside," and thus metaphorically move from "place-knowledge" to "space-knowledge." What this exercise has regularly brought about, most visibly over the last three centuries, conforms with what Claude Lévi-Strauss has harshly but justly called a "socialization of the *Cogito.*"

I have nothing against the thought of Habermas. I am just appalled by Rigby's imprudent use of it. In explaining his belief in "the transition from interpretation to action," he notes:

> The world of traditionally inherited meanings reveals itself to the interpreter only to the extent to which his own world thereby becomes transparent to himself at the same time. The man who understands the traditional meaning provides a link between the two worlds; he comprehends the factual content of what is handed down by applying the tradition to himself and his situation. If, however, the procedural rules thus combine interpretation with application, then the following explanation suggests itself; in revealing reality, interpretational research is guided by a concern for the maintenance and extension of possible intersubjective understanding which is necessary for the orientation of any symbolic interaction. Meaning is understood according to its structure with a view to a possible consensus of interacting individuals within the frame of a traditional or culturally patterned self-understanding. . . . A critical social science, however, is obviously not content with this; it tries in addition to discover which (if any) theoretical statements express unchangeable laws of social action and which, though they express relations of dependence, because they are ideologically fixed, are in principle subject to change. (Rigby 1985:35)

I am perturbed by such a statement without any discussion of its episte-mological context. Rigby is probably right when he reads in it a dynamic creativity from interpretation to action. But something else should be made explicit. Habermas speaks from within a given culture and expounds on the meanings of a junction between two worlds, a past and a present confronting the mystery of the future in the projection of a historical continuity. By trans-posing (with no discussion of its significance) this model of a "virtual con-tinuity" to an African "locus" or place, Rigby seems to silence something. In effect, the extension of the model could be seen as symbolizing the inevitability of a metonymic integration. Features of a well-localized African experience find sense in chronological determinations of European historical sequences, thus justifying the power of the "virtual totality." From this perspective, the Il-parakuyo reality would then witness to the tension existing between two abstract figures. It would incarnate, on the one hand, the European vision of a past (an unnamed savagery) for many, and, on the other hand, a project for modernity (defined also according to European paradigms), which might appear a night-mare. To modernize therefore implies, explicitly or implicitly, an evolutionary process through successive restructurations of the order of the socioeconomic as well as that of mythical and ideological configurations.

Thus, Rigby's text is interwoven with something like a terror of naming what is out there. It reconstructs its own ground, reinventing a "locus" in the most generous way, and looks for its raison d'être as a project in herme-neutical theories. Yet its real problem is simply one of describing the tension of a "tradition" vis-à-vis its "future," or modernity. One might then under-stand how and why in Rigby's Ilparakuyo context it becomes embarrassing to comment on the opposition between merits or values of the "world of tradition" vis-à-vis that of "the interpreter." If the first can be easily identified, then the second seems, at least to me, a question. In effect, since I take seriously Rigby's authority as an Ilparakuoni and as a social scientist thinker, I should also have to choose between (or at any rate to reconcile) the African elder who believes in the absolute pertinence of his "locus" and the credibility of a Marxist social scientist discoursing on it and intellectually "spatializing" it. Both are in the same person. This tension (should I say, this contradiction?) expresses some-thing simple: the future of the Ilparakuyo seems to reside in the rationality and the dream of the Marxist social scientist. In itself this does not seem to be anything shameful. Yet this very statement would appear scandalous to many American Africanists. On this topic, Marxism is ambiguous in its exposition of laws of historical materialism and, specifically, the succession of conflicting modes of production (Marx 1973). There is, in this dynamic, just one history. Why then does Rigby need to draw on the concept of "virtual continuity" to make his point?

A Practice of Anthropology

Rigby insists on another important methodological point: "Throughout my period with Ilparakuyo, and most particularly when I have been at Kwam-sanga, I have not asked a single formal question, except those relating to language or the identification and use of basic cultural objects. The questions I have asked have all arisen entirely out of the social context in which I happened to be at that moment; although I have, on occasion, attempted to tilt the discussion in one direction or another'' (Rigby 1985:26). He adds immediately that such a statement may "horrify" some people. I am not at all scandalized by Rigby's statement. To those who are "horrified," let me ask them to make explicit the real reasons of their discontent and then examine them in the context of Rigby's motives. In a recent book, *Veiled Sentiments* (1986), Leila Abu-Lughod makes a similar statement. Here is the framework. Her father, a "Jordanian," has accompanied his American-born and educated daughter to "her" fieldwork, a Bedouin milieu in Egypt. He introduces her to a Muslim culture, and she is confronted with the realization that she is not really one of "them." Her credentials are not solid:

> This introduction to the community profoundly affected my position and the nature of the work I could do. First, it identified me, despite my poor linguistic skills and my apparent foreignness, as a Muslim and an Arab. My Muslim credentials were shaky, as I did not pray and my mother was known to be an American. But most assumed that I shared with them a fundamental identity as a Muslim, and my father's speech was no doubt so sprinkled with religious phrases that they believed in his piety, which in turn rubbed off on me. Many times during my stay, I was confronted with the critical importance of the shared Muslim identity in the community's acceptance of me. As always, the old women and the young children bluntly stated what most adults were too polite to say. (Abu-Lughod 1986:13)

Yet she becomes a member of the community, mainly because of her father's commitment. His presence guaranteed the daughter's respectability according to Islamic canons and mobilized a familial obligation: males have to care about their female kin and make sure that they are situated in their proper sociological roles. Abu-Lughod notes:

> The other consequence of my introduction to the community as my father's daughter was that I was assigned and took on the role of an adoptive daughter. My protection/restriction was an entailment of this relationship, but so was my participation in the household, my identification with the kin group, and

the process by which I learned about the culture, a sort of socialization to the role. Although I never completely lost my status as a guest in their household, my role as daughter gradually superceded it. . . .

I should not give the impression that this role was forced on me. I was a willing collaborator. In a society where kinship defines most relationships, it was important to have a role as a fictive kinsperson in order to participate. I knew what was expected of an obedient daughter and found it hard to resist meeting those expectations. (Abu-Lughod 1986:15)

Two difficult questions could not but follow this *mise en place:* How should one behave authentically? How can one produce a credible knowledge about the experience? Indeed, the political structuration of a Bedouin place led to a young anthropologist's cultural ambiguity. This became the major level of the interplay between two arrangements, the local human place and its history, and the anthropologist's project for spatializing it as knowledge. I should here specify my understanding of the concepts of authenticity which, I suspect, is closer to Rigby's practice than to Abu-Lughod's exaggerated self-criticism. As Sartre put it, "The exercise of [a] freedom may be considered as *authentic* or *inauthentic* according to the choices made in the situation. Authenticity, it is almost needless to say, consists in having a true and lucid consciousness of the situation, in assuming the responsibilities and risks that it involves, in accepting it in pride or humiliation, sometimes in horror and hate" (Sartre 1965:90). In any case, inauthentic or not, Abu-Lughod emphasizes an important issue that Rigby simply reduces to the efficiency of a silent existential choice and a praxis.

My position of powerlessness in the community prevented me from coercing people into discussions in which they had no interest. Nor had I any desire to do so. I appreciated their perception of me as different from those researchers they had previously encountered. I heard stories of the "exams" these researchers had given them (questionnaires) and the hilariously wild tales the Bedouins had fed them. But because I wished to live with them, they assumed it must be on ordinary social terms. I was reluctant to violate these terms, and thus I rarely took notes or tape-recorded when they spoke (except later when I began collecting poetry) but rather wrote notes from memory at night or at odd moments during the day, and I tried to ask questions when people were already discussing a particular subject or event instead of out of the blue. (Abu-Lughod 1986:23–24)

Rigby's position draws its credibility from a similar, almost identical, argument. He writes: "It could be said with some accuracy that I am among those researchers who chose their specific area of research upon the grounds of an adoptive affinity and kinship rather than for strictly 'scientific' reasons; for personal interest rather than exclusively in the pursuit of knowledge" (Rigby 1985:26). Here he posits a personal and existential commitment as the road to authenticity. Yet it is essential to make it clearer and ponder its implications. Why, for example, should a social scientist connect parental affinity with his or her scientific practice? Rigby perceives the question in strictly political terms; he reduces it to a political project. His discourse decodes and recomposes an economy of everyday life and pastoral culture in order to think and propose modalities for a "socialist transformation." Specifically, he makes two main propositions. First, against the ongoing policies of "sedentarization," he defends the principle of "semi-sedentarization": "permanent villages [should have] reserved grazing for subsistence herds in the dry season . . . , related to relatively unlimited movement of the main herd, within the pattern of transhumance." Second, "the *present trend* in the division of labour and pastoral production relations (*Ilayiok,* youths who have to attend school and are still uncircumcised, versus *Ilmurran,* junior and senior) could be encouraged positively as a move towards socialist development, rather than the social category of *Ilmurran* being destroyed upon the dubious grounds of its anachronistic character" (Rigby 1985:163).

These political recommendations are presented as deductions from two critical interpretations of Marxist theses. The first exploits the notion of mediation from Marx's *Grundisse* and, in an Althusserian manner (*For Marx* 1977), emphasizes sociocultural factors as "crucial" in the transformation and development of processes of production. The second focuses on the utility of understanding the division of labor between sexes as dependent upon other frameworks: the cadre in which processes of production are related to social relations of production and defined as *de jure* and *de facto* in the organization of power on the basis of or in relation to age-set structures; and the reproduction of the domestic group, the local (pastoralist) definition of commodity relations (the herd being in this case a primary means of production). These are major issues in their theoretical meanings and in their concrete political implications.

Let us focus on the method first, and then address Rigby's political practice. Rigby calls his method "a Marxist phenomenology":

A Marxist phenomenology would thus contain the two procedural elements: 1) interpretation and translation of the "real world" of everyday life through the intersubjective situation in which the social scientist is involved, which illuminates the common and elemental link between knowledge and interest;

and 2) the translation in turn of the knowledge produced into action by theoretical reflexivity: this is what I have called "critical participation." Knowledge obtained through processes of mere observation or data collected upon the unsound assumption of ontological "objectivity" is ultimately alienated knowledge. (Rigby 1985:46)

There is more: the method also claims links with structuralism.

> The overall framework that I attempt to employ derives also from a Marxist epistemology. Structuralist and Marxist *methodologies* (whatever they may be as "Philosophical movements") are essentially complementary, since both postulate that the "reality" of social processes (structures and their transformations) is not manifestly accessible to the senses; rather, it is composed of a finite number of systematic, dialectical interrelationships which can only be arrived at by an analysis that "gets behind" the manifestation of social relations in any society (or social formation) at particular historical conjunctures, and also reveals the generation of new structural relations over time. (Rigby 1985:49)

That is a lot of references. What do they mean in workable terms? Certainly, a pastoral economy might illustrate a magnificent order of social and political obligations. But how can one know it? From the supposed certainty of the Cartesian cogito, such a knowledge is problematic. Indeed, it is possible to image a we-subject, a kind of collective body of consciousness. What is it really? The constituent individualities cannot be but tensions of an in-itself (a *res*, a thing) and a for-itself (a *res cogitans*, or consciousness). Thus, contrary to what Sartre expounded in his *Critique of Dialectical Reason*, the nightmare about the impossible union remains. It brings about two extreme yet very ordinary temptations. On the one hand, solipsism springs from my incapacity of thinking of myself as consciousness and of thinking simultaneously from within another's consciousness. Thus, a quite logical madness could impose itself upon me: since the existence of the other is ontologically an impossibility (see Sartre 1956), he or she does not exist. All colonialisms and imperialisms are predicated on a similar rational madness. They have been justifying themselves as means of bringing to life and to light the nonexistent other, or the incipient other who was still at the phase of an in-itself. Their normative policies used to expound ways and techniques of "inventing" a for-itself for the in-itself. What I am suggesting here is an immense paradox: there is a relation of congruence between the philosophical solipsism born from the Cartesian cogito and the expansion of the European space which actualized the conditions of possibility for arranging reasons and processes of converting non-Western peoples, reducing them to a European historicity, and promoting a universal will to truth.

On the other hand, the solidity of the cogito cannot resist and sustain itself vis-à-vis the existential presence of the other (Theunissen 1986). To negate the fact would be also, to use Schopenhauer's expression, sheer madness. Indeed, the other can always remind me of and prove the power and excesses of his or her liberty: rape, slavery, colonization are not only metaphors. They illustrate well Sartre's scandalous but pertinent statement in *No Exit:* "You remember all we were told about the torture-chambers, the fire and brimstone, the burning marl. Old wives' tales! There is no need for red-hot pokers. Hell is—other people!" In this experience of the violence that the other's existence can represent, it is the other's being and obvious existence that comes to light.

A threshold establishes itself, and I can, from this mysterious frontier, postulate the evidence of the other by conceiving in an empathic move which, negating the other's existence as my hell, assures my own I as the other. This reversal of the cogito suggested by Rousseau, in his *Discourse on the Origin and Foundation of Inequality,* would symbolize, as thinks Claude Lévi-Strauss, the best road to one's acceptance of oneself and "the goal assigned to human knowledge by the ethnologist" (Lévi-Strauss 1976:36). "What Rousseau means," writes Lévi-Strauss, "is that there exists a 'he' who 'thinks' through me and who first causes me to doubt whether it is I who am thinking [a surprising truth, before psychology and ethnology made us more familiar with it]. To Montaigne's 'What do I know?' (from which everything stems), Descartes believed it possible to answer that 'I know that I am, since I think.' To this Rousseau retorts with a 'What am I?' without a definite solution, since the question presupposes the completion of another more essential one: 'Am I?' Intimate experience provides only this "he" which Rousseau discovered and which he lucidly undertook to explore" (Lévi-Strauss 1976:37).

This experience manifests the pertinence of the identification with the other which, founding anthropology as a means of speaking about the other, brings to light a startling truth: the discourse on the other is essentially a discourse on oneself and one's own memory (see, e.g., Pagden 1982). But should one deduce "the end of the *Cogito*" from the value and the strength of this paradigm, as Lévi-Strauss noted (1976:38)? It would suffice to observe that the significance of the "I as an other" stems from two symbolic operations which transcend two logical principles, that of identity and that of noncontradiction. As Lévi-Strauss writes, "The process of language reproduces, in its way and on its plane, the process of humanity. The first stage is that of identification, here that of *the literal sense* and *the figurative sense;* the true name gradually comes out of *the metaphor which merges each being with other beings*" (Lévi-Strauss 1976:38–39).

We are dealing with a metaphoric terrain, that is, a space in which meaning is produced out of something else. What this space represents might seem to upset a philosophical tradition and its language. I do not see it ending the cogito. To refer to Maurice Merleau-Ponty's phenomenology, the true cogito or the origin of truth is a perceiving I (a *percipio*) who stands beneath or behind the thinking I (the cogito). It is a subject who does not, cannot, coincide nor identify with what it thinks. Let me quote Descombes' remarkable synthesis. "If the 'I' harbours an impersonal subject (as one sees, 'one is born,' as 'one begins'), then the same holds good for the 'we,' and this anonymous collective mind bridges the gulf that separates the *in-itself* and the *for-itself.*" In his inaugural lecture at the College de France in 1953, Merleau-Ponty said: "The theory of the sign, as elaborated by linguistics, may imply a theory of historical meaning which can cut across the alternative of *things* of *consciousness.* . . . Saussure may well have sketched a new philosophy of history."

Merleau-Ponty was probably the first to have actually demanded a philosophy from the *Course in General Linguistics.* Here he invokes its structuralism against Sartrian dualism. Ten years later, others (among them Lévi-Strauss) would invoke Saussure as they phased phenomenology into retirement (Descombes 1980:71). In any case, the I and the other seem to meet, reflecting and inventing each other in an anthropological locus. As Merleau-Ponty put it himself:

> The other, then, is a generalized I. He has his place not in objective space, which, as Descartes has said, is without mind, but in that anthropological "locality," that ambiguous space where nonreflective perception moves at its ease, though always on the margin of reflection, impossible to constitute, always already constituted. We find the other the same way we find our body. As soon as we look him in the face, the other is reduced to the modest condition of something innocent that one can hold at a distance. Moreover, he exists in the back of us, just as things acquire their absolute independence on the margin of our visual field. (1973:138)

> Myself and the other are like two *nearly* concentric circles which can be distinguished only by a slight and mysterious slippage. This alliance is perhaps what will enable us to understand the relation to the other that is inconceivable if I try to approach him directly, like a sheer cliff. . . .
> I make the other in my own image, but how *can there be for me an image of myself?* Am I not to the very end of the universe, am I not, by myself, coextensive with everything I can see, hear, understand, or feign?

How could there be an outside view upon this totality which I am? From where could it be had? Yet, that is just what happens when the other appears to me. To the infinity that was me something else still adds itself; a sprout shoots forth, I grow; I give birth, this other is made from my flesh and blood and yet is no longer me. How is that possible? How can the *cogito* emigrate beyond me, since it is me? (1973:134)

It could be remarked here how it becomes easy to understand the force of Rigby's methodological presuppositions and why his fusion of phenomenology and structuralism is sound despite its strangeness. It is, indeed, very strange from a Francophone viewpoint. But this combination of Marxism, phenomenology, and structuralism is quite logical (see Copans 1978). Where there had been traditionally a discourse of tension inherited from the Cartesian dualism (spirit versus matter, soul versus body) and its representations which have socialized the oppositions by transmuting them into cultural and historical metaphors (primitiveness unveiling the brutish being of the in-itself, and civilization coinciding with the liberty of the for-itself), phenomenologists have brought about a unifying interworld in which history speaks from language and its symbols; and structuralism has been interrogating the foundation of the dualism, its meaning and both the symbolic and political value of its social metaphorizations.

Marxism and an African Locus

Precisely because the major points made by Sartre, Merleau-Ponty, and Lévi-Strauss are very clear and often in conflict, they constitute problems that cannot be ignored when one decides to bring together their inspirations. For example, if, as Husserl and Merleau-Ponty thought, there is a *Sinngenesis* (genesis of meaning) which alone can teach us what the doctrine means, where can one find it in the practice of anthropology? What is the *body* of the history we should worry about according to Merleau-Ponty's reading of Marx? In the preface to his *Phenomenology of Perception,* he, indeed, writes that "it is true, as Marx says, that history does not walk on its head, but it is also true that it does not think with its feet. Or one should say rather that it is neither its 'head' nor its 'feet' that we have to worry about, but its body." In any case, on which basis can one reconcile the extreme subjectivism of phenomenology with the extreme objectivism of the Marxist method?

Interestingly enough, Rigby is magnificently clear in the manner in which he links his "phenomenology" to "Marxism" and "structuralism":

I have already argued that the application of phenomenological methodology in sociological and anthropological research can yield data which are essentially amenable to both structuralist and Marxist analysis. When Diamond, in an interesting but in many ways misguided critique of Lévi-Strauss, says the latter "had substantially dismissed phenomenology in *Tristes Tropiques,*" he is seriously in error. The critical interconnection between structuralist analysis and phenomenology has been admirably demonstrated by Boon . . . and Lewis . . . , among others. We may also note in passing that Lévi-Strauss dedicated his book, *La pensée sauvage* . . . , to Maurice Merleau-Ponty, and the common ground between structuralism and phenomenology in their mutual relationship to Gestalt psychology has frequently been indicated. . . .

The "debate" between Lévi-Strauss' "dialectical anthropology" and Jean-Paul Sartre's historical materialism is *not* representative of either structuralist views on history or Marxist views on structuralism. . . . Much of what antagonizes some Marxists in structuralism has been shown by Garaudy to be somewhat idiosyncratic in the work of Lévi-Strauss, rather than an integral element in structuralist methodology itself, although Garaudy may oversimplify to some extent. Lévi-Strauss . . . himself has certainly gone far in reconciling his views with Marxist criticism, in that he considers structuralist and Marxist methodologies as complementary.

Perhaps the clinching argument in all this debate, in support of the essential complementarity and compatibility of Marxism and structuralism, is provided by Maurice Godelier's brilliant article, "Système, structure, et contradiction dans *Le Capital.*" . . . Having noted that, "When Marx assumes that structure is not to be con ˑˑed with visible relations and explains their hidden logic, he inaugurates u. .nodern structuralist tradition," Godelier . . . goes on to demonstrate in a most convincing way how Lévi-Strauss' analysis of the Murngin kinship system . . . and his overall concept of social structure . . . are essentially comparable methodologically with historical materialism. . . .

Perhaps the part of Godelier's argument that is the most strikingly relevant to the present analysis is his concluding discussion of the nature and role of kinship relationships in societies with a relatively low level in the development of productive forces. The problem is, "How, within Marx's perspectives, can we understand both the *dominant role* of kinship and the *determinant role* of the economy in the last instance?" Godelier concludes that a solution to this problem is impossible "if economy and kinship are treated as base and superstructure." (Rigby 1985:50–52)

First, about Diamond's statement, I am really sorry, but it is Diamond who is right. Lévi-Strauss not only dismisses phenomenology in *Tristes Tropiques,* but he positively insults it (see Lévi-Strauss 1977:42–53). In the conclusion of *The Naked Man* it is "philosophy" which is rejected. That *La Pensée sauvage* is dedicated to Merleau-Ponty is a sign of contradiction in a philosopher converted to anthropology who, although hating philosophy, illustrates it in a most admirable manner. This should, indeed, vindicate Rigby's argumentation.

Claude Lévi-Strauss is very candid about this in his preface to *The Savage Mind*. He writes:

> No one will suppose that, by placing the name of Maurice Merleau-Ponty on the first page of a book whose final chapter is devoted to a work of Sartre, I have intended to oppose them to one another. Those who were close to Merleau-Ponty and myself during recent years know some of the reasons why it was natural that this book which develops freely certain themes of my lectures at the *Collège de France* should be dedicated to him. It would have been, in any case, had he lived, as the continuation of a dialogue whose opening goes back to 1930 when, in company with Simone de Beauvoir, we were brought together by our teaching activities, on the eve of receiving our final degrees. And, since death has torn him from us, may this book at least remain devoted to his memory as a token of good faith, gratitude and affection. (Lévi-Strauss 1966)

Second, thank God, Rigby can well identify a Marxist crux. If kinship were to be postulated as having a dominant role in the Ilparakuyo context, would this mean and imply that the economic space (defined by the dialectic between processes of production and social relations of production) would cease to have a determinant role in the last instance? By conceiving kinship more in terms of age-sets than in terms of relations of production, Rigby avoids facing the anti-Marxist character of his deduction: "Ilparakuyo . . . do not mean or represent exploitative relations of any kind; rather, they creatively represent relations of interdependence. . . . If these relations are exploitative in the current political economy of Ilparakuyo and the religious and symbolic structures involved have been transformed into such exploitative relations . . . they are the result of the colonial political economy, and do not have roots in an aggressive and exploitative precolonial, pre-capitalist situation" (Rigby 1985:64). What a wonderful Rousseauist picture! Indeed — and should we buy it? — colonialism is the only experience that could have induced exploitative violence from those peaceful social relations of production! But let us look carefully at the reasoning which makes possible such a conclusion. First, it insists that "Ilparakuyo belong historically and culturally to the eastern (or southern) Nilotic peoples of Eastern Africa, as do, of course, the pastoral Maasai" (Rigby 1985:52). Right. Second, Rigby invokes Southall's analysis of Eastern Nilotic age organization, particularly his interpretation according to which "where segmentary lineage organization is the major organizational principle . . . , there is no need for an elaborate structure of cross-cutting symbolic oppositions and identifications. Not only is there no need, but there is *nothing in the system likely to give rise to them*'' (Rigby 1985:52). Good. Yet how could one know that there is nothing in the system which might bring about these transformations and from the efficiency of which truthful grid? Third, the conclusion imposes itself if we were to follow Rigby: ''Hence, at similar level of the forces of production, where kinship relations for various . . . reasons, do not 'function as relations of production,' age-organization and symbolic dual organization do. Southall concludes, 'We do not therefore argue that age organization and segmentary lineage structure are incompatible, but the full and *dominant* development of the one is incompatible with the other' ''(Rigby 1985:52).

How Marxist this whole reasoning is (and consequently the socialist propositions expounded by the book) becomes an interesting question. That is the point I have been trying to make by taking a literalistic Marxist position. My aim was not to show how problematic Rigby is as a Marxist but instead to think about observable limitations of the Marxist method.

The problem is important and, I think, I should here specify the context from which I am speaking. I respect Marxism as a scientific method and discourse in its own right. Since the 1960s, when I was introduced to it, I have been trying to be serious about its demands and at the same time critical about its application. A member of the French Communist party, Yves Bénot, apropos of one of my novels written and finished in 1966 (*Entre les eaux,* Paris, 1973), insulted me in *La Pensée,* giving me the best compliment I could imagine. My knowledge of Marxism, despite or because of my credentials (I guess he knew that I got it principally from Althusserian seminars at Louvain), was too suspect to be trusted. He lumped the imaginary dream of a novel with Catholic anti-Communist programs which then were opposing socialist projects. He forgot or did not want to acknowledge that in Catholic circles I was seen as a Communist mole. The gratuitous naughtiness of all this stopped me from working with friends who were members of the Belgian or the French Communist party. More important, I began to interrogate Marxist dogmatist applications and their normative representations. In Africa, and about Africa, it was already clear that something was wrong, and fundamentally controversial. The debate on the Asiatic and lineage modes of production was a sign. The rewriting of African history by such Marxist luminaries as E. Sik (1963–65) and J. Suret-Canale (1961) was not convincing. African socialisms were a mystification and everyone knew it (Jewsiewicki 1985). Even the uprisings of peasants and rural peoples in Cameroon and in the Congo constituted a painful challenge for Marxist paradigms (e.g., Verhaegen 1969). I was in Kwilu (Congo) in 1964 and 1965 during the insurrection and can elaborate on its structural contradictions.

I am not a "professional" anti-Marxist. Moreover, what I question has nothing to do with the generosity, sincerity, and intelligence of those—such as Nyerere and Senghor—who promoted the African indigenization and dubious acculturation of Marxism. The problem and the reason of our failure was that all of us (Africans and Europeans, Communists and Marxists) thought in the 1960s that Africa was an absolutely virgin terrain on which we could experiment and succeed in organizing socialist societies. We were wrong in ignoring how colonialism, which had "invented" these societies in the nineteenth century, had also powerfully linked them to international capitalism.

From this background, Rigby's Marxism is romantically beautiful. I believe that two or three centuries from now some students of the African continent will find in his project a flavor and a beauty similar to what we are nowadays rediscovering in Rousseau's anthropology, thanks to Lévi-Strauss. That said, it is clear that Rigby could integrate today in his analysis another strand of evidence: the rules of historical transformation of modes of production as formulated by Marx constitute a hypothesis, and there is no reason to apologize about its shortcomings. That Rigby should struggle in order to prove theoretically and empirically that at certain levels kinship relations do not operate as relations of production and, at the same time, demonstrate at length that Ilparakuyo age-set and dual organization replace them (and thus should be integrated as variables of social relations of production in the analytic grid) is a problem which challenges Marxism as a universal science and not Rigby's reading of an African locus.

On the other hand, Rigby's critique of idealist models that have so far dominated Africanist discourses underscores the productivity of a Marxist evaluation of the history of African anthropology. In his chapter "History and Time," he carefully demonstrates the weaknesses and ideological preconceptions of theories on concepts of time. He singles out four approaches: the abstract mentalism represented by Lucien Lévy-Bruhl, the abstract empiricism of functionalism, the structural totalization based on analogical comparisons with linguistics as in Leach's studies, and finally the philosophical-theological orientation of Mbiti and other African scholars. They seem all to represent anti-Marxist stances and very subtly contribute to the controversial thesis of the ahistoricity of African experience of time.

Rigby's analysis of these trends is masterful. I shall emphasize here the perspectives of three writers (Lévy-Bruhl, Evans-Pritchard, and Mbiti) and indicate how in their conceptual stammerings they fuse in a scandalous hypothesis which still dominates the whole of African studies. Lévy-Bruhl manipulated and articulated "primitive" experiences as constituting a zero point of both a history of humankind and a chronology of knowledge. For him, the truth of Cartesian themes accounted for the immediacy and validity of his logical keys, specifically the principles of identity, noncontradiction and *tiers-exclu*. They confirmed the axiom according to which human nature is not identical through time (nor through space). His masterpiece, *Les Fonctions mentales dans les sociétés inférieures* (1911), claims to demonstrate this by elaborating on a primitive mentality completely governed by a natural determinism and thus different in nature from a philosophy ruled by logic. Lévy-Bruhl's work is generally singled out as the prototype of ethnocentrism and, despite his recantation (1949), as the best illustration of methodological reductionism. His hypotheses and theses have an intellectual context well qualified by Bergson in a brilliant metaphor: European logic is one which is adapted to schemata of acting and manipulating things in an Euclidean space. It is in the general configuration of such beliefs and ideas that, by subordinating a mentality to a philosophy, Lévy-Bruhl thought he could solve two problems, the question of human origin and that of a chronology of processes of knowledge. This was an extremely complex endeavor (that other scholars, such as Blondel, Durkheim, and Mauss, were facing from other presuppositions), if we accept Michel Foucault's proposition that there was then an alignment between human chronology (thus, biological evolution) and the human experience of things (thus, knowledge) and that, although the two are dependent upon each other, they could not be but fundamentally irreconcilible. As he put it, "This thought [on origin] brings into a final light and, as it were, into an essentially reticent clarity, a certain stratum of the original in which no origin was in fact present, but in which *man's time* (which has no beginning) made manifest, for a possible memory, the *time of things* which has no memory" (my emphasis, Foucault 1973:333). At least two temptations could impose themselves: a radical critique of positivism and a psychologization of knowledge. Indeed, Lévy-Bruhl psychologizes and brings about what Hountondji has rightly perceived and called an "ethnopsychology," that is, an atemporal rationale for primitive acts and deeds (Hountondji 1983b). Lévy-Bruhl's problematics simplified themselves by reducing the *primitive* to the time of things (that is, the silence of an in-itself, the inactual), considered as both a diseased, poor reflection of origins and the impossible memory of the civilized or historical for-itself.

Therefore, to lump together Lévy-Bruhl, Mauss, and Durkheim (as does Needham) is, to say the least, misleading. To claim, as Needham also adds, that Lévy-Bruhl "effectively inaugurated a comparative epistemology" (Rigby 1985:70) does not address the real issue: the "ratio" from which Lévy-Bruhl psychologizes about "primitive" experiences and utterances. Rigby correctly notes: "Both Lévy-Bruhl and Needham, following in the footsteps of the same philosophical tradition, fail to apprehend the fundamental epistemological break represented by Marx's much earlier critique of Hegel and Feuerbach, as it uncomfortably involves a self-critique of the historical and sociological grounds for their own ratiocination about time and other 'things' " (Rigby 1985:71). I shall add two points. First, the conceptual grid of Lévy-Bruhl magnifies as paradigm a reference which is both biological and psychological, as does Durkheim's grid. In comparing different systems, they can thus sort out gaps and comment on deviations (social pathologies, prelogical mentalities, primitive and morbid beliefs, etc.) that the normativity of the paradigm has strictly postulated and invented a priori. Second, the epistemological break represented by Marx has promoted a new model, an economic one, in which the concept of conflict becomes the major paradigm, and at least in principle, this new model weakens the pertinence of functional classifications (see Foucault 1973:344–73).

That functionalism, even in its most celebrated achievements, would still illustrate Lévy-Bruhl's perspective should not surprise a Marxist like Rigby. Apropos of categories of time bestowed by Evans-Pritchard upon the Nuer ("structural time," which is "entirely progressive," and "ecological time," which is "only progressive within an annual cycle," etc.), Rigby writes: "Evans-Pritchard strays, perhaps unconsciously, into Lévy-Bruhlian territory. In the middle of an incredibly rich ethnographic description, he suddenly states: 'Though I have spoken of time and units of time, it must be pointed out that, strictly speaking, the Nuer have no concept of time and, consequently, no developed abstract system of time reckoning' " (Rigby 1985:72). And after a brief analysis of Beidelman's perception of Kaguru time, Rigby concludes: "In sum, Beidelman and Evans-Pritchard, while not explicitly postulating a notion of 'primitive mentality' in the Lévy-Bruhlian sense, and differing in their notions of 'structural time,' both present us with an analysis of temporal concepts in which comparisons are made with a given notion of 'our' time, i.e., the time concepts of 'western' philosophical and 'scientific' investigation; but the implications of this comparison are not explored" (Rigby 1985:73).

Beidelman has recently published a book, *Moral Imagination in Kaguru Modes of Thought* (1986), in which he observes the impact of Arabic and European systems and chooses "to present some of the ways that Kaguru traditionally imagined the connections between different natural and social sequences of events and activities, and how these patterns relate to the other sides of Kaguru life and beliefs" (Beidelman 1986:84). There is nothing wrong in such a self-imposed limitation, which after a careful interpretation of data leads Beidelman to conclude that "Kaguru imagine time not in any abstract sense, such as Western intellectuals project it from time to time. Rather, and quite sensibly, they view it in terms of the events that fill it and the space in which these events take place" (Beidelman 1986:102). About Evans-Pritchard's connection with Lévy-Bruhl, I shall be brief and very clear. Here are three quotations from Evans-Pritchard:

> I think I may claim to be one of the few anthropologists here or in America who spoke up for him [Lévy-Bruhl], not because I agreed with him, but because I felt that a scholar should be criticized for what he said, and not for what he is supposed to have said. (Evans-Pritchard 1980:81)

> From my talks with him, I would say that in this matter, he [Lévy-Bruhl] felt himself in a quandary. For him, Christianity and Judaism were also superstitions, indicative of prelogical and mystical mentality, and on his definitions necessarily so. But, I think *in order not to cause offence, he made no allusion to them.* So he excluded the mystical in our own culture as rigorously as he excluded the empirical in savage cultures. (my emphasis, Evans-Pritchard 1980:95)

> How often have we been warned not to try to interpret the thought of ancient or primitive peoples in terms of our own psychology, which has been moulded by a set of institutions very different from theirs—by Adam Ferguson, Sir Henry Maine, and others, *including Lévy-Bruhl, who in this respect might be said to be the most objective of all the writers about primitive mentality.* (my emphasis, Evans-Pritchard 1980:109)

Evans-Pritchard's admiration for Lévy-Bruhl is a fact (see also Evans-Pritchard 1934). His critical objections which are strong go well along with a defense of Lévy-Bruhl's perspective. As he wrote himself: "For various reasons most writers about primitive peoples had tended to lay stress on the similarities, or what they supposed to be the similarities, between ourselves and them; and Lévy-Bruhl thought it might be as well, for a change, to draw attention to the differences" (Evans-Pritchard 1980:80). Evans-Pritchard's books on Azande and Nuer magnificently illustrate such a methodological *parti-pris*. Rigby is, I am afraid, too prudent when he states that "Evans-Pritchard strays, perhaps unconsciously, into Lévy-Bruhlian territory" (1985:72). Evans-Pritchard and Lévy-Bruhl share the same epistemological configuration and its functional presuppositions and speak the same language.

It is surprising that John Mbiti would actualize Lévy-Bruhl's ideas in his analysis of "African concepts of time." Yet, Rigby's critique is right.

> [Mbiti] maintains that "according to traditional concepts, time is a two-dimensional phenomenon, with a *long past,* a *present,* and virtually *no future*" (his emphasis). His generalization turns out to be based upon his understanding of the tense structures of two Bantu languages, Kikamba and Gikuyu, which in turn is further linguistically expanded into the Kiswahili concepts of *sasa* ("the now period") and *zamani* ("the long past"). The latter period has its own "past," "present," and "future." Mbiti's contention that "African" concepts of time encompass no *definite* future beyond six months to two years, and no *indefinite* future at all, is strongly suggestive of Lévy-Bruhlian influence. It has already been refuted for the Tiv by Bohannan . . . and it is unsupportable in numerous other cases. Despite the interesting and informative complexity of Mbiti's overall analysis, there *is a total lack of historical context in his discussion;* and explanatory comparison is further confounded by references to the lack in "African traditional thought" of concepts of history moving "towards a future climax, or towards an end of the world." *Why* anyone should wish to postulate history as moving towards an end of the world as a condition for a historical concept of the past and the future is a question not examined by Mbiti. (Rigby 1985:75)

Now all this analysis of Mbiti would not have been a serious matter coming from someone without Rigby's authority. Mbiti's general schema has caught the imaginations of a great number of people, principally outside African intellectual circles. To my dismay, I have been discovering during these last years uncritical echoes of Mbiti's model even in some colleagues' papers, and I would suspect that by now there are some university departments in which Mbiti's conception is canonical. There are reasons for this success. The credentials of the author (both intellectual and nationalist) and the comparatist juxtaposition of three African languages give credibility to the model. Its clarity, apparent coherence, and general correspondence with affirmations of functionalist anthropology, as well as its legibility (compared with technical studies on categories of time and grammatical tenses made by specialists of African languages), assured its circulation and intellectual impact and made it believable.

In any case, Rigby is fundamentally right in denouncing the incoherence that Lévy-Bruhl's influence still permits:

> It can be stated without too much distortion that all of these anthropological and philosophical approaches to the understanding of time and temporal concepts, even when they do make reference to "historical" time and the nature of historical reality, treat the latter as a separate dimension of time; a separate

"entity" which may, or more often may not, be like "our" conception of history, which is taken as a self-evident truth. History is thus treated as either non-existent in African (and other so-called "primitive") societies, or as an analytically distinct conceptual element amongst other such elements in "cosmology" of time. There is seldom any attempt to place all these elements or "levels" of time reckoning, even where their existence is noted, in a total and specific historicity arising from the nature of the specific social formation under consideration, which in turn is itself a product of that specific historical development. (Rigby 1985:75)

Here one could also choose to meditate on Mbiti's case and its significance. His whole enterprise can be defined as simultaneously political and religious. One should relate his well-known *African Religions and Philosophy* (1969) to his lesser-known *New Testament Eschatology in an African Background* (1971), an offshoot of his doctorate at Cambridge, which had made the first book possible. In both books, one finds two guiding theses which are political postulations: the cultural unity of African cultures (a reconstitution of pan-Africanism) and the metaphoric investment of the African past into Christian eschatology (which redescribes the secret of revelation). Philosophy is then conceived as a foundation for responsible action. The project is difficult, but appealing. The African present (*sasa*) can be cleansed in the biblical God's revelation (whose signs were already there in a localized tradition or *zamani*). It is promoted into a modernity to be invented which should be capable of creating its cultural and regional consciousness. By sprinkling his demonstration with pan-Africanist themes, Mbiti safeguards his argument from any critique from empiricist researchers. To question it would seem to be politically suspect. On the other hand, by inserting the being of the African present condition into a mythical African future which is an absolute "eschatological" and "Christian" emergence, he pretends not to confuse it with European history and thus achieves a nationalist dream which challenges the African past as the invention of today and interrogates European ethnocentrism from its own Christian basis.

That Lévy-Bruhl's dichotomy might be here operating silently should be obvious. The passivity of a vague *zamani* vis-à-vis a quasi inexistent future could authorize such a deduction. From a Marxist viewpoint, no doubt, the topographical politics and its objectives are idealist. Mbiti, I would suspect, is a great theologian. He is not much of a linguist, and in any case, his project does not seem really similar to those of anthropologists, particularly functionalists. Yet I personally see in it the potential for a radical departure which might be helpful even to Marxism. Mbiti would probably admit that his model does not oppose the possibility of thinking in African contexts about the complementarity of historicities such as those described by Paul Ricoeur (1974:46) and which I tend to think are present in all human cultures. There is, first, the historicity of founding events, which mixes mythical and historical experiences of all human beginnings and developments. Then comes, at a second level, the historicity of discourses on a living tradition which comment upon and actualize genealogies, seasonal and temporal habits, cycles of rituals, order and disorder, and the meaning of the regional domestic economies. Finally, there is the historicity of hermeneutics, that is, of a discourse such as Mbiti's (or Rigby's), which after locating (wrongly or rightly; that is a different issue) social signs of a tradition, tries to make them speak.

I am, personally, immensely grateful to Rigby. He forced me to rethink in the field of African social science the links between emancipatory project and scientific rationality, individual autonomy and the priority of a critical self-reflection. His own scrupulous, yet utopian, investment in Marxism bears witness to the usefulness of reformulating new requirements and principles of practical action, as well as both the principle of the requirements and the epistemological exigencies of the principle.

It has become obvious that beyond the dichotomy entertained by evolutionists, Lévy-Bruhl's and Evans-Pritchard's disciples, between rudimentary and scientific knowledge, illusion and truth, there is another problem concerning the very conditions of knowledge. Most of us would agree with Michel Foucault that two steps should be distinguished. On the one hand, there is the fact of necessary distinctions about the truth itself: ''a truth that is of the same order as the object—the truth that is gradually outlined, formed, stabilized, and expressed through the body and the rudiments of perceptions''; ''the truth that appears as illusions''; and ''a truth that is of the order of discourse—a truth that makes it possible to employ, when dealing with the nature of history of knowledge, a language that will be true'' (Foucault 1973:320). Such distinction should have a universal application. On the other hand, there is an important question that concerns the status of a true discourse. As noted by Foucault, ''Either this true discourse finds its foundation and model in the empirical truth whose genesis in nature and in history it retraces, so that one has an analysis of the positivist type . . . , or the true discourse anticipates the truth whose nature and history it defines . . . , so that one has a discourse of the eschatological type'' (Foucault 1973:320).

The predicament as well as the real significance of the so-called crisis of social sciences in general and African studies in particular is here. As Verhaegen saw it (1974), it resides in the tension between the claim and will to truth of empirical discourses (in which supposedly reality determines the credibility and objectivity of the discourse) and the claims of eschatological discourses (in which the value of a hope and promise is supposed to actualize a truth in the process of fulfilling its being). As noted by Foucault, in this tension, Marxism comes in contact with phenomenology and posits the human being as a disturbing object of knowledge. More prosaically, one also discovers that Auguste Comte and Karl Marx witness to an epistemological configuration in which "eschatology (as the objective truth proceeding from man's discourse) and positivism (as the truth of discourse defined on the basis of the truth of the object) are indissociable" (Foucault 1973:320–21).

The awareness that Rigby's book brings about imposes itself as an epistemological demand. Most African Marxist projects ignore the complexity of their own epistemological roots and thus erase the paradoxes of their own discourse and practice. On the other side, non-Marxist works, by ignoring history (as a framework of their own discourses and the conflicting historicities of their "objects" of knowledge), tend to privilege the allegory of closed, nonexistent societies reduced to mythical pasts; or, as in the case of Mbiti's project, they postulate a subjunctive mood (Que je sois! Que l'Afrique soit!) accounted for by an uncritical leap out of history into a Christian eschatology.

I have questioned Rigby's Marxism. Yet he is fundamentally right in insisting on the fact that there is a relation of necessity between the practice of social science and politics. One might oppose his political deductions, but there is no way of ignoring their significance and the evidence they unveil: the cost (or price) of social mythologies (development, modernization, etc.) invented by functionalism, applied anthropology, colonialism is such that a redefinition of the anthropological practice should be isomorphic with that of our political expectations and actions. Here again, contrary to what one might think, a realistic analysis shows that in the long run, the issue seems both real and very probably universal. In effect, the "performance principle" and its capitalist paradigms of unlimited expansion and development may become very soon problematic and so costly that realistic alternatives should be found.

In any case, we should thank Rigby for reminding us, in a magnificent fashion, of this basic lesson. The anthropologist's action and confession (that we consider scientific knowledge) spatializes a place. If there is in it any truth, this should be accounted for by its isomorphism with a basic construct made of dreams and traces, functioning in the materiality of a locus.

7
Coda

An interpretation of the relation between a lived experience and an oral or written narrative witnessing to it can only be a reduction to a theoretical synthetic unit. It signifies both a simplification of the complexity of the dynamics of the lived in the real place and jumps from the rules of the place to those of an intellectual space in which observed facts and behaviors are submitted to a context of theory and the logic of a scientific discourse and its procedures. This jump constitutes, indeed, a questionable translation of the lived and, simultaneously, aestheticizes it. In effect, the apparent agreement between the two orders actualizes a capacity of ordering the complex dynamics of the place from the viewpoint of a theoretical context. Such an exercise may be a decorative one, as in the case of some post-functionalist Africanist works which have been, since the 1960s, reinterpreting the body of African cultures in an antithetical reaction to the ''masters of primitivism,'' their predecessors. Between these two trends, there is now a third possibility, one that can transcend them and pave the way for possibly going beyond these two extremes.

Since the early 1980s, it is clear that one can think of the possibility of a critical and historical reading of Africanism, as did Alfons J. Smet with his *Histoire de la philosophie africaine* (1980); and even of analyzing the insights of a history of histories of Africanist trends. My *Invention of Africa* (1988) explored this possibility. Most clearly, my dialogue with Peter Rigby illustrates the fact that it is feasible to turn our analyses to the complexity of meanings coming out of aestheticized paradigms and propositions in Africanist discourses.

In this collection of subjective essays, instead of substituting positive images for the negative ones of yesterday that are still actual in today's medias, I chose to expound my own reading and situate it at a very specific level. This level is not one of recording founding events and their supposed objectivity, as anthropologists and African historians claim to do; it is also not the classical level that some Africanist social scientists interrogate, challenge, and reflect upon, about the fundamentals of the African founding events and their intellectual pertinence. I contend that a critical search for and meditation on the meanings coming out of these two preliminary levels is now the best way to understand simultaneously what African cultures are and are not, and on the other hand to face the predicament of scientific investigations in the social and human sciences.

I would hope that my contribution is pertinent. Concretely, I wanted to show that it is almost impossible—even about Africa(s)—to liberate completely a description or an interpretation from a context of methodological debates framed, to refer to Thomas Kuhn, by the analogical model of natural sciences. How then could one postulate a faithful translation of the dynamics of the real place? In my discussion what comes to light most visibly is that, in Africanisms, we have today a critical descriptive function and the possibility of a complex intellectual history of African cultures as well as that of a context from which one, finally, could write a history of histories of African anthropology, history, sociology, philosophy, or theology.

My objective was to reinforce this descriptive function by critically rereading prejudicial and ornamental descriptions of African experiences. For illustrative reasons, I decided to focus on Central Africa and Luba-Songye. What comes out of this choice, now that I can look at it as a definite object, is an obsessive theme on otherness and a statement about the reader, that is, myself. Yet what my text indicates and designates is our common and subjective freedom: we can read and comment about the passions present in transcribed oral traditions, written texts, and performances in African or European languages and, indeed, reconstruct and/or deconstruct the history, arguments, and paradigms of the anthropological and colonial libraries.

Appendix

Bibliography

Index

Appendix
Peter Rigby's Response to "Anthropology and Marxist Discourse"

I wrote my critique of Peter Rigby's book Persistent Pastoralists *(chapter 6) five years ago and submitted it to Peter Rigby. We intended to publish his response along with my critique in an Africanist journal, but we didn't succeed in doing so. (V. Y. Mudimbe)*

First, I must note that your critique has been thoroughly stimulating to me, and will certainly have a strong influence on the future course of my studies on Ilparakuyo society, history, and culture. I am currently working on a second book, to be submitted for publication this summer. I would be most grateful for your comments (if you have the time) on the manuscript; I will send it to you anyway, as soon as it is ready!

Responses to Major Issues

In the following, I will begin by selecting a few of the issues that struck me as the most crucially important for the present and future trajectories of my work; I then conclude with a few notes, comments and queries on statements by specific pages, paragraphs, and lines.

In *Persistent Pastoralists,* I make the point that the work is a product basically of two "intellectual Odysseys," one which took me "into" Ilparakuyo culture and conceptualizations, the other through a number of theoretical problematics. The convergence of these two streams, as far as I could go with them in this book (I trust I will now go further, both because of your critique as well as the problems with which I have been struggling since its publication) led to a number of insights which I attribute specifically to this Odyssey.

By "convergence" I mean precisely that my theoretical movement from functionalism, through structuralism, to historical materialism, is both the *result* and the *cause* of my (claimed) ability to "re-present" (or "interpret") the Ilparakuyo social formation. In other words, the dialectical relation between the illumination given me by my education into Ilparakuyo culture and my adoption of a Marxist problematic is simultaneously analogous to the relation between *praxis* and *theory.* This, perhaps, accounts for what you call my "romantically beautiful" Marxism; but more of that later.

In relation to the issue of the "authenticity" of the cultural knowledge produced, I would not take account of other developments: for example, Fabian's superb rendering of the two mechanisms of "distancing" in anthropology, which exploit respectively the notions of time and place. While it is possible epistemologically to avoid (or reduce to a minimum) the inauthenticity produced by the former, it seems to be virtually impossible to transcend the latter. The inequality, and hence the relation of power, established by both forms of distancing *must* be minimized before there can be a *true* dialectic of theory and practice. The attempt I make in this book to juxtapose (if not fully *integrate*) phenomenology, structuralism and, ultimately, historical materialism, represents an effort to create the *co-evality* essential to the production of authentic knowledge in terms of distancing. As Fabian notes (1983:30), "To recognize *Intersubjective Time* would seem to preclude any sort of distancing almost by definition."

In this regard, I may have achieved partially one of the two conditions to establish authenticity and hence the relation between *theory* and *praxis*. The other, as you point out, is much more perplexing: "the best translation is always a reflection; or, more specifically, a metaphoric construct. . . . What a competent translation such as Rigby's does is not apprehending the *being there,* not even unveiling it, but organizing a reflection, and specifying a commentary, a new order of meaning."

Following your distinction between *place* and *space,* we cannot *but* recognize that a transposition from one to the other involves a distancing; but this is as true for the metapower involved in transforming an *Ilparakuyo* place into "a discursive invented space" as it is in transforming a "*class* place" and the notion of the "privileged knowledge" of the proletariat (Merleau-Ponty, Lukacs, etc.) into the conceptual space of revolutionary theory and *praxis* within *one* (capitalist, bourgeois) social formation and its culture. The possibility of transcending *this* form of distancing-produced power lies only at the level of revolutionary *praxis* itself, and hence *historical* (not epistemological) substantiation?

Although you disagree with Sartre, I am still extremely worried by the implications of your discussion concerning the "rational (but logical) madness" upon which "all colonialism and imperialism are predicted." It is not at all clear to me whether you are commenting upon (including) my work in this "logical madness," or whether you are continuing your interpretation of Sartre?

My attempts to construct an epistemology out of the convergence (or is it a collision?) between the logic of Ilparakuyo history, culture, and apprehension of the *transparency* of socio-political relations in society on the one hand, and a specific form of "Marxist phenomenology" on the other may not achieve the *equality* necessary for authenticity; but I do hope that I have escaped the conditions upon which I may be guilty of *imposing* an Ilparakuyo "For-Itself" upon a "passive" and invented other "In-Itself." If I *am* guilty of this, then I have failed completely in (our) enterprise. I would be grateful if you could clarify these passages dealing with Sartre and Theunissen in relation to *Persistent Pastoralists*. Perhaps you could refer the discussion of this issue to the later context in which you approve my seemingly contradictory fusion (?) of phenomenology, structuralism, and Marxism? I am very glad that you refer to Jean Copans in regard to this issue, since my attempt is, indeed, "very strange from a Francophone viewpoint"! But could we not also ask, surely this "metapower" *emerges from the very act of writing itself* ? Or even from *any* form of "intellectual production"?

Thus, while I stand corrected in that my transposition of Habermas's model of the movement from interpretation to action is insufficiently conscious of its epistemological dangers (and hence its significance), I feel that the problem here is much more general (universal?) than that of discourses created in a conceptual space which is not historically and culturally congruent with the "original locus." But, when I (as Olparakuoni) reject the historical grounds for a (European-imposed) "project for modernity," I am simultaneously rejecting the second of your "two abstract figures," a "European vision of a past (an unnamed savagery)," *as well as* the notion of "an evolutionary process." If this is so, would it not be helpful, when you note that "the future of the Ilparakuyo seems to reside in the rationality and dream of the social scientist" and that "in itself this does not seem to be anything shameful," to specify *who* are the "many" to which "this very statement would appear scandalous"? And although, as you correctly indicate, I have under-theorized the use of the Habermas model at this point in the book, I think that I make up a little for this lapse (in a different way) in later discussion, particularly in the chapter on Time and History; or do you think not?

At any rate, most of this seems unavoidable; and this brings me to that issue of *political commitment*. You raise the question of political commitment and its epistemological implications in a number of places and in different ways, all of which are fundamentally important. First, you ask the question, "Why . . . should a social scientist connect his parental affinity to his scientific practice." And your answer is, "Rigby perceives the question in strictly political terms; he reduces it to a political project. His discourse decodes and recomposes an economy of everyday life and pastoral culture in order to think and propose modalities for a 'socialist transformation.' "

I have two reasons for this. First, the *historical* fact is that contemporary Ilparakuyo and other Maasai communities are part of the political economy of post-colonial states, in one of which, Tanzania, "socialism" is *defined for them* by those who have, in this locus, *power* over both Ilparakuyo *and me,* as Olparakuoni brother (son, etc.) *and* as social scientist, whether or not I am physically *there.* Second, I maintain, from my discussions and involvement in the political *praxis* of Ilparakuyo, that the *goals* of this State are not antithetical to Ilparakuyo or myself, even if we can see that they are applied in the fashion of a misguided and authoritarian discourse and practice so common in many post-colonial states. I deal with this issue in some more detail in several places in my forthcoming book. In Kenya, on the other hand, Maasai are subjected to vastly more Draconian measures under the name of "development," and where the myth of "African socialism" is seen, by Maasai as much as by other Kenyans, to be what it actually is: the commoditization of their means of existence. I return to the implications of this for my work in the Ilparakuyo community and other sections of Maasai.

But you raise the issue of the reflexivity of political commitment in two other contexts, in relation to my critique of Mbiti and the basis of your own authority in discourse upon the nature of Marxist theory and its relevance to Africa. You note correctly that Mbiti's "whole enterprise can be defined as simultaneously *political and religious,*" a position in which there are "two guiding theses which are political postulates: the cultural unity of African cultures (a reconstitution of pan-Africanism); with the metaphoric investment of the African past into Christian eschatology (which redescribes the secret of revelation)." That Mbiti's model has had enormous influence rests upon his authority as theologian, philosopher, and African scholar, so much so that "to question it would seem to be politically suspect." But I think you agree with me that my critique of Mbiti holds *not* because of the claim to existential authority by either party (he or I), but to epistemological differences which *involve* political commitments?

The third context in which you discuss political commitment as crucial to theoretical understanding and epistemology relates to your own position *vis-à-vis* the various *forms* of Marxism and their relevance to Africa. As a result of your own experiences, you begin "to interrogate Marxist *dogmatic applications* and their normative representations" (my emphasis). Certainly, the "dogmatic" Marxism of the Second International and Stalinism was (and is) totally inappropriate for any contemporary applications, whether in the "Third World" *or* in "advanced" capitalism. As Perry Anderson beautifully demonstrates (1984:15–18), these dogmatisms led, in Europe, to a virtually unbridgeable chasm between the *praxis* of communist parties on the one hand, and the *philosophical* discourse of Marxism, "itself centered on questions of method — that is, more episte-mological than substantive in character" (Anderson 1984:16). The epis-temological significance of this philosophical discourse (in the work, e.g., of Adorno, Althusser, Gramsci, Korsch, Lukacs, Marcuse, Bloch, Colletti and, eventually, Sartre) was in creating an historical materialist theory of *cultural processes,* language, and history, a theoretical develop-ment of "brilliance and fertility . . . as if in glittering compensation for their neglect of the structures and infrastructures of politics and economics" (Anderson 1984:17).

The transformations of this philosophical tradition and the rebirth of Marxist political *praxis,* mainly since the 1960's, has two strands: First, within the capitalist West from the late 1960's (in France, Portugal, etc.); and second, in the Third World. Despite the influence of such scholars as Althusser and Sartre upon the latter (the relevance of this being brilliantly assessed by yourself), the European strand of Marxism is at least partially shut out by the continuity of Third World Marxisms of scholars and revolutionaries from the 1920's to the 1940's (e.g., C. L. R. James, Mao, Ho Chi Minh, Cabral, and the mature Nkrumah, for example) up to the contemporary applications by, e.g., Samir Amin, Hountondji, Walter Rodney, Clive Thomas, Mafeje, Nabudere, etc., together with other Blacks of the African diaspora, such as Oliver Cox and Manning Marable. The strength of Marxist *cultural critique* in Africa, as you know, can be seen in the writings of such major figures as Ngugi wa Thiong'o, Sembene Ous-mane, Onoge, Nazareth, and numerous others (see, e.g., Ngara 1985; Gugelberger 1985).

The point of this over-extended digression is that I am not sure what you mean by "a literalistic Marxist position" or "the African indigenization and *dubious* inculturation of Marxism" (my emphasis) as a basis for your otherwise stimulating critique of my own use of an historical materialist problematic. In the light of this, I do not see *why* you have to "defend" yourself by stating that you are "not" a "professional anti-Marxist"?

Perhaps the "romanticism" in *my* Marxism can be traced not only to the deep intellectual and emotional commitment I have for "Ilparakuyo-ness" (or "Maasai-ness," I trust without the colonialist exploitation of the latter as false consciousness), but also to the conviction that at the heart of Marxism lies an essentially "humanistic project," and that its most bril-liant applications are to be seen in the works of such authors as Ngugi wa Thiong'o and Raymond Williams. The real question that arises for me is, can *any* epistemological position *not* involve, or imply, a *political position*? It seems that your need to discuss such a commitment in at least three places would suggest that the answer to this question for both of us is "No"!

More mundanely, let me now list some of the other crucial points from *Persistent Pastoralists* which I attribute to the synthesis of Ilparakuyo consciousness and historical materialism, some of which you most penetratingly rephrase for me in your paper.

1. It is absolutely crucial that, for Ilparakuyo and other pastoralists, the herd be considered a *means of production* and not a product. This has a number of consequences.

2. First, this realization led to debates among my Ilparakuyo brothers, age-mates, friends, and acquaintances of the *absolute* illogicality of the entire range of "development" policies they had experienced from "above," both during the colonial period and in the post-1967 (Arusha Declaration) "socialist" and *ujamaa* period. But it also illuminated, I think, for "all parties," that some *education* for the agents of "development" was urgently required. To some extent, perhaps for the first time in this community, Ilparakuyo saw that "others," the western-educated agents of government policies, could be criticized as *ignorant* (or *mistaken*) in their efforts to bring about change, rather than as being merely "bloody-minded"!

3. This, in turn, opened up debates on the fact that the implementation of *ujamaa vijijini* policies was supposed to come from Ilparakuyo villagers themselves, and not from local government functionaries.

4. All of this involved two things: (a) that there was a *conceptual* problem involved in "bringing about socialism," and (b) that there were grounds to question the unequal *relations of power* between the local community and national-regional government in the post-colonial era. It might be pertinent to note here that, during my 1987 visit home to my Ilparakuyo *enkang'* (homestead), many families were moving *out* of the government-designated villages, with no apparent consequences.

5. You feel that both Ilparakuyo concepts and Marxist theory converge to produce my (perhaps insufficiently elaborated) point about the mode of production, the *nature* of the means of production, and the unique form taken by the lack of "objectification of the world" by Ilparakuyo, other Maasai, and (by extension), other pastoral social formations, and the implications of this for the relative "transparency of social relations" (Rigby 1985:101–3, *et passim*) in Ilparakuyo society. Not only are Ilparakuyo at the *opposite pole* from capitalist society in their "temporary appropriation of the world," in which the concept of "private

property" (or even the very notion of "property" itself) does not arise, but also they can be differentiated on this basis from agricultural and agro-pastoral societies with similar development of the forces of production (a point upon which you comment), thus indicating the "specificity" of pastoralism.

6. These facts have enormous implications for Ilparakuyo and Maasai *Weltanschauungen,* an issue which I explore in more detail in the second volume of Ilparakuyo/Maasai studies now in preparation.

7. I think also that my discussion of time and history would not have been possible without the resolution I derived from Althusser-Balibar on the conditions for the production of specific forms of historicity (Rigby 1985:76–80, *et passim*).

8. Apropos of your comment that "I am not convinced *at all* that Rigby's book is *meaningful* to his Ilparakuyo friends and parents in the manner it might be to his American and English colleagues," I hope that in my responses I have gone some way towards illustrating that it *may* have some meaning to the former. For what it is worth, and although it does not really add to my competence as interpreter and translator of Ilparakuyo-Maasai culture, let me add that I have *always* sought comments from fellow-Ilparakuyo and Maasai on *everything* I write (see Rigby 1985:ix). I have also heard from "reliable sources" that the book is circulating in Tanzania and Kenya Maasai-land, in the latter with some political risk to its readers since the present Kenya regime is, as you know, rabidly anti-Marxist.

References

Anderson, Perry. 1984. *In the Tracks of Historical Materialism.* Chicago: University of Chicago Press.

Bourdieu, Pierre. 1984. *Distinction: A Social Critique of the Judgement of Taste.* Cambridge, Mass.: Harvard University Press.

Fabian, Johannes. 1983. *Time and the Other: How Anthropology Makes its Object.* New York: Columbia University Press.

Gugelberger, Georg M., ed. 1985. *Marxism and African Literature.* Trenton, N.J.: Africa World Press.

Ngara, Emmanuel. 1985. *Art and Ideology in the African Novel: A Study of the Influence of Marxism on African Writing.* London: Heinemann.

Rigby, Peter. 1985. *Persistent Pastoralists: Nomadic Societies in Transition.* London: Zed Books.

Bibliography

Abanda Ndengue, M. J. 1970. *De la négritude au négrisme*. Yaoundé: Clé.

Abraham, W. E. 1962. *The African Mind*. Chicago: University of Chicago Press.

Abu-Lughod, L. 1986. *Veiled Sentiments: Honor and Poetry in a Bedouin Society*. Berkeley: University of California Press.

Actes du Colloque sur la Théologie Africaine. 1969. *Renouveau de l'église et nouvelles églises*. Mayidi.

Adotevi, S. 1972. *Négritude et négrologues*. Paris: Plon.

Agblemagnon, F. N. 1957. "Du 'temps' dans la culture Ewé." *Présence africaine* 14–15:222–32.

Agblemagnon, F. N. 1958. "Personne, tradition et culture." In *Aspects de la culture noire*, 22–30. Paris: Fayard.

Agblemagnon, F. N. 1960. "L'Afrique noire: La Métaphysique, l'éthique, l'évolution actuelle." *Comprendre* 21–22:74–82.

Agblemagnon, F. N. 1962. "Totalités et systèmes dans les sociétés d'Afrique noire." *Présence africaine* 41:13–22.

Allier, R. 1929. *The Mind of the Savage*. London: G. Bell and Sons.

Althabe, G. 1972. *Les fleurs du Congo*. Paris: Maspero.

Althusser, L. 1977. *For Marx*. Norfolk: Thetford Press.

Amselle, J. L. 1976. *Les Migrations africaines*. Paris: Maspero.

Arendt, H. 1968. *Imperialism*. Part 2 of *The Origins of Totalitarianism*. New York: Harcourt Brace Jovanovich.

Asad, T., ed. 1973. *Anthropology and the Colonial Encounter*. London: Ithaca Press.

Asch, S. 1983. *L'Eglise du Prophète Kimbangu*. Paris: Karthala.

Atal, D. 1972. *Structures et signification des cinq premiers versets de l'hymne Johannique*. Kinshasa: Recherches Africaines de Théologie.

Atangana, N. 1971. *Travail et développement*. Yaoundé: Clé.

Avermaet, E. Van. 1954. *Dictionnaire Kiluba-Français*. Tervuren: Koninklijk Museum van Belgisch-Kongo.

Ba, A. H. 1972. *Aspects de la civilisation africaine*. Paris: Présence Africaine.

Ba, A. H. 1976. *Jésus vu par un Musulman*. Dakar-Abidjan: Nouvelles Editions Africaines.

Bahoken, J. C. 1967. *Clairières métaphysiques africaines: Essai sur la philosophie et la religion chez les Bantu de Sud-Cameroun*. Paris: Présence Africaine.

Bal, W. 1963. *Le Royaume du Congo aux XVe et XVIe siècles: Documents d'histoire*. Léopoldville: Institut National d'Etudes Politiques.

Barrett, D. B. 1968. *Schism and Renewal in Africa*. London: Oxford University Press.

Baudrillard, J. 1981. *For a Critique of the Political Economy of the Sign*. St. Louis: Telos Press.

Beauvoir, S. de. 1980. *The Ethics of Ambiguity*. Secaucus, N.J.: Citadel Press.

205

Beidelman, T. O. 1986. *Moral Imagination in Kaguru Modes of Thought*. Bloomington: Indiana University Press.

Bénot, Y. 1975. *Indépendances africaines*. Paris: Maspero.

Bimwenyi, O. 1968. "Le Muntu à la lumière des ses croyances en l'Au-delà." *Cahiers des religions africaines* 8:137–51; 9 (1971):59–112.

Bimwenyi, O. 1980. *Discours théologique négro-africain*. Paris: Présence Africaine.

Bimwenyi, O. 1981. "Inculturation en Afrique et attitude des agents de l'évangélisation." In *Aspects du catholicisme au Zaïre*. Kinshasa: Faculté de Théologie Catholique.

Blier, S. 1982. *Gestures in African Art*. New York: L. Kahan Gallery.

Blyden, E. W. 1967 [1887]. *Christianity, Islam and the Negro Race*. Edinburgh: Edinburgh University Press.

Bontinck, F. 1964. *Brève Relation de la fondation de la mission des Frères Mineurs Capucins de Séraphique Père Saint François au Royaume de Congo*. Publications de l'Université Lovanium de Léopoldville 13. Paris: Béatrice-Nauwelaerts.

Bontinck, F. 1969. "Les deux Bula Matari." *Etudes congolaises* 12, no. 3:83–97.

Bontinck, F. 1970. *Diaire congolaise (1690–1701) de Fra Luca de Caltanisetta*. Louvain: Nauwelaerts.

Bontinck, F. 1972. *Histoire du royaume du Congo*. In *Etudes d'histoire africaine IV*. Louvain: Nauwelaerts.

Bontinck, F., and D. N. Nsasi. 1978. *Le Catéchisme Kikongo de 1624*. Brussels: Académie Royale des Sciences d'Outre-Mer.

Bouillon, A. 1954. "La Corporation des chasseurs Baluba." *Zaïre* 8:563–94.

Bourdieu, P. 1977. *Outline on a Theory of Practice*. Trans. R. Nice. Cambridge: Cambridge University Press.

Bowman, A. A. 1958. *The Absurdity of Christianity and Other Essays*. New York: Liberal Arts Press.

Braudel, F. 1980. *On History*. Chicago: University of Chicago Press.

Brelsford, V. 1935. *Primitive Philosophy*. London: John Bale.

Brelsford, V. 1938. "The Philosophy of the Savage." *Nada* 15:62–65.

Bryan, M. A., comp. 1959. *The Bantu Languages of Africa*. London: Oxford University Press.

Buakasa, T. K. M. 1973. *L'Impensé du discours: Kindoki et nkisi en pays Kongo du Zaïre*. Kinshasa: Presses Universitaires du Zaïre.

Buakasa, T. K. M. 1981. "L'Environment social et culturel du christianisme: Le Zaïre à l'heure de deuxième centenaire de l'église catholique." In *Aspects du catholicisme au Zaïre*, 191–98. Kinshasa: Faculté de Théologie Catholique.

Bujo, B. 1981. "Pour une éthique africano-christocentrique." In *Combats pour un christianisme africain*, 21–32. Kinshasa: Faculté de Théologie Catholique.

Burton, W. F. P. 1961. *Luba Religion and Magic in Custom and Belief*. Tervuren: Musée Royal de l'Afrique Centrale.

Bwanga, A. 1981. "Le Pacte de sang africain." In *Aspects du catholicisme au Zaïre*, 151–90. Kinshasa: Faculté de Théologie Catholique.

Certeau, M. de. 1969. *L'Etranger; ou, L'Union dans la différence*. Paris: Desclée de Brouwer.

Certeau, M. de. 1984. *The Practice of Everyday Life*. Berkeley: University of California Press.

Clifford, J., and G. Marcus. 1986. *Writing Culture: The Poetics and Politics of Ethnography*. Berkeley: University of California Press.

Cohn, N. 1957. *The Pursuit of the Millennium*. London: Secker and Warburg.

Colle, P. 1913. *Les Baluba*. 2 vols. Brussels: Albert Dewitt.

Comaroff, J. L. and S. A. Roberts. 1981. *Rules and Processes: The Cultural Logic of Dispute in an African Context*. Chicago: University of Chicago Press.

Comité-Zaïre. 1978. *Zaïre: Le Dossier de la recolonisation*. Paris: L'Harmattan; Brussels: Editions Vie Ouvrière.

Copans, J. 1978. "A Chacun sa politique." *Cahier d'études africaines* 18, no. 69:93–122.

Coquery-Vidrovitch, C. 1969. *Recherches sur un mode de production africaine. La Pensée* no. 144:61–78.

Craemer, W. de. 1977. *The Jamaa and the Church: A Bantu Catholic Movement in Zaire*. Oxford: Clarendon Press.

Crahay, F. 1965. "Le 'Décollage' conceptuel: Conditions d'une philosophie bantoue." *Diogène* 52:61–84.

Cuvelier, J. 1946. *L'Ancien Royaume du Congo*. Brussels: Desclée de Brouwer.

Cuvelier, J., and L. Jadin. 1954. *L'Ancien Congo d'après les Archives Romaines, 1518–1640*. Brussels: Académie Royale des Sciences Coloniales.

Danquah, J. B. 1968. *The Akan Doctrine of God*. London: Cass.

Davis-Roberts, C. 1980. "Mungu na Mitishambe: Illness and Medicine among the Batabwa of Zaire." Ph.D. diss., University of Chicago, Dept. of Anthropology.

Davis-Roberts, C. 1981. "Kutambuwa Ugonjwua: Concepts of Illness and Transformation among the Tabwa." *Social Science and Medicine* 15B:309–16.

Delcommune, A. 1922. *Vingt années de vie africaine*. 2 vols. Brussels: Larcier.

Deleuze, G., and F. Guattari. 1977. *Anti-Oedipus: Capitalism and Schizophrenia*. Minneapolis: University of Minnesota Press.

De Maret, P., and F. Nsuka. 1977. "History of Bantu Metallurgy: Some Linguistic Aspects." *History in Africa* 4:43–65.

Demunter, Paul. 1972. "Structure de classes et lutte de classes dans le Congo colonial." *Contradictions* (Brussels) January–June: 67–109.

Derrida, J. 1978. *Writing and Difference*. Chicago: University of Chicago Press.

Deschamps, H. 1954. *Les Religions de l'Afrique noire*. Paris: Presses Universitaires de France.

Descombes, V. 1980. *Modern French Philosophy*. Cambridge: Cambridge University Press.

De Sousberghe, L. 1966. "L'Immutabilité des relations de parenté par alliance dans les sociétés matrilinéaires du Congo ex-belge." *L'Homme* 6, no. 1:82–94.

Détienne, M., and J. P. Vernant. 1974. *Les Ruses de l'intelligence: La Métis des Grecs*. Paris: Flammarion.

Deutsch, Karl W. 1968. *Nationalism and Social Communication*. Cambridge: MIT Press.

Diagne, M. 1976. "Paulin J. Hountondji; ou, La Psychanalyse de la conscience ethnophilosophique." *Psychopathologie africaine* 3:xii.

Diagne, P. 1967. *Pouvoir politique traditionnel en Afrique occidentale*. Paris: Présence Africaine.

Diagne, P. 1972. Pour l'unité ouest-africaine. Paris: Anthropos.

Diagne, P. 1981. *L'Europhilosophie face à la pensée du négro-africain*. Dakar: Sankoré.

Dickson, K. A. 1978. "Assumption of African Civilization Values as Christian Values." In *Civilisation noire et église catholique*, 389–402. Paris: Présence Africaine.

Dickson, K. A. 1984. *Theology in Africa*. New York: Orbis.

Dieng, A. L. 1979. *Hegel, Marx, Engels et les problèmes de l'Afrique noire*. Dakar: Sankoré.

Dieng, A. L. 1983. *Contribution à l'étude des problèmes philosophiques en Afrique noire*. Paris: Nubia.

Dieterlen, G. 1951. *Essai sur la religion Bambara*. Paris: Presses Universitaires de France.

Diop, C. A. 1954. *Nations nègres et culture*. Paris: Présence Africaine.

Diop, C. A. 1960a. *L'Afrique noire précoloniale*. Paris: Présence Africaine.

Diop, C. A. 1960b. *Les Fondements culturels, techniques et industriels d'un futur état fédéral d'Afrique noire*. Paris: Présence Africaine.

Diop, C. A. 1960c. *L'Unité culturelle d'Afrique noire*. Paris: Présence Africaine.

Diop, C. A. 1967. *Antériorité des civilisations nègres*. Paris: Présence Africaine.

Diop, C. A. 1981. *Civilisation ou barbarie*. Paris: Présence Africaine.

Donohugh, A., and Berry, P. 1932. "A Luba Tribe in Katanga." *Africa* 5, no. 2:176–83.

Douglas, M. 1963. *The Lele of the Kasai*. London: Oxford University Press.

Douglas, M. 1966. *Purity and Danger*. New York: Praeger.

Douglas, M. 1970. *Natural Symbols: Explorations in Cosmology*. London: Cresset Press.

Douglas, M. 1975. *Implicit Meanings*. London: Routledge and Kegan Paul.

Dubois, J. 1981. "Les Kimbanguistes vus par eux-mêmes." In *Combats pour un christianisme africain*, 127–32. Kinshasa: Faculté de Théologie Catholique.

Dumont, L. 1971. "Religion, Politics and Society in the Individualistic Universe." In *Proceedings of the Royal Anthropological Institute for 1970*. London: Royal Anthropological Institute.

Dupré, G. 1982. *Un Ordre et sa destruction*. Paris: Office de la Recherche Scientifique et Technique Outre-Mer.

Durkheim, E., and M. Mauss. 1963. *Primitive Classification*. Trans. R. Needham. London: Cohen and West.

Eboussi-Boulaga, F. 1968. "Le Bantu Problématique." *Présence Africaine* 66:4–40.

Eboussi-Boulaga, F. 1977. *La Crise du Muntu*. Paris: Présence Africaine.

Eboussi-Boulaga, F. 1981. *Christianisme sans fétiche*. Paris: Présence Africaine.

Elungu, A. P. 1973a. "Authenticité et culture." *Revue zairoise de psychologie et de pédagogie* 2, no. 1:71–74.

Elungu, A. P. 1973b. *Etendue et connaissance dans la philosophie de Malebranche.* Paris: Vrin.

Elungu, A. P. 1977. "La Philosophie, condition du développement en Afrique aujourd'hui?" *Présence africaine* 103:3–18.

Elungu, A. P. 1978. "La Philosophie africaine hier et aujourd'hui." In *Mélanges de philosophie africaine,* 9–32. Kinshasa: Faculté de Théologie Catholique.

Evans-Pritchard, E. E. 1934. "Lévy-Bruhl's Theory of Primitive Mentality." In *Bulletin of the Faculty of Arts.* Egyptian University (Cairo), vol. 2.

Evans-Pritchard, E. E. 1956. *Nuer Religion.* London: Oxford University Press.

Evans-Pritchard, E. E. 1971. *The Azande.* London: Oxford University Press.

Evans-Pritchard, E. E. 1980. *Theories of Primitive Religion.* Oxford: Clarendon Press.

Fashole-Luke, E., ed. 1978. *Christianity in Independent Africa.* Bloomington: Indiana University Press.

Feierman, S. 1973. *The Shambaa Kingdom.* Madison: University of Wisconsin Press.

Fernandez, J. 1978. "African Religious Movements." *Annual Review of Anthropology* 7:198–234.

Fernandez, J. 1982. *Bwiti: An Ethnography of the Religious Imagination in Africa.* Princeton: Princeton University Press.

Finnigan, R. 1970. *Oral Literature in Africa.* Oxford: Oxford University Press.

Fleischman, E. 1970. *Le Christianisme "mis à nu."* Paris: Plon.

Forde, D., ed. 1976. *African Worlds: Studies in the Cosmological Ideas and Social Values of African Peoples.* Oxford: Oxford University Press.

Fortes, M., and G. Dieterlen, eds. 1965. *African Systems of Thought.* London: Oxford University Press.

Foucault, M. 1973. *The Order of Things.* New York: Random.

Foucault, M. 1982. *The Archaeology of Knowledge.* New York: Pantheon.

Fouda, B. J. 1967. *La Philosophie africaine de l'existence.* Ph.D. diss. Université de Lille, Faculté des Lettres.

Fourche, T., and H. Morlighem. 1973. *Une Bible noire.* Brussels: Max Arnold.

Freud, S. 1953–74. *The Complete Psychological Works.* 24 vols. Ed. and trans. J. Strachey. London: Hogarth Press.

Frobenius, L. 1899. *Die Geschichte des afrikanischen Kultur.* Leipzig. (French ed. 1936. *Histoire de la civilisation africaine.* Paris: Gallimard.)

Frobenius, L. 1933. *Kulturgeschichte Afrikas.* Zürich: Phaidon.

Fu-Kiau, A. 1969. *Le Mukongo et le monde qui l'entourait.* Kinshasa: Office National de la Recherche Scientifique.

Furet, F. 1984. *In the Workshop of History.* Chicago: University of Chicago Press.

Ganay, S. de. 1949. "Notes sur la théodicée Bambara." *Revue de l'histoire des religions* 125:187–213.

Ganay, S. de. 1951. "Etudes sur la cosmologie des Dogon et des Bambara du Soudan français." *Africa* 21:20–23.

Girard, R. 1979. *Violence and Sacred.* Baltimore: Johns Hopkins University Press.

Godelier, M. 1977. *Horizons, trajets Marxistes en anthro-pologie.* Paris: Maspero.

Gohring, H. 1970. *BaLuba: Studie zur Selbstzuordnung und Herrschaftsstruktur der baLuba.* Studia Ethnologica 1. Meisenheim am Glan: Hain.

Goody, J. R. 1977. *The Domestication of the Savage Mind.* Cambridge: Cambridge University Press.

Gran, G. 1976. "Policy Making and Historic Process: Zaire's Permanent Development Crisis." Paper presented at the annual meeting of the African Studies Association, Boston, Nov.

Gravrand, H. 1962. *Visage africain de l'église.* Paris: Orante.

Grévisse, F. 1956–58. "Notes ethnographiques relatives à quelques populations autochtones du Haut Katanga Industriel." *Bulletin du Centre d'Etudes des Problèmes Sociaux Indigènes* 32:65–207; 33:68–150; 34:53–136.

Griaule, M. 1948. *Dieu d'eau: Entretiens avec Ogotommeli.* Paris: Chêne.

Griaule, M. 1950. "Philosophie et Religion des Noirs." *Présence africaine* 8–9:307–12.

Griaule, M. 1952. "Le Savoir des Dogon." *Journal de la Société des Africanistes* 22:27–42.

Guthrie, M. 1948. *The Classification of the Bantu Languages.* Oxford: Oxford University Press.

Habermas, J. 1971. *Knowledge and Human Interests.* Boston: Beacon Press.

Hama, B. 1969. *Kotia-Nima.* Paris: Présence Africaine.

Hama, B. 1972. *Le Retard de l'Afrique: Essai philosophique.* Paris: Présence Africaine.

Hastings, A. 1979. *The History of African Christianity.* Cambridge: Cambridge University Press.

Hauser, M. 1982. *Essai sur la poétique de la négritude.* Lille: Université de Lille III.

Hazoume, P. 1935. *Doguicimi.* Paris: Larose.

Hebga, M. 1958. "Plaidoyer pour les logiques de l'Afrique noire." In *Aspects de la culture noire,* 104–16. Paris: Fayard.

Hebga, M. 1982. "Eloge de l'ethnophilosophie." *Présence africaine* 123:20–41.

Henroteaux, M. 1945. "Notes sur la secte des Bambudye." *Bulletin des juridictions indigènes et du droit coutumier congolais* 13, no. 4:98–107.

Hertz, R. 1973. "The Pre-Eminence of the Right Hand: A Study in Religious Polarity." In *Right and Left.* Ed. R. Needham, 3–31.

Heusch, L. de. 1972. *Le Roi ivre; ou, L'Origine de l'état.* Paris: Gallimard.

Heusch, L. de. 1982. *The Drunken King; or, The Origin of the State.* Bloomington: Indiana University Press.

Heusch, L. de. 1985. *Sacrifice in Africa.* Bloomington: Indiana University Press.

Hiernaux, J., E. Maquet, and J. De Buyst. 1968. "Excavations at Sanga, 1958." *South African Journal of Science* 64:113–17.

Hodgen, M. T. 1971. *Early Anthropology in the Sixteenth and Seventeenth Centuries.* Philadelphia: University of Pennsylvania Press.

Holas, B. 1965. *Le Séparatisme religieux en Afrique noire.* Paris: Presses Universitaires de France.

Holas, B. 1968. *Les Dieux d'Afrique noire.* Paris: Geuthner.

Horton, R. 1967. "African Traditional Thought and Western Science." *Africa* 37, no. 1:50–71; no. 2:155–87.

Horton, R. 1971. "African Conversion." *Africa* 41, no. 2:85–108.

Hountondji, P. 1977. *Sur la philosophie africaine.* Paris: Maspero.

Hountondji, P. 1980. "Distances." *Recherche, pédagogie et culture* 49, no. 9:27–33.

Hountondji, P. 1981. "Que peut la philosophie?" *Présence africaine* 119:47–71.

Hountondji, P. 1983a. *African Philosophy: Myth and Reality.* Bloomington: Indiana University Press.

Hountondji, P. 1983b. "Reason and Tradition." In *Philosophy and Cultures.* Nairobi: Bookwise Limited.

Howlett, J. 1974. "La Philosophie africaine en question." *Présence africaine* 91:14–25.

Hubert, H., and M. Mauss. 1964. *Sacrifice: Its Nature and Function.* Chicago: University of Chicago Press.

Hulstaert, G. 1950. *Carte linguistique du Congo Belge.* Brussels.

Hulstaert, G. 1961. *Les Mongos: Aperçu general.* Tervuren: Musée Royal de l'Afrique Centrale.

Hulstaert, G. 1971. "Sur quelques croyances magiques des Mongos." *Cahiers des religions africaines* 9:145–67.

Hulstaert, G. 1980. "Le Dieu des Mongo." In *Religions africaines et christianisme* 2:33–84. Kinshasa: Faculté de Théologie Catholique.

Isaacman, A., and B. Isaacman. 1977. "Resistance and Collaboration in Southern and Central Africa, ca. 1850–1970." *International Journal of African Historical Studies* 10, no. 1:31–62.

Jacobson-Widding, A. 1979. *Red-White-Black as a Mode of Thought.* Uppsala Studies in Cultural Anthropology 1. Stockholm: Almquist and Wikseu.

Jahn, J. 1958. *Muntu: Umrisse der neoafrikanschen Kultur.* Köln: E. Diedericks.

Jahn, J. 1961. *Muntu: An Outline of the New African Culture.* New York: Grove Press.

Janzen, J. M. 1977. "The Tradition of Renewal in Kongo Religion." In *African Religions: A Symposium.* Ed. N. S. Booth, 69–115. New York: Nok.

Janzen, J. M. 1978. *The Quest for Therapy in Lower Zaire.* Berkeley: University of California Press.

Janzen, J. M. 1982. *Lemba, 1650–1930.* New York: Garland.

Janzen, J. M., and W. MacGaffey. 1974. *An Anthropology of Kongo Religion.* Lawrence: University of Kansas Press.

Jewsiewicki, B. 1979. "Zaire Enters the World System: Its Colonial Incorporation as the Belgian Congo, 1885–1960." In *Zaire: The Political Economy of Underdevelopment.* Ed. G. Gran, 29–53. New York: Praeger.

Jewsiewicki, B. 1983. "Présentation." *Récits de vie et mémoire.* Paris: L'Harmattan.

Jewsiewicki, B. 1985. *Marx, Afrique et occident.* Montreal: McGill University Centre for Developing Area Studies.

Jousse, M. 1925. "Le Style oral rythmique et mnémotechnique chez les Verbo-Moteurs." *Archives de philosophie* 2.

Jung, C. G. 1972. *Two Essays on Analytical Psychology.* Princeton: Princeton University Press.

Jung, C. G. 1980. *The Archetypes and the Collective Unconscious.* Princeton: Princeton University Press.

Kachama-Nkoy, S. 1963. "De Karl Marx à Pierre Teilhard de Chardin dans la pensée de L. S. Senghor et Mamadou Dia." In *Voies africaines du socialisme*, 63–83. Léopoldville: Bibliothèque de l'Etoile.

Kagame, A. 1956. *La Philosophie bantu-rwandaise de l'être*. Brussels: Académie Royale des Sciences Coloniales.

Kagame, A. 1968. "La Place de Dieu et de l'homme dans la religion des Bantu." *Cahiers des religions africaines* 4:213–22; 5:5–11.

Kagame, A. 1971. 'L'Ethno-Philosophie des Bantu.' In *La Philosophie contemporaine*. Ed. R. Klibansky, 4:589–612. Florence: La Nuova Italia.

Kagame, A. 1976. *La Philosophie bantu comparée*. Paris: Présence Africaine.

Kalanda, M. 1967. *La Remise en question: Base de la décolonisation mentale*. Brussels: Remarques Africaines.

Kamitatu-Massamba, C. 1977. *Zaïre: Le Pouvoir à la portée de peuple*. Paris: L'Harmattan.

Kankwenda, M. 1978. "Sous-Développement de l'agriculture et pauvreté d'un pays riche: Le Cas du Zaïre." *Etudes zaïroises*.

Kanyo, E. 1979. "Political Power and Class Formation in Zaire." Ph.D. diss. Yale University, Dept. of Political Science.

Kaoze, S. 1907–11. *La Psychologie des Bantus et quelques lettres*. Anastatic reproduction by A. J. Smet (1979). Kinshasa: Faculté de Théologie Catholique.

Katuala, J. G. 1979. "Blockage Mechanisms, Disincentives and Financial Crisis in Zaire." Ph.D. diss. University of California, Berkeley, Dept. of Political Science.

Kimoni, I. 1975. *Destin de la littérature négro-africaine; ou, Problématique d'une culture*. Kinshasa: Presses Universitaires du Zaïre.

Kinyongo, J. 1970. *Origine et signification du nom divin de Yahvé*. Bonn: Bonner Biblische Beiträge.

Kinyongo, J. 1973. *L'Etre manifesté: Méditation philosophique sur l'affirmation de soi, la participation et l'authenticité au Zaïre*. Lubumbashi: Synthèse.

Kinyongo, J. 1979. "Essai sur la fondation épistémologique d'une philosophie herméneutique en Afrique: Le Cas de la discursivité." *Présence africaine* 109:12–26.

Koffi, N. 1976. "L'Impensé de Towa et de Hountondji." Paper presented at the international seminar on African Philosophy, Addis-Ababa, Dec.

Kristeva, J. 1980. *Desire in Language*. New York: Columbia University Press.

Kristeva, J. 1982. *Power of Horror: An Essay on Abjection*. New York: Columbia University Press.

Lacan, J. 1966. *Ecrits*. Paris: Seuil.

Laleye, P. I. 1975. *La Philosophie? Pourquoi en Afrique?* Bern: Peter Lang.

Laleye, P. I. 1977. *Pour une anthropologie repensée*. Paris: La Pensée Universelle.

Laleye, P. I. 1982. "La Philosophie, l'Afrique et les philosophes africains: Triple malentendu ou possibilité d'une collaboration féconde?" *Présence africaine* 123:42–62.

Lanternari, V. 1963. *Religions of the Oppressed*. New York: Alfred Knopf.

Leach, E. R. 1961. *Rethinking Anthropology*. London: Athlone.

Leach, E. R. 1980a. *Claude Lévi-Strauss*. New York: Penguin Books.

Leach, E. R. 1980b. "Genesis as Myth." In *Myth and Cosmos*. Ed. J. Middleton, 1–13. Austin: University of Texas Press.

Leclaire, S. 1971. *Démasquer le réel*. Paris: Seuil.

Leiris, M. 1941. "La Notion d'Awa chez les Dogons." *Bulletin de la Société des Africanistes* 11:219–30.

Le Roy, A. 1909. *La Religion des primitifs*. Paris: Beauchesne.

Lévi-Strauss, C. 1958. *Anthropologie structurale*. Paris: Plon.

Lévi-Strauss, C. 1966. *The Savage Mind*. Chicago: University of Chicago Press.

Lévi-Strauss, C. 1967. *Structural Anthropology*. New York: Doubleday.

Lévi-Strauss, C. 1969. *The Raw and the Cooked*. New York: Harper and Row.

Lévi-Strauss, C. 1976. *Structural Anthropology, Vol. II*. New York: Harper and Row. (French original: 1973. *Anthropologie structurale II*. Paris: Plon.)

Lévi-Strauss, C. 1977. *Tristes Tropiques*. New York: Washington Square Press.

Lévi-Strauss, C. 1979. *The Origins of Table Manners*. New York: Harper and Row.

Lévi-Strauss, C. 1981. *The Naked Man*. New York: Harper and Row.

Levy-Bruhl, L. 1911. *Les Fonctions mentales dans les sociétés inférieures*. Paris: Alcan.

Levy-Bruhl, L. 1949. *Les Carnets de Lucien Lévy-Bruhl*. Paris: Presses Universitaires de France.

Lienhardt, G. 1961. *Divinity and Experience*. Oxford: Clarendon Press.

Livingstone, D. 1857. *Missionary Travels and Researches in South Africa*. London: Murray.

Lokadi, L. 1979. "Différence entre la généralité II du matérialisme dialectique et la généralité II du matérialisme historique: Contribution à la critique de l'epistémologie althussérienne." Ph.D. diss. Université Nationale du Zaïre, Campus de Lubumbashi, Faculté des Lettres.

Lucas, S. A. 1966–67. "L'Etat traditionnel Luba." Pts. 1, 2. *Problèmes sociaux congolais* 74:83–97; 79:93–116.

Lufuluabo, F. M. 1962. *Vers une théodicée bantoue*. Paris: Tournai.

Lufuluabo, F. M. 1964a. *Orientation préchrétienne de la conception bantoue de l'être*. Léopoldville: Centre d'Etudes Pastorales.

Lufuluabo, F. M. 1964b. *La Notion Luba-bantoue de l'être*. Tournai: Casterman.

Lufuluabo, F. M. 1966. *Perspective théologique bantoue et théologie scholastique*. Malines.

Lwakale, C. M. 1966. *Initiation africaine et initiation chrétienne*. Kinshasa: Centre d'Etudes Pastorales.

Mabika, K. N.d. *Baluba et Lulua*. Brussels: Remarcques Congolaises.

MacGaffey, W. 1975. "Oral Tradition in Central Africa." *Journal of African Historical Studies* 7, no. 3:417–26.

MacGaffey, W. 1977. "Cultural Roots of Kongo Prophetism." *History of Religions* 17, no. 2:177–93.

MacGaffey, W. 1978. "African History, Anthropology, and the Rationality of Natives." *History in Africa* 5:101–20.

MacGaffey, W. 1981. "Ideology and Belief." *African Studies Review* 24, nos. 2–3:227–74.

MacGaffey, W. 1983. *Modern Kongo Prophets*. Bloomington: Indiana University Press.

MacKnight, J. D. 1967. "Extra-Descent Group Ancestor Cults in African Societies." *Africa* 37, no. 1:1–21.

Mahieu, W. de. 1970. "Anthropologie et théologie africaine." In *La Revue du clergé indigène* 25:378–87.

Makarakiza, A. 1959. *La Dialectique des Barundi*. Brussels: Académie Royale des Sciences Coloniales.

Maquet, J. 1986. *The Aesthetic Experience: An Anthropologist Looks at Visual Arts*. New Haven: Yale University Press.

Marks, S. 1970. *Reluctant Rebellion: An Assessment of the 1906–08 Disturbance in Natal*. Oxford: Clarendon Press.

Martin, M. L. 1971. *Kirche ohne Weisse*. Basel: Reinhardt.

Marx, K. 1959. *Economic and Political Manuscripts of 1844*. Trans. M. Milligan. Moscow: Progress Publishers.

Marx, K. 1967. *Capital: A Critique of Political Economy*. 3 vols. New York: International Publishers.

Marx, K. 1973. *Sur les sociétés précapitalistes*. Paris: Editions Sociales.

Marx, K., and F. Engels. 1970. *The German Ideology*. New York: International Publishers.

Masamba Ma Mpolo. 1976. *La Libération des envoûtés*. Yaoundé: Editions Sociales.

Maurier, H. 1975. *Philosophie de l'Afrique noire*. Studia Instituti Anthropos 27 St. Augustin: Anthropos-Institut. (2d ed., 1985.)

Mauss, M. 1968. *Sociologie et anthropologie*. 4th ed. Paris: Presses Universitaires de France.

Mbiti, J. S. 1969. *African Religions and Philosophy*. London: Heinemann.

Mbiti, J. S. 1970. *Concepts of God in Africa*. London: S.P.C.K.

Mbiti, J. S. 1971. *New Testament Eschatology in an African Background*. Oxford: Oxford University Press.

Meester, P. de. 1980. *Où va l'église d'Afrique?* Paris: Cerf.

Meeussen, A. 1956. "Statistique lexicographique en Bantu: Bobangi et Zulu." *Kongo-Overzee* 22:86–89.

Meillassoux, C. 1964. *Etude de l'anthropologie économique des Gouro de Côte d'Ivoire*. Paris: Mouton.

Meillassoux, C. 1972. "From Reproduction to Production." *Economy and Society* 1, no. 1:93–105.

Meillassoux, C. 1975. *Femmes, greniers et capitaux*. Paris: Maspero.

Meillassoux, C. 1981. *Maidens, Meal and Money*. London: Cambridge University Press.

Melone, T. 1962. *De la négritude dans la littérature négro-africaine*. Paris: Présence Africaine.

Memel-Fote, H. 1962. "Rapport sur la civilisation animiste." In *Colloque sur les religions*, 31–58. Paris: Présence africaine.

Memel-Fote, H. 1965. "De la Paix perpétuelle dans la philosophie pratique des Africains." *Présence africaine* 55:15–31.

Merleau-Ponty, M. 1962. *Phenomenology of Perception*. New York: Humanities Press.

Merleau-Ponty, M. 1973. *The Prose of the World*. Evanston: Northwestern University Press.

Merriam, A. P. 1974. *An African World: The Basongye Village of Lupupa Ngye*. Bloomington: Indiana University Press.

Middleton, J. 1960. *Lugbara Religion*. London: Oxford University Press.

Middleton, J. ed. 1980 [1963]. *Myth and Cosmos*. Austin: University of Texas Press.

Middleton, J., and E. H. Winter. 1963. *Witchcraft and Sorcery in East Africa*. London: Routledge and Kegan Paul.

Molena, S. M. 1920. *The Bantu, Past and Present*. Edinburgh: Green.

Monguya-Mbenge, Daniel. 1962. *Histoire secrète du Zaïre: L'Autopsie de la barbarie au service du monde*. Brussels: Editions Actuelles.

Monsengwo, L. P. 1973. *La Notion de nomos dans le pentateuque grec*. Rome and Kinshasa: Recherches Africaines de Théologie.

Mouralis, B. 1981. ''Mudimbé et le savoir ethnologique.'' *L'Afrique littéraire et artistique* 58, no. 1:112–25.

Mpinga-Kasenda, and D. J. Gould. 1975. *Les Réformes administratives au Zaïre (1972–1973)*. Kinshasa: Presses Universitaires du Zaïre.

Mpongo, L. 1968. *Pour une anthropologie chrétienne du mariage au Congo*. Kinshasa: Centre d'Etudes Pastorales.

Mpongo, L. 1981. ''La Liturgie de demain au Zaïre.'' In *Aspects du catholicisme au Zaïre*, 83–96. Kinshasa: Faculté de Théologie Catholique.

Mudimbe, V. Y. 1970. ''Matérialisme historique et histoire immédiate.'' *Cahiers economiques et sociaux* 8, no. 3.

Mudimbe, V. Y. 1974. *L'Autre Face du royaume: Une Introduction à la critique des langages en folie*. Lausanne: L'Age d'Homme.

Mudimbe, V. Y. 1981a. ''Regards sur l'église catholique du Zaïre.'' In *Aspects du catholicisme au Zaïre*, 73–81. Kinshasa: Faculté de Théologie Catholique.

Mudimbe, V. Y. 1981b. *Visages de la philosophie et de la théologie contemporaines au Zaïre*. Brussels: Cedaf.

Mudimbe, V. Y. 1982a. ''La Pensée africaine contemporaine, 1954–1980: Répertoire chronologique des ouvrages de langue française.'' *Recherche, pédagogie et culture* 56, no. 9:68–73.

Mudimbe, V. Y. 1982b. *L'Odeur du père*. Paris: Présence Africaine.

Mudimbe, V. Y. 1988. *The Invention of Africa*. Bloomington: Indiana University Press.

Mujynya, E. N. C. 1972. *L'Homme dans l'univers des Bantu*. Lubumbashi: Presses Universitaires du Zaïre.

Mulago, V. 1956a. ''L'Union vitale bantu; ou, Le Principe de cohésion de la communauté chez les Bashi, les Banyarwanda et les Barundi.'' *Annali Lateranensi* (Rome) 20:61–263.

Mulago, V. 1956b. ''L'Union vitale bantu.'' *Rythmes du monde* (Abbaye de S. André, Bruges) 4, nos. 2–3:133–41.

Mulago, V. 1957a. ''Nécessité de l'adaptation missionnaire chez les Bantu du Congo.'' In *Des prêtres noirs s'interrogent*, 2d ed., 19–40. Paris.

Mulago, V. 1957b. "Le Pacte du sang et la communion alimentaire, pierres d'attente de la communion eucharistique." In *Des prêtres noirs s'interrogent*, 171–87; *Perspectives de la catholicité* (Brussels) 15, no. 4:79–92.

Mulago, V. 1958. "Dialectique existentielle des Bantu et sacramentalisme." In *Aspects de la culture noire*, 146–71. Paris: Fayard.

Mulago, V. 1959. "La Théologie et ses responsabilités." In *Deuxième congrès des ecrivains et artistes noirs*, 188–205. Paris: Présence Africaine.

Mulago, V. 1962. "Le Christianisme face aux aspirations de l'âme bantu." *Antennes* (Louvanium) 6:475–86.

Mulago, V. 1965a. *Un Visage africain du christianisme: L'Union vitale bantu face à l'unité vitale ecclésiale*. Paris: Présence Africaine.

Mulago, V. 1965b. "Mariage africain et mariage chrétien: Perspectives liturgico-pastorales." *Revue de clergé africain* 20, no. 6:547–64.

Mulago, V. 1966. "Sauver la vérité des sacrements dans nos jeunes chrétientés." *Revue du clergé africain* 21, no. 3:274–91.

Mulago, V. 1967a. "La Conception de Dieu dans la tradition bantu." *Revue du clergé africain* 22, no. 3:272–99.

Mulago, V. 1967b. "Naturalisation du christianisme en dehors de l'occident à la lumière de Vatican II." *Euntes Docete* (Rome) 20:241–62.

Mulago, V. 1968a. "Le Dieu des Bantu." *Cahiers des religions africaines* 2, no. 3:23–64.

Mulago, V. 1968b. "Christianisme et culture africaine: Apport africain à la théologie." In *Christianity in Tropical Africa: Studies Presented and Discussed at the Seventh International African Seminar at the University of Ghana*, April 1965, pp. 308–28. Oxford: Oxford University Press.

Mulago, V. 1968c. "Die lebensnotwendige Teilhabe." In *Theologie und Kirche in Afrika*, 54–72. Stuttgart.

Mulago, V. 1969a. "La Participation vitale." In *Pour une théologie africaine*, 191–216. Yaoundé.

Mulago, V. 1969b. "Vital Participation: The Cohesive Principle of the Bantu Community." In *Biblical Revelation and African Beliefs*, 137–58. London.

Mulago, V. 1969c. "Le Problème d'une théologie africaine revu à la lumière de Vatican II." *Revue du clergé africain* 24, nos. 3–4:277–314, and *Renouveau de l'église et nouvelles églises* (Mayidi) pp. 115–152.

Mulago, V. 1969d. "Le Culte de Lyangombe chez les Bashi et les Banya-rwanda." *Cahiers des religions africaines* 3, no. 6:299–314.

Mulago, V. 1971a. "Le Mariage traditionnel bantu." *Revue du clergé africain* 26, nos. 3–4:5–61.

Mulago, V. 1971b. "Symbolisme dans les religions traditionnelles africaines et sacramentalisme." *Bulletin of "Secretariatus pro non-Christianis"* (Città del Vaticano) 18:169–203, and *Revue du clergé africain* 27, nos. 4–5:467–502.

Mulago, V. 1972. "La Religion traditionnelle, élément central de la culture africaine." In *Colloque international sur les religions africaines comme source de civilisation*, 115–55. Paris.

Mulago, V. 1973a. *La Religion traditionnelle des Bantu et leur vision du monde.* Bibliothèque du Centre d'Etudes des Religions Africaines, no. 1. Kinshasa.

Mulago, V. 1973b. *Endagano Mpyahya* (Nouveau Testament en mashi, traduit par un groupe de prêtres du clergé diocésain sous la direction de Mulago). 2d ed. Kinshasa: Société Missionaire de St. Paul pour l'Archidiocèse de Bukavu.

Mulago, V. 1976. "Evangélisation et cultures." (*Congrès International de Missiologie,* Rome, 5–12 October 1975.) *Cahiers des religions africaines,* 10, no. 19:107–24.

Mulago, V. 1978a. "Mariage africain et mariage chrétien." *Studia Missionalia* 27:53–134.

Mulago, V. 1978b. "Le Langage de l'église missionnaire." (Atti del Simposio Internazionale di Missiologia, Rome, 24–28 October 1977.) *La Formazione del missionario oggi,* 51–76. Rome.

Mulago, V. 1978c. "Solidarité africaine et corresponsabilité chrétienne." (Colloque International de Kinshasa, 9–14 January 1978.) *Religions africaines et christianisme,* 43–63. Kinshasa.

Mulago, V. 1979a. "Initiation africaine et initiation chrétienne." (Colloque organisé par le Centre de Recherches Universitaires du Kivu de l'I.S.P., May 1976.) *Le Mythe et les rites de Lyangombe,* 29–75. Bukavu: Editions du Ceruki.

Mulago, V. 1979b. *Simbolismo religioso africano: Estudio comparativo con el sacramentalismo cristiano.* Madrid: Biblioteca de Autores Cristianos.

Mulago, V. 1979c. "L'Avenir des ministères dans l'église catholique." (Actes de la VIII Semaine Théologique de Kinshasa, 23–28 July 1973.) *Ministères et services dans l'église,* 60–62. Kinshasa.

Mulago, V. 1980a. "Le Nouveau Rituel de la pénitence." (Actes de la IXe Semaine Théologique de Kinshasa, 22–27 July 1974.) *Péché, pénitence et réconciliation,* 143–48. Kinshasa.

Mulago, V. 1980b. "Religions traditionnelles et christianisme." (Actes de la Xe Semaine Théologique de Kinshasa, 21–26 July 1975.) *L'Evangélisation dans Afrique aujourd'hui,* 77–83. Kinshasa.

Mulago, V. 1980c. *La Religion traditionnelle des Bantu et leur vision du monde.* Bibliothèque du Centre d'Etudes des Religions Africaines, no. 5, 2d ed. Kinshasa.

Mulago, V. 1981. "Evangélisation et authenticité." In *Aspects du catholicisme au Zaïre,* 7–55. Kinshasa: Faculté de Théologie Catholique.

Mulago, V., et al. 1964. *Mkono mkononi: Ndoa ya heri.* Bukavu: Editions du Centre de Pastorale Liturgique.

Mulago, V., and T. Theuws. 1960. *Autour du mouvement de la "Jamaa."* Cahier no. 1 d'Orientations Pastorales. Limete-Léopoldville.

Murdock, G. P. 1959. *Africa.* New York: McGraw-Hill.

Mveng, E. 1964. *L'Art d'Afrique noire.* Paris: Mame.

Mveng, E. 1978. "De la sous-mission à la succession." In *Civilisation noire et église catholique,* 267–76. Paris: Présence Africaine.

Mveng, E. 1981. "Un Visage africain du christianisme: Pour une Ecclésiologie africaine." In *Combats pour un christianisme africain.* Ed. A. M. Ngindu, 133–35. Kinshasa: Faculté de Théologie Catholique.

Mwabila-Malela. 1973. "Proletariat et conscience de classe au Zaïre: Essai d'explication de la prolétarisation incomplète des travailleurs de Lubambashi." Ph.D. diss. Université Libre de Bruxelles.

Mwamba, N. 1972. "De Quelques Mythes Luba du Shaba." *Cahiers de religions africaines* 12, no. 6:201–13.

N'Daw, A. 1966. "Peut-on parler d'une pensée africaine?" *Présence africaine* 58:32–46.

N'Daw, A. 1983. *La Pensée africaine: Recherches sur les fondements de la pensée négro-africaine*. Dakar: Nouvelles Edititions Africaines.

Neckebrouck, V. 1971. *L'Afrique noire et la crise religieuse de l'occident*. Tabora: T.M.P.

Needham, R., ed. 1973. *Right and Left: Essays on Dual Symbolic Classification*. Chicago: University of Chicago Press.

Nenquin, J. 1963. *Excavations at Sanga, 1957: The Protohistoric Necropolis*. Tervuren: Koninklÿk Museum van Belgisch-Kongo.

Ngindu, A. M. 1974. "La Recours à l'authenticité et le christianisme au Zaïre." *Cahiers des religions africaines* 8:16.

Ngindu, A. M. 1978. *Le Problème de la connaissance religieuse d'après Lucien Laberthonière*. Kinshasa: Faculté de Théologie Catholique.

Ngindu, A. M. 1980. "L'Eglise de la chrétienté face aux cultures nouvelles." In *Concilium*, Projet X, 166:89–100.

Ngindu, A. M., ed. 1981a. *Combats pour un christianisme africain: Mélanges en l'honneur du Professeur V. Mulago*. Kinshasa: Faculté de Théologie Catholique.

Ngindu, A. M. 1981b. "L'Inculturation du christianisme comme problème théologique." In *Combats pour un christianisme africain*, 9–19. Kinshasa: Faculté de Théologie Catholique.

Ngindu, A. M. 1981c. "La Théologie africaine en marche." In *Aspects du catholicisme au Zaïre*, 61–72. Kinshasa: Faculté de Théologie Catholique.

Ngoma, B. 1978. "La Récusation de la philosophie par la société africaine." In *Mélanges de philosophie africaine*, 85–100. Kinshasa: Faculté de Théologie Catholique.

Ngubane, H. 1977. *Body and Mind in Zulu Medicine*. Cambridge: Cambridge University Press.

Nguvulu, A. 1971. *L'Humanisme négro-africain face au développement*. Kinshasa: Okapi.

Njoh-Mouelle, N. 1970a. *De la médiocrité à l'excellence*. Yaoundé: Clé.

Njoh-Mouelle, N. 1970b. *Jalons: Recherches d'une mentalité neuve*. Yaoundé: Clé.

Njoh-Mouelle, N. 1975. *Jalons II*. Yaoundé: Clé.

Nkombe, O. 1977. "Méthode et point de départ en philosophie africaine: Authenticité et libération." In *La Philosophie africaine*, 68–87. Kinshasa: Faculté de Théologie Catholique.

Nkombe, O. 1978. "Essai de sémiotique formelle: Les Rapports différentiels." In *Mélanges de philosophie africaine*, 131–48. Kinshasa: Faculté de Théologie Catholique.

Nkombe, O. 1979. *Métaphore et métonymie dans les symboles parémiologiques: L'Intersubjectivité dans les proverbes Tetela*. Kinshasa: Faculté de Théologie Catholique.

Nkombe, O. 1981. "La Métaphysique vive et la métaphysique morte." In *Combats pour un christianisme africain*, 149–58. Kinshasa: Faculté de Théologie Catholique.

Nkombe, O., and A. J. Smet. 1978. "Panorama de la philosophie africaine contemporaine." In *Mélanges de philosophie africaine*, 263–82. Kinshasa: Faculté de Théologie Catholique.

Nkrumah, K. 1964. *Consciencism: Philosophy and Ideology for Decolonization with Particular References to the African Revolution*. London: Heinemann.

Nothomb, D. 1965. *Un Humanisme africain*. Brussels: Lumen Vitae.

Ntedika, J. 1966. *L'Evolution de la doctrine du purgatoire chez Saint-Augustin*. Paris: Etudes Augustiennes.

Ntedika, J. 1971. *L'Evocation de l'au-delà dans la prière des morts: Etude de patristique et de liturgie latines*. Louvain-Paris: Béatrice Nauwelaerts.

Ntedika, J. 1977. "Les Responsabilités du département de philosophie et religions africaines de la Faculté de Théologie." In *La philosophie africaine*, 9–20. Kinshasa: Faculté de Théologie Catholique.

Nyeme, T. 1975. *Munga: Ethique en milieu africain. Gentilisme et christianisme*. Ingenbohl: Imprimerie du P. Théodose.

Nzege, A. 1980. "Intelligence et guerre: Essai sur la philosophie politique de Bergson." Ph.D. diss. Université Nationale du Zaïre, Campus de Lubumbashi, Faculté des Lettres.

Nzongola-Ntalaja. 1975. "Urban Administration in Zaire: A Study of Karanga, 1971–1973." Ph.D. diss. University of Wisconsin–Madison, Dept. of Political Science.

Okolo, O. 1979. "Tradition et destin: Essai sur la philosophie herméneutique de P. Ricoeur, M. Heidegger, et II. G. Gadamer." Ph.D. diss. Université Nationale du Zaïre, Campus de Lubumbashi, Faculté des Lettres.

Orjo de Marchovelette, E. de. 1950. "Historique de la Chefferie Kabongo." *Bulletin des juridictions indigènes et du droit coutumier congolais* 12:354–68.

Ortigues, E. 1962. *Le Discours et le symbole*. Aubier: Editions Mantaigne.

Pagden, A. 1982. *The Fall of Natural Man*. Cambridge: Cambridge University Press.

Parrinder, G. 1961. *West African Religion*. London: Epwort Press.

Parrinder, G. 1970. *Religion in Africa*. London: Pall Mall Press.

Peel, J. D. Y. 1968. *Aladura: A Religious Movement among the Yoruba*. Oxford: Oxford University Press.

Phillipson, D. W. 1984. "Early Food Production in Central and Southern Africa." In *From Hunters to Farmers*. Ed. J. D. Clark and S. A. Brandt, 272–80. Berkeley: University of California Press.

Phillipson, D. W. 1985. *African Archaeology*. Cambridge: Cambridge University Press.

Possoz, E. 1945. Preface to *La Philosophie bantoue*. By P. Tempels. Elisabethville: Lovania. English version, 1959.

Radin, P. 1957. *Primitive Man as Philosopher*. New York: Dover Publications.

Randles, W. G. L. 1968. *L'Ancien Royaume du Congo des origines a la fin du XIXe siecle*. Paris: Mouton.

Reefe, T. Q. 1981. *The Rainbow and the Kings*. Berkeley: University of California Press.

Rey, P. P. 1970. *Colonialisme, néo-colonialisme et transition au capitalisme*. Paris: Maspero.

Rey, P. P. 1973. *Les Alliances des classes: Sur l'articulation des modes de production*. Paris: Maspero.

Ricoeur, P. 1965. *History and Truth*. Evanston: Northwestern University Press.

Ricoeur, P. 1974. *The Conflict of Interpretations*. Evanston: Northwestern University Press.

Ricoeur, P. 1984. *The Reality of the Historical Past*. Milwaukee: Marquette University Press.

Riesman, P. 1977. *Freedom in Social Life: An Introspective Ethnography*. Chicago: University of Chicago Press.

Rigby, P. 1985. *Persistent Pastoralists: Nomadic Societies in Transition*. London: Zed Books.

Roberts, A. 1979. "The Ransom of Ill-Starred Zaire: Plunder, Politics, and Poverty in the OTRAG Concession." In *Zaire: The Political Economy of Underdevelopment*. Ed. G. Gran, 211–36. New York: Praeger.

Roberts, A. 1980. "Heroic Beasts, Beastly Heroes: Principles of Cosmology and Chiefship among the Lakeside BaTabwa of Zaire." Ph.D. diss. University of Chicago, Dept. of Anthropology.

Roberts, A. 1981. "Passage Stellified: Speculation upon Archaeoastronomy in Southeastern Zaire." *Archaeoastronomy* 4, no. 4:27–37.

Roberts, A. 1982. "Comets Importing Change of Times and States: Ephemerae and Process among the Tabwa of Zaire." *American Ethnologist* 9, no. 4:712–29.

Roberts, A. 1983a. " 'Perfect' Lions, 'Perfect' Leaders: A Metaphor for Tabwa Chiefship." *Journal de la Société des Africanistes* 53, nos. 1–2:93–105.

Roberts, A. 1983b. "Anarchy, Abjection and Absurdity: A Case of Metaphorical Medicine among the Tabwa of Zaire." In *The Anthropology of Medicine: From Theory to Method*. Ed. L. Romanucci-Ross, D. Moerman, and L. Tancredi, 119–33. New York: Praeger.

Roberts, A. 1984. "Fishers of Men: Religion and Political Economy among Colonized Tabwa." *Africa* 54, no. 2:49–70.

Roberts, A. 1986a. "Social and Historical Contexts in Tabwa Arts." In *The Rising of a New Moon: A Century of Tabwa Art*. Eds. A. Roberts and E. Maurer, 1–48. Ann Arbor: University of Michigan Museum of Art.

Roberts, A. 1986b. "Duality in Tabwa Art." *African Arts* 19, no. 4:26–35, 86–87.

Roberts, A. (MS1). "Where the King is Coming From." In *Body, Gender and Space: African Folk Models of Social and Cosmological Order*. Ed. A. Jacobson-Widding. Washington, D.C.: Uppsala University and the Smithsonian University Press. Forthcoming.

Roberts, A. (MS2). "History, Ethnicity and Change in the 'Christian Kingdom' of Southeastern Zaire." *The Creation of Tribalism in South and Central Africa.* Ed. L. Vail. London: James Currey. Forthcoming.

Sahlins, M. 1976. *Culture and Practical Reason.* Chicago: University of Chicago Press.

Sartre, J. P. 1948. "Orphée noir." *Les Temps modernes* 4:577–606.

Sartre, J. P. 1956. *Being and Nothingness.* New York: Washington Square Press.

Sartre, J. P. 1964. *Nausea.* New York: New Directions.

Sartre, J. P. 1965. *Anti-Semite and Jew.* New York: Schocken Books.

Sartre, J. P. 1967. *Essays in Existentialism.* New York: Citadel Press.

Sartre, J. P. 1968. *Search for a Method.* New York: Random House.

Sartre, J. P. 1969. *The Devil and the Good Lord.* New York: Vintage Books.

Sartre, J. P. 1976. *No Exit.* New York: A. A. Knopf.

Sartre, J. P. 1982. *The Critique of Dialectical Reason.* London: Verso.

Schebesta, P. 1923. "Die religiose Anschauungen Süd-Afrikas." *Anthropos* 18–19:114–24.

Schebesta, P. 1963. *Le Sens religieux des primitifs.* Paris: Mame.

Schmidt, W. 1933-49. *Die Ursprung der Gottesidee.* Munster: Aschendorff.

Sebag, L. 1967. *Marxisme et structuralisme.* Paris: Payot.

Sene, A. 1966. *Sur le chemin de la négritude.* Cairo: Imprimerie Catholique de Beyrouth.

Senghor, L. S. 1961. *Nation et voie africaine du socialisme.* Paris: Présence Africaine.

Senghor, L. S. 1962. *Pierre Teilhard de Chardin et la politique africaine.* Paris: Seuil.

Senghor, L. S. 1964. *Liberté I: Négritude et humanisme.* Paris: Seuil.

Senghor, L. S. 1967a. *Négritude, arabisme et francité.* Beirut: Dar Al-Kitab Al-lubnani.

Senghor, L. S. 1967b. *Les Fondements de l'africanité ou négritude et arabité.* Paris: Présence Africaine.

Senghor, L. S. 1971. *Liberté II: Nation et voie africaine du socialisme.* Paris: Seuil.

Senghor, L. S. 1972. "Pourquoi une idéologie négro-africaine?" *Présence africaine* 82:11–38.

Senghor, L. S. 1976a. *Pour une relecture africaine de Marx et d'Engels.* Dakar-Abidjan: Nouvelles Editions Africaines.

Senghor, L. S. 1976b. "Authenticité et négritude." *Zaïre-Afrique* 102:81–86.

Senghor, L. S. 1977. *Liberté III: Négritude et civilisation de l'universel.* Paris: Seuil.

Senghor, L. S. 1980. *La Poésie de l'action: Conversations avec Mohamed Aziza.* Paris: Stock.

Senghor, L. S. 1983. *Liberté IV: Socialisme et planification.* Paris: Seuil.

Senghor, L. S. 1988. *Ce que je crois.* Paris: Grasset.

Shorter, A. 1977. *African Christian Theology.* New York: Orbis.

Sik, E. 1963–65. *Histoire de l'Afrique noire.* 3 vols. Budapest: Akademiai Kiado.

Sine, Babakar. 1975. *Imperialisme et théories sociologiques du développement.* Paris: Anthropos.

Slade, R. 1959. *English-Speaking Missions in the Congo: Independent State, 1878–1908.* Brussels: Académie Royale des Sciences Coloniales.

Smet, A. J. 1975a. "Bibliographie sélective des religions traditionnelles de l'Afrique noire." *Cahiers des religions africaines* 9, nos. 17–18:181–250.

Smet, A. J., ed. 1975b. *Philosophie africaine.* 2 vols. Kinshasa: Presses Universitaires du Zaïre.

Smet, A. J. 1977. "Histoire de la philosophie africaine: Problèmes et méthode." In *La Philosophie africaine*, 47–68. Kinshasa: Faculté de Théologie Catholique.

Smet, A. J. 1978a. "L'Oeuvre inédite du Père Placide Tempels." In *Philosophie et libération*, 331–46. Kinshasa: Faculté de Théologie Catholique.

Smet, A. J. 1978b. "Bibliographie sélective de la philosophie africaine: Répertoire chronologique." In *Mélanges de philosophie africaine*, 181–262. Kinshasa: Faculté de Théologie Catholique.

Smet, A. J. 1980. *Histoire de la philosophie africaine contemporaine.* Kinshasa: Faculté de Théologie Catholique.

Smith, E. W. 1950. *African Ideas of God.* London: Edinburgh House Press.

Souza, G., de. 1975. *La Conception de "vie" chez les Fons.* Cotonou: Editions du Bénin.

Sow, I. D. 1977. *Psychiatrie dynamique africaine.* Paris: Payot.

Stahl, A. B. 1984. "A History and Critique of Investigations into Early African Agriculture." In *From Hunters to Farmers.* Ed. J. D. Clark and S. A. Brandt, 9–21. Berkeley: University of California Press.

Stefaniszyn, B. 1954. "African Reincarnation Re-Examined." *African Studies* 13, nos. 3–4:131–46.

Sundkler, B. 1961 [1948]. *Bantu Prophets in South Africa.* London: Oxford University Press.

Sundkler, B. 1976. *Zulu Zion.* Oxford: Oxford University Press.

Suret-Canale, J. 1961. *L'Afrique noire, occidentale et centrale.* Paris: Editions Sociales.

Suret-Canale, J. 1971. *Le Marxisme et les sociétés africaines.* Paris: Editions Sociales.

Suret-Canale, J. 1973. *Afrique noire: De la colonisation aux indépendances.* Paris: Editions Sociales.

Tastevin, C. 1934. "Les Idées religieuses des Africains." *Géographie* 62:243–70.

Taylor, J. G. 1970. *From Modernization to Modes of Production.* Atlantic Highlands, N.J.: Humanities Press.

Taylor, J. V. 1963. *The Primal Vision: Christian Presence amid African Religion.* London: SCM Press.

Tegnaeus, H. 1954. *La Fraternité du Sang.* Paris: Payot.

Tempels, P. 1936. "Hoe de Baluba-shankadi zich de wereld voorstellen." *Kongo-Overzee*, 129–38.

Tempels, P. 1938. "Raadsels in Midden-Katanga." *Kongo Overzee*, 203–9.

Tempels, P. 1945. *La Philosophie bantoue: Traduit du néerlandais par A. Rubbens.* Elisabethville: Lovania.

Tempels, P. 1946. *Bantoue-Filosofie.* Antwerpen: De Sikkel.

Tempels, P. 1959. *Bantu Philosophy.* Paris: Présence Africaine.

Tempels, P. 1961. *La Philosophie bantoue.* 2d ed. Paris: Présence Africaine.

Tempels, P. 1962. *Notre rencontre.* Léopoldville: Centre d'Etudes Pastorales.

Tempels, P. 1979. *Philosophie bantoue.* Introduction and revision of the Rubbens translation by A. J. Smet. Kinshasa: Faculté de Théologie Catholique.

Terray, E. 1969. *Le Marxisme devant les sociétés "primitives."* Paris: Maspero.

Theunissen, M. 1986. *The Other: Studies in the Social Ontology of Heidegger, Sartre and Buber.* Cambridge, Mass.: MIT Press.

Theuws, T. 1951. "Philosophie bantoue et philosophie occidentale." *Civilisations* 1, no. 3:54–63.

Theuws, T. 1954. "Textes luba (Katanga)." In *Bulletin trimestriel du Centre d'Etude des Problèmes Sociaux Indigènes* 27:1–153.

Theuws, T. 1960. *Naître et mourir dans le rituel luba.* In *Zaïre* 14(2–3):115–73.

Theuws, T. 1961. *Le Réel dans la conception luba.* In *Zaïre* 15(1):3–44.

Theuws, T. 1965. *Rites et religion en Afrique.* In *Revue du clergé africain* 205–40.

Theuws, T. 1983. *Word and World: Luba Thought and Literature.* St. Augustin: Anthropos-Instituts.

Thomas, L. V., R. Luneau, and J. L. Doneux. 1969. *Les Religions d'Afrique noire.* Paris: Fayard.

Thompson, R. 1983. *Flash of Spirit.* New York: Random House.

Thompson, R. F. 1974. *African Art in Motion.* Berkeley: University of California Press.

Thomson, J. 1968 [1881]. *To the Central African Lakes and Back.* 2 vols. London: Cass.

Tobner, O. 1982. "Cheikh Anta Diop, l'hérétique." *Peuples noirs, peuples africains* 30:85–91.

Towa, M. 1971a. *Léopold Sédar Senghor: Négritude ou servitude.* Yaoundé: Clé.

Towa, M. 1971b. *Essai sur la problématique philosophique dans l'Afrique actuelle.* Yaoundé: Clé.

Tshiamalenga, N. T. 1973. "La Vision ntu de l'homme: Essai de philosophie linguistique et anthropologie." *Cahiers des religions africaines* 7:176–99.

Tshiamalenga, N. T. 1974. "La Philosophie de la faute dans la tradition luba." *Cahiers des religions africaines* 8:167–86.

Tshiamalenga, N. T. 1977a. "Qu'est-ce que la 'philosophie africaine'?" In *La Philosophie africaine,* 33–46. Kinshasa: Faculté de Théologie Catholique.

Tshiamalenga, N. T. 1977b. "Langues bantu et philosophie: Le Cas du Ciluba." In *La Philosophie africaine,* 147–58. Kinshasa: Faculté de Théologie Catholique.

Tshiamalenga, N. T. 1981. "La Philosophie dans la situation actuelle de l'Afrique." In *Combats pour un christianisme africain,* 171–88. Kinshasa: Faculté de Théologie Catholique.

Tshibangu, T. 1964. "Melchior Cano et la théologie positive." Ph.D. diss. Louvain University.

Tshibangu, T. 1965. *Théologie positive et théologie spéculative.* Paris-Louvain: Béatrice Nauwelaerts.

Tshibangu, T. 1974. *Le Propos d'une théologie africaine.* Kinshasa: Presses Universitaires du Zaïre.

Tshibangu, T. 1980. *Théologie comme science au XXème siècle*. Kinshasa: Presses Universitaires du Zaïre.

Tshibangu, T., and A. Vanneste. 1960. "Débat sur la théologie africaine." *Revue de clergé africain* 15.

Turner, V. 1967. *The Forest of Symbols: Aspects of Ndembu Ritual*. Ithaca: Cornell University Press.

Turner, V. 1968a. *The Drums of Affliction*. Oxford: Clarendon Press.

Turner, V. 1968b. "Myth." In *International Encyclopedia of the Social Sciences*. New York: Macmillan.

Turner, V. 1969. *The Ritual Process*. Chicago: Aldine.

Turner, V. 1975. *Revelation and Divination in Ndembu Ritual*. Ithaca: Cornell University Press.

Ugirashebuja, O. 1977. *Dialogue entre la poésie et la pensée dans l'oeuvre de Heidegger*. Brussels: Lumen Vitae.

Van Caeneghem, P. R. 1956. *La Notion de Dieu chez les Baluba du Kasai*. Brussels: Académie Royale des Sciences d'Outre Mer.

Van Gennep, A. 1960. *The Rites of Passage*. Chicago: University of Chicago Press.

Van Lierde, J. 1963. *La Pensée politique de Patrice Lumumba*. Paris: Présence Africaine.

Vansina, J. 1958. "Les Croyances religieuses des Kuba," *Zaïre* 12, no. 7:725–58.

Vansina, J. 1965. *Les Anciens Royaumes de la savane*. Kinshasa: Institut de Recherches Economiques et Sociales.

Vansina, J. 1966. *Introduction à l'ethnographise du Congo*. Brussels: Editions Universitaires du Congo.

Vansina, J. 1973a. "Lukoshi/Lupambula: Histoire d'un culte religieux dans les régions du Kasai et du Kwango (1920–1970)." *Etudes d'histoire africaine* 5:51–97.

Vansina, J. 1973b. *The Tyo Kingdom of the Middle Congo, 1880–1892*. London: Oxford University Press.

Vatican II. 1966. *Gaudium et Spes*. Rome: Acta Apost. Sedes 58.

Verbeke, F. 1937. "Le Bulopwe et Kutomboka par le sang humain chez les Baluba-Shankaji." *Bulletin des juridictions indigènes et du droit coutumier congolais* 5, no. 2:52–61.

Verhaegen, B. 1969. *Rébellions au Congo*. Vol. 2. Brussels: Editions Universitaires du Congo.

Verhaegen, B. 1974. *Introduction à l'histoire immédiate*. Gembloux: Duculot.

Verhulpen, E. 1936. *Baluba et Balubaïsés du Katanga*. Anvers: Editions de l'Avenir Belge.

Veyne, P. 1984. *Writing History*. Middletown: Wesleyan University Press.

Vilasco, G. 1972. "La Philosophie négro-africaine face aux idéologies." In *Annales de l'Université d'Abidjan*, Series D, no. 12. Abidjan: Faculté des Lettres.

Wagner, R. 1981. *The Invention of Culture*. Chicago: University of Chicago Press.

Wallerstein, I. 1974. *The Modern World System*. New York: Academic Press.

Wamba-dia-wamba, E. 1980. "La Philosophie en Afrique; ou, Les Défis de l'Africain philosophe." In *Les Faux Prophètes de l'Afrique; ou, L'Afr(eu)canisme.* Ed. A. Schwarz, 225–44. Québec: Presses de l'Université Laval.

Wendorf, F., and R. Schild. "The Emergence of Food Production in the Egyptian Sahara." In *From Hunters to Farmers,* Ed. J. D. Clark and S. A. Brandt, 93–107. Berkeley: University of California Press.

Willame, J. C. 1972. *Patrimonialism and Political Change in the Congo.* Stanford: Stanford University Press.

Willams, D. 1978. *Sacred Spaces: A Preliminary Enquiry into the Latin High Mass.* Paper presented to the Canadian Sociology and Anthropology Association Conference.

Womersley, H. 1984. *Legends and History of the Luba.* Los Angeles: Crossroads Press.

Yai Olabiyi, J. 1977. "Theory and Practice in African Philosophy: The Poverty of Speculative Philosophy." *Second Order* 2:3–20.

Young, C. 1965. *Politics in the Congo.* Princeton: Princeton University Press.

Young, C. 1976. *The Politics of Cultural Pluralism.* Madison: University of Wisconsin Press.

Young, C. 1978. "Zaire: The Unending Crisis." *Foreign Affairs* (Autumn).

Zahan, D. 1970. *Religion, spiritualité et pensée africaine.* Paris: Payot.

Index

227